Waiting for the Workers

Waiting for the Workers

A History of the Independent
Labour Party 1938–1950

BY PETER THWAITES

THE CHOIR PRESS

First published in the United Kingdom in 2020 by
The Choir Press

ISBN 978–1–78963–130–2

To the memory of Thomas James Thwaites (1908–1971),
Doris Ellen Thwaites (1910–1997)
and Stephanie Joan Thwaites (1945–2016)

Contents

Acknowledgements

———————

This book is based on a thesis which was approved for the degree of PhD by the University of London and I owe a debt of gratitude to my first supervisor, Lord Donoughue of Ashton, for his advice on research methods, and to Professor Emeritus Rodney Barker, Government Department at LSE, who took over as my supervisor in 1974, guided me through my research, and even unwittingly suggested the title for this book.

Needless to say I am indebted to all those listed in my bibliography who granted me interviews or wrote me letters, but my greatest debt is to the late Dr Don Bateman who allowed me access to the ILP's papers, answered many questions and put me in touch with a number of other ILPers and former party members. My greatest regret in not publishing this book until over 40 years after completing my PhD thesis is that those ILPers who helped me with information and hospitality are not alive to see it.

My thanks are also due to the staff of the British Library of Political and Economic Science; of the Modern Records Centre, University of Warwick; of the Public Record Office; of The Keep, East Sussex Record Office; of the British Museum Newspaper Library; of the British Library; of the Bristol University Library Special Collections; as well as the Archivists of the Labour Party, and finally Mrs D. Fiddick of the Dorset County Library Service for her help with my original bibliography.

I should also mention the assistance I received with the typing of the first draft of this book from Jan Nicholson in 1997, and also the generous help from Mike Noyce and Jon Gundry of the ORS Group in turning that transcript into a Word document in 2017. Finally I should like to thank Miles Bailey and The Choir Press for turning my manuscript into a published book.

As always my family have been my major prop. My late mother, Doris Thwaites, my brother David, and my sister, Margaret Roberts, encouraged me throughout my studies, and my late wife Stephanie supported me financially and emotionally during the writing of the original thesis and I am very sorry that she did not live to see its publication. My daughter Jane has given me considerable moral support, while my son, Simon, has provided invaluable advice and help in the production of this final version. I could not have done it without them.

Preface

There have been a number of excellent studies of the Independent Labour Party produced over the last 50 years. But the majority end with the ILP's disaffiliation from the Labour Party in 1932, or with the outbreak of the Second World War and they do not consider in any depth the ILP's activities during and just after that war, even though the ILP retained representation in Parliament until November 1947 and played a part in the local government of some towns and cities until 1950. The Second World War is touched on briefly in the several biographies of the ILP's emblematic leader, James Maxton, and in slightly more detail in the autobiographies of the leading wartime ILPers Fenner Brockway and John McGovern. But in all these works the treatment of the period is episodic and no attempt is made to describe the Party's activities in any detail or to discuss the effect of the war on the ILP's history. I hope that this book will fill in that gap and show that the ILP, though small and weak in those years, still had an interesting part to play in the political history of this country.

This book is divided into two main sections. The first acts as an introduction by giving a very brief history of the ILP from its foundation in 1893 until 1938 and then discussing the ILP's organisation, underlying political philosophy and policies; while the second section takes a chronological look at the history of the ILP during the period 1938 to 1950.

This is a story of ultimate failure but of honest, if naive, endeavour and of supreme faith in the judgement and latent political sense of the ordinary working man and woman, which is not, perhaps, a bad epitaph for a socialist party.

Abbreviations

BUF	British Union of Fascists
CAB	Cabinet Minutes and Papers
CIA	Central Intelligence Agency
CND	Campaign for Nuclear Disarmament
CPGB	Communist Party of Great Britain
CW	Common Wealth (Party)
DBC	Don Bateman Collection
EC	Executive Committee of the ILP
FJC	Francis Johnson Correspondence
HC	House of Commons Debate Reports 5th Series
HO	Head Office
ILL	Independent Labor League of America
ILP	Independent Labour Party
ILPer	Member of the ILP
ISP	Independent Socialist Party
LAB	Ministry of Labour Papers
LSI	Labour and Socialist International
MFGB	Miners' Federation of Great Britain
MO	Mass Observation
MP	Member of Parliament
NAC	National Administrative Council of the ILP
NCF	No-Conscription Fellowship
NEC	National Executive Committee of the Labour Party
NUDAW	National Union of Distributive and Allied Workers
NUR	National Union of Railwaymen
NUWM	National Unemployed Workers' Movement
PLP	Parliamentary Labour Party
POUM	Partido Obrero de Unificación Marxista
PPU	Peace Pledge Union
PSOP	French Socialist Party of Workers and Peasants

RCP	Revolutionary Communist Party
RPC	Revolutionary Policy Committee
SLP	Socialist Labour Party
SOs	(PLP) standing orders
SPGB	Socialist Party of Great Britain
TUC	Trades Union Congress
UNRAA	United Nations Rehabilitation and Relief Agency
USDAW	Union of Shop, Distributive and Allied Workers
USSE	United Socialist States of Europe
WIL	Workers' International League

SECTION 1

Introduction

———

1

The ILP 1893 to 1938

———————

The Independent Labour Party (ILP) was founded in Bradford in 1893 with a socialist programme and the declared aim of securing the election of working men to Parliament independent of the Liberal Party. In 1897 it sought to forge a political alliance with the trades unions and in 1900 it was one of the founding organisations of the Labour Representation Committee, which became the Labour Party in 1906.[1] Although affiliated to the Labour Party the ILP retained its own membership (ILPers), organisation and policies while at the same time acting as one of the main conduits through which individuals could work within the Labour Party. At the end of the First World War, however, the Labour Party adopted a new constitution which seemed to commit it to a socialist programme and allowed individual members to join local Labour parties. This 1918 constitution spelt the end of the ILP's special position within the Labour Party. The ILP lost its guaranteed seats on the Labour Party's governing body, the National Executive Committee (NEC), but more importantly it was no longer the main avenue for individuals wishing to join the Labour Party nor could it now claim to offer a unique socialist path to the future.[2]

Clearly the ILP needed to find a new role if it was to remain a distinctive organisation, particularly after the Labour Party adopted many of the ILP's policies in the early 1920s.[3] But it gradually became apparent that there were two visions within the ILP of what this future role should be and this created in turn two groups pulling in different directions. One group, led, after November 1922, by the Parliamentary Labour Party (PLP) leader, James Ramsay MacDonald,[4] argued that in future the ILP would have no need of its own policies and programmes or separate electoral organisation, and should become instead a think tank, socialist educational body and propaganda machine for the Labour

Party.[5] The other group, spearheaded in the 1920s by the Scottish and Lancashire ILP branches and in Parliament by the Clydeside group of ILP MPs including John Wheatley,[6] James Maxton,[7] David Kirkwood[8] and Campbell Stephen,[9] refused to envisage a purely propaganda role for the ILP. Some within this latter group, who have been accused of adopting a patronising posture regarding the Labour Party,[10] were fundamentally opposed, for historical, political or personal reasons, to subordinating the ILP to the Labour Party, while others were 'radicals' influenced by Marxism or Guild Socialism.[11] This increasingly influential radical faction regarded Parliament as 'territory occupied by the class enemy'[12] and, while ready to use the House of Commons as one weapon in the fight to achieve a social revolution, were highly suspicious of MacDonald and the others they saw as 'reformists' or 'gradualists' who believed that socialism could be achieved over time by parliamentary means. These radicals would not accept, therefore, a passive supporting role for the (Independent Labour) Party and believed instead that the ILP was more suited than the reformist Labour Party to be the vanguard party which would lead the socialist revolution in Britain.

Clashes were inevitable between these two groups, with their very different views on the future of the ILP and on the way ahead for socialism, and these came to the fore during the Labour Party's two periods of minority government in the 1920s. The cautious approach of both the first and second Labour governments to social change and to the relief of unemployment, during what appeared to many to be a time of major crisis for capitalism, particularly dismayed the radical ILP faction. They were also incensed by the fact that many of the 'reformist measures' to which they objected were both introduced into Parliament and subsequently supported by MPs and government ministers who claimed to be members of the ILP, despite the fact that official ILP policy, as laid down at the ILP's annual conferences, now often reflected the views of the more radical elements of the Party.[13] Indeed the pro-Labour-Party ILPers, who wanted the Party to become purely a propaganda body, had begun to move away from the ILP and to work within the Labour Party's new organisation. That left the ILP's main organs in the hands of those who still believed that the ILP had an independent political role to play. This was symbolised at the April 1926

ILP annual conference both by the election of James Maxton, the most prominent member of the radical ILP faction in Parliament, as Chairman of the Party, and by the adoption of a new programme called *Socialism in Our Time* which, though possibly more proto-Keynesian than pure socialist, was quite distinct from the Labour Party's official policies.[14] This programme, which was initiated by the ILP Treasurer, Clifford Allen[15] and popularised by H. N. Brailsford,[16] the editor of the ILP's newspaper the *New Leader*, had as its main plank the creation of a living wage. According to the economist and ILPer J. A. Hobson,[17] raising the spending power of the working class would end the under-consumption of goods and services, which, he believed, was creating unemployment, and that in turn would mean the end of poverty.[18]

The radical faction in the ILP attacked the Labour Party and the trade unions for not supporting the 'Socialism in Our Time' policy and was also incensed by what it saw as those organisations' inter-class collaboration after the failure of the General Strike in May 1926. In June 1928 James Maxton produced, along with A. J. Cook, the General Secretary of the Miners' Federation of Great Britain, a manifesto calling for 'an unceasing war against poverty and working-class servitude', which was a thinly disguised attack on the Labour Party's co-operation with capitalism, and may have been a response to the talks taking place at that time between the industrialist Sir Alfred Mond and the President of the TUC, Ben Turner, which aimed at finding common ground for co-operation between owners and workers. The Cook–Maxton Manifesto proposed a series of meetings and conferences throughout the country to discuss its aims. The meetings were a failure, but the manifesto worsened the split within the ILP between the radicals and the reformists and widened the rift between the ILP and the Labour Party.[19]

But the quarrel between the two groups, with their differing concepts of socialism and of the future of the ILP, finally came to a head during the second Labour government. The radical ILPers, usually led in Parliament by Maxton and Wheatley (until his death in May 1930), continuously attacked the Labour government's domestic and foreign policies and called for a bolder set of socialist policies, to deal with unemployment and economic depression, based upon the nationalisation of key industries and the introduction of a living wage.

Those ILPers remaining loyal to the government, orchestrated by Emanuel Shinwell,[20] tried to curb the activities of the radical ILP MPs in the Commons by taking control of ILP Parliamentary Group policy meetings, and endeavouring to prevent the adoption by the Group of an anti-government stance on any proposed legislation. The radical ILPers retaliated by attempting to ensure that only MPs who accepted ILP conference decisions could continue to call themselves ILPers and attend those ILP Group meetings.[21]

That struggle reached its climax in 1930 when the ILP annual conference in Birmingham instructed the ILP's administrative body, the National Administrative Council (NAC), to reconstruct the ILP Parliamentary Group to include only those MPs who accepted ILP policies as laid down by annual conference.[22] At the same time the Labour Party re-emphasised the standing orders (SOs) of the PLP which insisted that Labour Party MPs should accept and support majority decisions of the PLP and so effectively prevented them from voting against the Labour government.[23] In other words, just as the ILP was forcing its MPs to decide whether their loyalty lay with the ILP or the Labour Party, the Labour Party was attempting to stop the radical ILPers from continuing their attacks on the Labour government. Of the 140 or so MPs who were nominally members of the ILP, all but 18 refused to accept the ILP's hard line on the Labour Party and were expelled from the Party. The remaining ILP Parliamentary Group then informed the PLP at the end of 1930 that it could no longer accept the PLP's standing orders without amendment.[24] The NEC had in the meantime begun refusing to endorse ILP parliamentary candidates who would not commit to the PLP's SOs.[25] Meanwhile the clashes between the radical ILP MPs and the government in the Commons became even more acrimonious, as the ILP Group insisted that the Labour government should stand or fall on a radical socialist programme.

In August 1931 the Labour government did fall when the Cabinet split over further public spending cuts and was replaced by a National Government which was led by Ramsay MacDonald and included a select few of his erstwhile Cabinet colleagues. In the subsequent general election in October both the Labour Party and the ILP lost a large number of seats. The Parliamentary Labour Party was reduced to 46

MPs, and the ILP Group now consisted of just five MPs.[26] Far from bringing the ILP and the Labour Party together, though, this disaster seemed to drive them further apart. The ILP radicals claimed that the actions of MacDonald and his Labour Party colleagues who joined the National Government merely proved that the Labour Party was reformist at heart. The Labour Party, on the other hand, argued that the defection of MacDonald demonstrated the necessity for unity and discipline. For that reason it refused to countenance any continuation of the attacks on Labour Party policies by the ILP MPs while the ILP remained under the Labour Party's umbrella and so would not consider revising the PLP's SOs to accommodate the ILP MPs. For their part the ILP MPs now considered that they represented an independent group outside of the PLP and were no longer bound by its SOs.

That position became a reality in July 1932 when an ILP special conference held in Bradford voted by 241 votes to 142 in favour of disaffiliating the ILP from the Labour Party.[27] This rupture between the two parties had been precipitated by the question of the enforcement of the PLP's SOs but clearly the causes of the disagreement went far deeper than that. The Labour Party was now a mass party with its own policies, its own branches and with the knowledge that it had become a party of government. It had no further need for the ILP and was embarrassed and angered by the ILP radicals who attacked its social and economic policies in Parliament and who competed against it in the country for working-class support. Meanwhile, the ILP no longer had any faith in the Labour Party's ability or inclination to deliver the social changes which the ILP believed were necessary to achieve a socialist Britain. The ILP now argued that it was the only party capable of bringing about the transition to socialism and it believed that within a short time the working people of Britain were certain to realise this and to turn to it.[28] The Party felt moreover that it had become independent at just the right time because it was believed by many socialists that the Great Depression proved that capitalism had reached a crisis point. This was bound, the Party argued, to produce a revolutionary consciousness amongst the British workers[29] and they in turn would look for a revolutionary party to guide them to the socialist utopia. Free from the shackles of the Labour Party the ILP could now become that revolutionary party.

Unfortunately for the Party, the special conference decision on disaffiliation had not been accepted by all elements of the ILP. Moreover some ILPers were particularly unhappy about the Bradford conference's allied decisions to cut off relations with the Co-operative Movement and to forbid ILPers to pay their union levy if it was to be sent to the Labour Party. The implications of both these decisions were to drive a further wedge between the ILP and the wider Labour Movement.[30] Many moderate ILPers did not want to cut their ties with the Labour Party or that wider Labour Movement, and as a result three months after disaffiliation the NAC admitted that 10 per cent of ILP branches had disappeared and by November 1932 203 branches had been lost out of a pre-disaffiliation total of 653. The Party suffered particularly serious losses in its previous strongholds in Scotland, Lancashire and Yorkshire and even those branches which remained suffered catastrophic declines so that within a year the ILP had lost half its pre–1932 membership and one of its five MPs, David Kirkwood,[31] while another, Richard Wallhead, resigned in September 1933. Any influence the Party had enjoyed within the trade union movement had also drained away and its representation in local government had been decimated. It was only the presence of the very small but highly vocal group of ILP MPs in the Commons which now kept the Party in the public eye.

These losses in branches and membership were soon exacerbated by the factional fighting which developed within the ILP after disaffiliation. Disaffiliation had been passionately advocated by a group of London-based communist ILPers which called itself the Revolutionary Policy Committee (RPC).[32] The RPC wanted the ILP to become a revolutionary socialist party and it (along with the influential ILPer Fenner Brockway[33] and others) strove to persuade the 1933 and 1934 ILP annual conferences to adopt a more revolutionary socialist programme, which downplayed the role of Parliament and advocated instead the formation of workers' councils that the RPC believed would be the main weapon of the working class in establishing socialism. This programme was opposed within the Party by the self-styled Unity Group, based in Lancashire, East Anglia and London, and by both the much-loved ILP veteran F. W. Jowett[34] and the respected writer and leading ILPer John Middleton Murry.[35] These ILPers were antipathetic to the existence of organised party factions and wanted the ILP to remain committed to the parliamentary road, and to an ethical rather than revolutionary socialism. When the Unity Group's position failed to carry the 1934 ILP annual conference, its members left the ILP and formed the Independent Socialist Party (ISP).[36] In October of the following year the RPC, frustrated and weakened by its failure to persuade the ILP to affiliate to either the Communist Third International (the Comintern) or to the Communist Party of Great Britain (CPGB), left the ILP and joined the CPGB.[37]

During that period, moreover, approximately 100 Trotskyists joined the ILP and in 1934 formed the Marxist Group. They opposed the RPC, and unsuccessfully attempted to persuade the ILP to help form the (Trotskyist) Fourth International. The Marxist Group, with the support of Fenner Brockway, also tried to get the ILP to support the use of 'workers' sanctions' against Italy after Italian forces had invaded Abyssinia in October 1935. But this policy was opposed by the ILP Parliamentary Group, of James Maxton, George Buchanan, John McGovern, and the newly re-elected Campbell Stephen, who argued that sanctions of any kind were a prelude to war and that there was little to choose between the Abyssinian and Italian dictatorships; and the ILP 1936 annual conference, despite initially voting in favour of workers' sanctions, was subsequently persuaded, by Maxton's threat to resign on this issue, to accept the Parliamentary Group's position.[38] Shortly afterwards the highly vocal, but largely unsuccessful, Marxist Group split and most of its members left the ILP to form a new Trotskyist party.[39] Dr Charles Smith,[40] the Party Chairman, wrote in the July 1939 edition of the ILP's internal typescript magazine *Between Ourselves*, that during the mid–1930s, 'loyal Party members' had become fed up with and disheartened by the incessant intrigue and bickering caused by this succession of party factions, and he claimed that an enormous amount of energy had been diverted 'from our fight against capitalism to our fights with one another'.[41]

However, despite, or perhaps because of, this internal wrangling, it became clear to the ILP's leaders that the Party would have to strengthen its contacts within the Labour Movement if it was to retain any influence and credibility while it waited for the workers to abandon the Labour Party. The ILP had little hope of joining with the smaller socialist parties, the Socialist Party of Great Britain (SPGB) or the Socialist Labour Party (SLP), as they were exclusive sects which would have no truck with other political parties whether or not they claimed to be socialist.[42] The Trotskyist parties were at that time too small to have much influence on British politics and were in any case busy trying to gain strength by working within the ILP and the Labour Party. But the CPGB seemed a much more likely candidate for joint action with the ILP as both were now avowedly revolutionary socialist parties, were of similar size and had established links in the wider Labour Movement. The ILP had indeed welcomed the Russian Bolshevik Revolution in October 1917, and continued to broadly support the Soviet Union as the first workers' state. Moreover in both 1920 and 1933 the ILP had briefly considered working with the Comintern.[43] The ILP and CPGB now began an uneasy period of collaboration which was to last for the next six years. They appeared together during demonstrations and public meetings on behalf of the National Unemployed Workers' Movement and against the Means Test.[44] From March 1933 they formed a United Front against the fascists' regimes which were then springing up in Europe, and collaborated in struggles against the British Union of Fascists (BUF), including during the famous Battle of Cable Street on 4 October 1936. But throughout this time their joint campaigns were marred by mutual suspicion and political intrigue as both parties jockeyed for position within the left of the Labour Movement and attempted to attract members from each other.[45]

The mutual hostility between these two socialist parties, which was never far below the surface, erupted in 1937 into open political warfare both over the parties' support for rival Republican elements in the Spanish Civil War, and the Communists' call for a Popular Front against fascism. In July 1936 civil war broke out in Spain between on one side the Nationalist Coalition, led by General Francisco Franco, consisting of the bulk of the armed forces and the National Front of monarchists, Catholics and landowners, and supported militarily by Benito Mussolini, the Italian prime minister and Adolf Hitler, the German Chancellor, and on the other the Republican government which included communists and revolutionary socialists amongst its supporters, and was aided by Joseph Stalin, the leader of the Soviet Union. The ILP sent food, medical supplies and later a small contingent of fighting men to help its sister party, the Partido Obrero de Unificación Marxista (POUM), which was holding part of the Republican front line in Aragon.[46] Meanwhile the CPGB was supplying men and material to the International Brigade which was fighting for the Republican government in the region around Madrid. Both British parties were in theory supporting the same side, but the political situation in Spain was complicated by the different aims of some of those fighting for the Republic. In Catalonia the outbreak of war had resulted in a quasi-socialist revolution in that region, led by the anarchist trade unions and supported by the POUM. As a result, in Catalonia the Republican forces became bitterly divided. The communist and liberal forces believed that the defeat of Franco and his allies should take precedence over the introduction of revolutionary social change, while the anarchists and POUM argued that their first priority was to save the gains of the socialist revolution in Catalonia.[47] Fighting between these two Republican factions broke out in Barcelona in May 1937 and this led to the disarming of the anarchists and the suppression of the POUM by the Republican government. Some members of the POUM and a few of their comrades from the ILP contingent were arrested and the communist parties in Spain and in Britain accused the POUM and the ILP of being Trotskyists and agents of fascism.[48] The ILP violently denied these charges and accused the Communists in turn of putting the interests of the Soviet Union before those of the Spanish workers. This led to bitter hostility and mutual recriminations which poisoned relations between the two parties.

This occurred in the middle of the most important campaign that the ILP and CPGB had organised together. In January 1937 the two parties, in collaboration with the left-wing Socialist League drawn from the Labour Party, began the Unity Campaign against fascism and in favour of building a mass movement for socialism.[49] The three groups held a number of well supported joint public meetings but the campaign was undermined by the Labour Party's decision to disaffiliate the Socialist League and to make any sort of association with this campaign incompatible with membership of the Labour Party.[50] The CPGB responded by trying to form a Popular Front against fascism, like those already established in France and Spain, to include not only communists and socialists but also Liberals and radical members of the Conservative Party. The ILP bitterly attacked the idea of co-operating with non-socialists, calling it political opportunism and a betrayal of socialist principles, and the Party withdrew its support from the campaign.[51] Moreover, the ILP had begun openly criticising the foreign policy of the Soviet Union, and attacking what it saw as a lack of democracy and equality within Russia. In particular it protested about the trials of old Bolsheviks which were then taking place in Moscow. It called the proceedings a fraud and demanded an international commission to investigate the allegations against the accused.[52] The CPGB was furious and repeated its claims that the ILP had fallen into the hands of the Trotskyists and was in danger of becoming a wing of fascism.[53]

Because of the vehemence of their attacks on each other, and the deep-seated political differences these disputes revealed, it became impossible for the two parties to continue working together. As a result, the ILP's participation in the quest for a broad unity of left-wing forces in Britain ended and the ILP was forced to reconsider its place within the Labour Movement and in particular its relationship with the Labour Party. Disaffiliation had not, as Maxton was forced to admit to the NAC in August 1939, brought the expected benefits for the Party so eagerly awaited in 1932.[54] The ILP had failed to attract large numbers of new recruits; indeed it was steadily losing members to the Labour Party, to the CPGB and to the small Trotskyist parties. Its attempt to replace the Labour Party as the party of the working class had failed, as its disastrous showing in the 1935 general election clearly proved, when it only managed to hold on to its four seats in Scotland despite fielding 17 candidates in specially targeted constituencies across Britain. The Party was becoming increasingly weak, isolated and impotent just as socialism's nemesis, fascism, was beginning to spread its evil tentacles throughout Europe. It was apparently going to need a new direction and sense of purpose if it was to survive and continue to play a part in British politics.

2

The ILP's
Organisation and Membership

The basic organisational unit of the ILP was always the local branch. The Party had originally grown from the bottom up[1] and so the pattern of branch distribution was far from regular, and branch demarcations bore little relationship to constituency boundaries.[2] In the Shettleston constituency in the East End of Glasgow, for example, the Party had four branches covering an area divided up into two municipal wards,[3] while in Norwich there was only one ILP branch although the Party was electorally active in several wards. Branches also varied in size. In 1945 the Neath ILP branch had only four members while at the same time Norwich ILP claimed to have nearly 1,000 on its books. But the available evidence suggests that by 1942 most branches had fewer than 25 members.[4]

Ideally local branches were organised together into Federations. The branches in a Federation sent representatives to monthly or sometimes quarterly meetings where local problems were discussed, campaigns and demonstrations organised and general tactics co-ordinated. However, these Federations usually only functioned properly when several branches were sited close together so that communications were quick and easy. Therefore, in those areas like Wales and the West Country where the ILP was weak and its branches thinly spread, Federations, which might have had a useful part to play in welding these weak elements into a stronger unit, could not be maintained. It was only in the large cities where communications were good that Federations flourished and even there they were subject to serious disruption as travel became difficult during the Second World War.[5]

However, all the branches, and their Federations, were organised into

Divisions. There were nine of these: Scotland, the North East, Yorkshire, Midlands, East Anglia, London and the South East, the South West, Wales, and Lancashire.[6] Before 1932 Scotland and Lancashire were the two strongest Divisions. Disaffiliation seriously weakened both of them, and then in 1934 the defection to the ISP of Elijah Sandham, the NAC's Lancashire representative, and his followers practically destroyed the Lancashire ILP.[7] East Anglia now boasted the largest number of members on its books,[8] though Scotland remained the Division with the greatest number of active ILPers, followed closely by London. Lancashire, Yorkshire, and the Midlands Divisions were numerically roughly the same size. The South West Division was slightly smaller and its ILPers were mainly concentrated in a few blocks leaving the rest of the Division's geographical area unmanned. The North East Division had even fewer members who were even more geographically concentrated, but they included a hard core of extremely active ILPers, particularly in the industrial field, making this Division a strong Party centre. The Welsh Division after 1932, however, was in a sad state. Less than two-score ILPers huddled together in a handful of branches cut off from the main areas of ILP strength by poor communications. A strong branch survived in Merthyr but the rest of the Division was stagnant, and it defied repeated attempts by the ILP's Head Office to revive it.[9]

Branches sent delegates to annual divisional conferences where resolutions for submission to the ILP's annual conference were discussed and voted on, branch reports were given, and a Divisional Council elected. These Divisional Councils, which consisted of an elected chairman, secretary, and any other officers that were considered necessary,[10] plus, usually, representatives from each of the branches in the Division, met at regular intervals to co-ordinate activity, arrange propaganda campaigns, and organise municipal or parliamentary election contests. In Divisions where a large number of branches made the composition of the Divisional Council unwieldy an Executive Committee was sometimes appointed which met frequently and transacted much of the routine business arising between meetings of the full council.

Ideally Divisions appointed a full-time Divisional Organiser. His[11] many functions included following up enquiries received by ILP Head

Office or the Divisional Secretary from people living in the Division who were interested in joining the ILP but who were not within the catchment area of an existing branch. The Organiser would contact the enquirer and, as long as the Organiser was convinced that this potential convert was a genuine socialist who understood what joining a small party like the ILP would entail, attempt to persuade him or her to form a local branch.[12] If the new recruit did agree to form a branch, the Organiser would assist him or her with the initial arrangements and propaganda work, sometimes taking on the job of branch secretary himself until the branch was firmly established. His other duties included ensuring that the existing branches in his Division were carrying out their work to the best of their ability, arranging for people to sell the ILP's newspaper in places where the Party did not have a branch, and addressing public meetings, as well as helping the branches in any way he could. All in all being an Organiser could be a difficult and onerous job.[13] However, it was also expensive to have a full-time Organiser and occasionally branches complained about the cost and argued about the Organiser's duties,[14] and only the Scottish Division was able to maintain one on a full-time basis throughout most of this period. During financially difficult times, some Divisions had part-time Organisers for short periods, or shared an Organiser with another Division, but most often had to rely on either the efforts of volunteers acting as unpaid Organisers during the evenings and weekends, or the occasional loan of the General Secretary, John McNair, from Head Office.[15]

ILP policy was decided at the Party's annual conference at Easter. Every branch, which had been in existence since before the previous 31 December and had paid in full its affiliation fee to the National Administrative Council, was eligible to send at least one delegate with voting powers.[16] Branches which could not for some reason send their own representative might empower either a delegate from another branch, or from the Division, to carry their vote for them. In practice this system of voting, which guaranteed at least one vote for each branch whatever its size, made little allowance for differences in actual branch membership or financial contributions to the Party. The Scottish Division, therefore, which generally contained the largest number of both branches and members of any Division and consistently made the greatest contributions to the Party's funds (often more than all the other Divisions put together), did not automatically have the dominant voice at the conference, though it could usually have relied on controlling about one quarter of the conference votes if it had so wished. But that Division rarely presented a united front on any issue and so clashes between it and the rest of the Party did not normally occur, though it did occasionally lead revolts against the NAC's actions.[17]

Resolutions passed at the annual conference became ILP policy at once, though a two-thirds majority was needed to make any changes to the Party's constitution and rules, which enshrined the aims and objectives of the ILP and the rules governing how it should be organised and run. However, if on any serious matter a delegate or delegates believed that the conference was unrepresentative of the Party as a whole they could ask for a special conference to be held on that particular issue (and indeed individuals or branches could ask for such a conference to consider any 'special business' at any time). The special conference would then be called by the NAC if two thirds of its members or one third of the ILP's branches requested it. It was also possible to call for a plebiscite or ballot of the whole party membership to decide an issue. However, it was not easy to obtain and collate the opinions of every single member of the party[18] (particularly during the war), and so this expedient was rarely used, except to fill NAC National Member vacancies between conferences.

Most problems which arose between annual conferences were dealt with by the NAC. This body consisted of one representative from each Division, elected at the relevant divisional conference or by specially convened branch meetings, plus four National Members and a Chairman and National Treasurer elected by the delegates at the ILP's annual conference. The Party's General Secretary,[19] a paid official, also acted as a non-voting ex-officio member of the council, as did the Political Secretary.[20] As its name suggests the NAC was intended as an administrative rather than an executive body. The structure of the NAC had been revised in 1906 in an attempt to decentralise power in favour of the Divisions because of the vital importance given to local ILP identity and autonomy[21] and this had left the council pitifully weak in comparison with the National Executive Committee of the Labour Party or the executive committees of the various communist parties. Attempts between 1923 and 1925 to enhance the position of the NAC had been defeated through the resistance of the Divisions, but at the 1934 and 1935 annual conferences, in line with the Party's move at that time towards a more revolutionary socialist stance, reforms were passed which were intended to strengthen the central management of party policy and activity.[22] To implement this so-called democratic centralist control, the Executive Committee (EC) was reinstated.[23] This was elected from the NAC and usually consisted of a representative of the Parliamentary Group, plus the Party Chairman, Treasurer, the General and Political Secretaries and one or two other NAC members. The EC was intended to meet every six weeks and to have an explicitly executive role, to be responsible for the operational activity of the ILP, and to decide the NAC's agenda. At the same time an Inner Executive, elected by the EC, was established to be responsible for financial, organisational and disciplinary matters and to lead the ILP if the Party was ever declared illegal. The composition of this body is unclear, but it seems to have been made up of the Parliamentary Group together with the Political Secretary and one leading member of the NAC. It generally met in a House of Commons Committee Room.[24] Unfortunately for this democratic centralist experiment, both the EC and Inner Executive became dominated by the Parliamentary Group, and after that Group clashed with the rest of the Party over the question of workers' sanctions during the Abyssinian crisis, the Inner Executive gradually lost its leadership role and withered away,[25] and the EC became an ad hoc committee which met when the Party Chairman or the General Secretary thought fit, to take decisions on matters which had arisen between any of the six annual meetings of the NAC.[26] The EC was answerable to the NAC and the NAC was answerable to the annual conference. The NAC also elected from amongst its own members (though it could also call on other ILPers if necessary) a series of sub-committees to tackle particular parts of its duties. There were, for example, permanent sub-committees dealing with the Party's finances, its organisation, and its publications. Ad hoc sub-committees might also spring up on occasion to deal with such subjects as the ILP's by-election contests, or a specific political campaign. In 1939 there were 26 such sub-committees and, in addition, boards containing NAC members were appointed to manage the ILP newspaper; the Blackfriars Press, and the ILP Trust funds. Moreover, NAC members might also be expected to represent the ILP on the councils of other organisations domestic or international.[27] Being a member of the NAC could, therefore, involve a substantial time commitment above and beyond that required by its six annual meetings.

The NAC could not make policy decisions so could only implement those taken by conference, though the council would occasionally interpret its instructions in such a way that it would try to lead the ILP in a particular direction; and after the 1934 reforms it set the annual conference Agenda, which gave it the opportunity to control what subjects would be debated. It was also empowered to make rule changes with the support of two thirds of its members, though any changes could be overruled if either a third of branches or two thirds of Divisional Councils objected within two months. This power was rarely if ever used.[28] Moreover, the Party's constitution guaranteed branches full autonomy in the direction of their own affairs as long as they observed the rules and constitution of the ILP and abided by conference decisions.[29] Branches were very jealous of their rights, generally resisted centralising tendencies, and were likely to react angrily to any interference, however well-intentioned, from the NAC, the Divisional Councils or the Federation Committees.[30] They (and the Divisions) would also reprimand the NAC at the Party conference if it had acted contrary to their wishes.

The NAC's democratic centralist control was effectively lost after 1936, partly because of its own failure to present a united front on key issues.[31] However, the NAC did retain certain useful powers. It could adjudicate in disputes between branches and expel branches or individuals who had broken the ILP's rules (although those expelled could appeal to the next annual conference). It exercised a determining voice in the selection of parliamentary campaigns, and parliamentary candidates. But most usefully it had the right to 'raise and disburse funds for general or by-elections and for other objects of the Party'.[32] This meant that the NAC controlled the purse strings. Every member of the

ILP in employment was expected to pay 6d (2½p) per month in affiliation fees (unemployed members and housewives paid 3d). Of this 6d, 2d was kept by the branch, 2d was paid to the relevant Division and 2d was sent to Head Office for the NAC's use. In addition each branch was expected to pay a levy, called the Quota Fund, based on its membership numbers, which was also shared between the NAC and the Divisions.[33] Moreover, after the Derby conference of 1933 the ILP introduced a new device for raising money, The Power For Socialism Fund (also known as the Power Fund), which was based on a personal levy on the individual members, related to their income, and collected via a donation box kept in each ILPer's house. Usually half of this money also went to Head Office and was partly used to subsidise the Party's newspaper.[34] In the Great Depression and during the Second World War it was obviously not possible for all ILPers to contribute as much to party funds as the NAC expected. It was already an expensive party to belong to as some branches asked for an affiliation fee of 1/- (5p) per month instead of 6d.[35] There were frequent complaints from the NAC that branches were not meeting their financial obligations,[36] and direct appeals had to be made in the ILP's newspaper for donations to keep that party organ going, or for money to cover operating and election expenses. However, the NAC was still receiving a relatively large sum of money from the branches while they were often in financial difficulties.

Moreover, the NAC had access to additional sources of income not open to the branches. During the ILP's early years it had found it difficult to gain access to meeting halls and printing facilities. Thereafter, money donated to the Party by sympathisers had been used to acquire suitable buildings and a printing business. In 1901 the ILP had established Labour Leader Limited, a company designed to control the printing of the party newspaper, the *Labour Leader*.[37] Seven years later the ILP set up National Labour Press Limited with its printing offices in Blackfriars Street, Manchester. This limited company bought out the Labour Leader Limited and proceeded to print the *Labour Leader* and to undertake some private printing work.[38] In August 1915 E. Whitley (Blackfriars Press) Limited, of the same address as the National Labour Press Limited, changed its name to the Blackfriars Press Limited and came directly under the control of the ILP, only ILP members being eligible to buy its shares.[39] This company was a very successful printing concern, having contracts to print amongst other things Nestlé products' labels and the *Municipal Year Book*. In 1922 these two companies moved to Leicester, although the name Blackfriars Press was retained. After disaffiliation the ILP founded a subsidiary company to the Blackfriars Press called Fiction House Limited, which was apparently used to print a series of 'rather shabby', but profitable, paperbacks for one of the chain stores.[40] The profits made by the Blackfriars Press and its subsidiary allowed those concerns to provide free printing (and a supply of paper) for the *New Leader*, as the Party's paper was now called, and the ILP's various pamphlets during some of the most difficult periods of the war.

To protect its investments, as neither the NAC nor the ILP itself were legal entities, the council decided in 1915 to set up ILP Trust Limited.[41] This company was empowered to buy or acquire in any legal way property, real or personal,[42] and to use the capital and income 'to aid and further the work of the ILP, and the interest of the workers in general, particularly in the field of electoral activity and in the acquisition of halls and social clubs'. The articles of association specified that if the company should be wound up, the assets could only be transferred to the ILP or used in the interests of the working class.[43] A number of ILP branches had also acquired their own property and there had been a danger that in some instances this could be lost to the Party after disaffiliation. However, in a test case concerning the Hamilton branch of the ILP, Lord Pitman, Senator of the College of Justice in Scotland, decided that disaffiliation was not against the constitution of the ILP and therefore the pro-affiliation majority in the Hamilton ILP had no right to seize the branch property and take it into the Labour Party with them.[44] In the same way the property of defunct ILP branches could usually be claimed by the Party and passed to the ILP Trust Limited.[45] The money from the sale of such property or the profits from investments made by the ILP Trust Limited could be put directly to use by the ILP, as directed by the NAC. The profits made by the commercial printing concerns could not be used so freely, though the Blackfriars Press would usually make an annual donation to the ILP via the ILP Trust Limited.[46] Moreover, those companies' boards of directors were largely composed of NAC members who received salaries which they gave to party funds.[47] These sums appeared in the ILP's financial statements under the general heading 'donations', and in some years the money acquired in this way, along with the money raised by the Party's frequent appeals for funds, amounted to many times more than that sent in by the branches as affiliation fees; and for much of the period under discussion both Head Office and the Party newspaper were heavily dependent on donations to meet their day-to-day costs.[48]

Although the NAC had access to sums of money far in excess of those available to the individual branches or the Divisions, one or two branches remained self-sufficient,[49] and the Divisional Councils had income from their share of the affiliation fees and the Quota and Power funds which they could use to assist branches in defraying the cost of propaganda campaigns or election contests.[50] But generally any large expenditure required additional financial support from the NAC. This meant that the council had the initiative in all the major activities of the ILP. Yet it would be wrong to assume that the NAC was able to dominate the rest of the ILP. The flirtation with democratic centralist control in the mid-1930s had not been a success, and many ILPers were proud of the fact that under the Party's constitution 'the ILP had Officers, not leaders'[51] and they were very suspicious of any attempts by the NAC to give the Party a strong lead. This suspicion may have been heightened by an apparent difference in the class makeup of the NAC compared with the Party as a whole.[52] The ILP seems to have had a predominantly working-class membership and its main electoral support came from staunchly working-class wards in Glasgow, Great Yarmouth, Merthyr and Norwich.[53] The NAC on the other hand contained a large proportion of people in middle-class occupations.[54] In 1939–1940, for example, of the 14 NAC members whose occupations can now be established, only three were manual workers still employed in their industry, one was a full-time union official and one a railway clerk, and all the rest were in what would normally be described as middle-class professions, including one manager, two journalists and no less than four schoolteachers. This NAC is fairly typical in composition of the various councils elected between 1933 and 1946; indeed there was a considerable continuity of personnel. During 1946 and 1947, however, a number of leading ILPers left the Party through death or resignation and the composition of the

NAC altered, the balance swinging much more in favour of manual workers. Until that time, though, many ILPers may have agreed with J. T. Abbot, a veteran ILPer from Lancashire, that the NAC was composed mainly of 'petite bourgeoisie with no training and actual experience of working class conditions of life'.[55]

Yet class antagonisms were seemingly not a vital factor in the relationship of the NAC to the rest of the Party. Some ILP working-class members who managed to attend one of the Party's (political) summer schools left appalled at the end of the week having come in contact there with many middle-class 'cranks'.[56] And the Scottish and North Country ILPers were fond of attacking London 'intellectuals' who, they claimed, had an unhealthy effect on the Party's Head Office and NAC.[57] But there is no evidence that there were any political repercussions from these apparent class differences and the same men and women were elected to the NAC year after year as National Members and party officials which would seem to suggest that they retained the confidence of the rank and file of the Party. Moreover, the NAC did not dominate the ILP partly because the leading members of the council had no desire to do so. Maxton, for example, the ILP's charismatic, much-loved and emblematic leader, was generally reluctant to impose his will on the Party, and Brockway, though influential, was too much the libertarian socialist to try.[58] Most NAC members had spent many years in the Party and seem to have valued, as much as the rank and file did, the libertarian constitution and structure of the ILP. This was to mean, though, that the NAC was frequently hesitant and divided and the ILP faced the difficult years from 1938 to 1950 without firm direction,[59] the consequences of which were often vacillation and weakness.

3

The ILP's Political Beliefs

———————

The Objective of the ILP, as stated in its constitution, was the establishment of a socialist commonwealth. From its birth in 1893 until 1932 one of the Party's principle methods of trying to achieve this objective was through an attempt to secure for the working class control of both national and local government. And it has been claimed that for many ILP branches the electoral side of their activities, especially in the parliamentary field, was a 'constant stimulus underlying three quarters of the fine work' they did for the Party.[1] However, the experience of two Labour governments in the 1920s reinforced the belief of the radical ILPers, and, indeed, convinced many other ILPers, that a policy of gradual reform would not work and that socialism would never be achieved through Parliament. The 1933 annual conference, therefore, partly under the influence of Fenner Brockway, the Party's Political Secretary; the Party's General Secretary John Paton, and the RPC, adopted a resolution calling for the formation of workers' councils. Seemingly analogous to the Russian Soviets of Workers' and Soldiers' Deputies, these were to act as the primary instrument in the workers' struggle both for the protection of their rights against encroachment by the capitalists and for carrying through the revolutionary takeover of power.[2] The bulk of the ILP, including James Maxton, was convinced at that time that even if the working class should achieve a majority in Parliament it would still have to fight the forces of reaction if it was to make any progress towards socialism; and this could be done by the workers' councils, not by socialist MPs.[3] Parliamentary action was therefore, 'relegated to the sphere of lesser activities'[4], though it was not abandoned altogether. It was recognised by the Party that it was possible, for example, to use Parliament as a means of wringing some concessions from the capitalist class, and for obtaining information during the course of debates and question times that would not normally be available to a small political party[5]. Moreover, the Commons had the added attraction of being a prominent public platform from which the ILP believed revolutionary socialists might use the publicity which always surrounded parliamentary debates to expose the capitalist system and the futility of gradualism and thereby spread the socialist message to a wider audience.[6] This viewpoint was accepted by the majority of ILPers and remained the orthodox ILP line until the Party lost its last MP in 1947.[7]

At the same time, the disaffiliated ILP adopted a revolutionary socialist stance on the question of social reform,[8] and this move away from gradualism was accompanied by a declaration that the ILP was now a Marxist party.[9] At this time the Party was still inspired by the Soviet Union, which had, after all, carried through what appeared to be the first successful socialist revolution and, moreover, now seemed to be the only major power not affected by the world slump.[10] Appropriately James Maxton wrote a book about Lenin in 1932 and made him the subject of his lecture to that year's ILP summer school. The Party now believed it was becoming a revolutionary socialist party, and toyed with the idea of joining, or at least co-operating with, the CPGB in the face of the supposed imminent collapse of capitalism and the growing fascist threat.[11]

Many ILP branches organised classes in Marxist theory, and some even required applicants to show knowledge of this theory before they could be accepted into the branch.[12] The *New Leader* carried articles on Marxism, and the Party's correspondence course on socialism run by some of the ILP's leading academics had a high Marxist content.[13] But the ILP's propaganda, public utterances and internal debates show little real Marxist influence. For the majority of members of the ILP, Marxism seems to have played a relatively small part in the formation or expression of their political ideas. Most of them appear to have arrived at their convictions through their own personal experiences and then used odd bits of Marxist terminology to give them a verbal tool to explain some of these beliefs.[14] The ILP's spokesmen often treated Marxism in the same cavalier fashion. Maxton, for instance, insisted that the British workers should be wary of adopting Marxism wholesale, and once told an audience that the dictatorship of the proletariat meant simply majority rule; and Brockway claimed that he 'accepted a good deal of Marxism *but not its materialism*'.[15] And at the 1943 ILP annual conference one amendment to a resolution stating party policy attempted to commit the ILP to the 'materialist conception of history as the basis of its socialist activity' but was overwhelmingly defeated.[16] What the ILP did accept from Marxism was the belief that 'all the social, political and economic evils which face us ... are the inevitable accompaniment of capitalism, and that the fight against capitalism must be conducted on the basis of the class struggle, nationally and internationally'.[17]

The ILP, however, even during the height of its revolutionary socialist phase, never defined satisfactorily what it meant by revolution, or agreed on whether it expected a socialist revolution to be accompanied by violence.[18] In 1933, during the debate on workers' councils, Brockway stated that the ILP did not support the 'insurrectionary view', although he did qualify that statement by hinting that the situation might be different if the Army supported the revolution.[19] But John McGovern MP and Dr Charles Smith amongst others in the ILP seemed at that time to be willing to advocate a violent takeover of the government if the workers could somehow obtain arms.[20] Yet on the day the Second World War broke out the Yarmouth ILP Press Correspondent informed the local newspaper that the ILP only used the term 'revolution' in a philosophical and economic sense.[21] Meanwhile Maxton was calling on the British people to rise spontaneously without any guidance or preparation and overthrow the government, thus ending capitalism and the war in one great act.[22]

Maxton's call for spontaneous action on the part of the workers was in keeping with what seems to have been the underlying political philosophy of the ILP at this time. It appeared above all else a party with strong libertarian socialist leanings and a respect for the freedom of individuals and of political units which was reflected in its own ultra-democratic structure and constitution and which arguably made it an unsuitable party to lead the socialist revolution.[23] Indeed Maxton claimed that there would be 'no revolution in this country until revolution appeals to the mass of the people as an intelligent and common sense thing to do',[24] which seemed to limit the ILP to a propaganda role while it waited for the workers to come round to its point of view. Moreover, this libertarian socialist tendency was strengthened in the late 1930s by the entry into the Party of Walter Padley who rapidly became the ILP's Industrial Organiser and the NAC representative for London. Padley was a disciple of the Polish Marxist Rosa Luxemburg,[25] and shared her belief in the creative energies of the ordinary people and her distrust of highly centralised parties which attempt to dictate to the people how they should act. He propagated Luxemburg's theories whenever he could in both speeches and pamphlets, and he and those who thought like him managed to exert enough influence within the Party to add the names of Luxemburg and her German colleague Karl Liebknecht to the ILP's roll of heroes.

However, it was the ILP's contact with Spanish anarchism which was probably the main cause of the accentuation in the late 1930s of the Party's libertarian socialist strain. Some ILPers, including Maxton, counted the writings of the anarchist Peter Kropotkin[26] amongst their earliest influences.[27] They now had the opportunity to see anarchist theories being put into practice in Catalonia where the local anarchists were dominating the social revolution which had followed the outbreak of the Spanish Civil War in 1936. The ILPers who fought in Catalonia during the civil war and their colleagues who visited the area brought back glowing reports of the tremendous strides made by the Catalonian anarcho-syndicalists[28] towards the creation of a communistic community despite the dislocations caused by the war.

At this time the ILP was particularly receptive to these libertarian socialist and anarchist ideas because it was becoming increasingly disillusioned with state socialism as practised in the Soviet Union. This was partly the result of the loss of the influence of the communist RPC, which had left the Party in 1934, but the Moscow Trials of so-called Trotskyists, and the activities of the Communist Party in Spain[29] helped convince the ILP that the Russian Revolution had produced, not the socialist commonwealth it had dreamed of, but a totalitarian state run by a rigid bureaucracy.[30] Moreover, the Party's loss of faith in parliamentary action and its adoption of the concept of workers' councils caused it to revive its interest in industrial action. The ILP had supported the concept of workers' control of industry since 1922 when it had officially endorsed the Guild Socialism programme.[31] Now it began to show an interest in the use of the general strike as the main working class weapon against any attempt by a capitalist government to take the country to war.[32] The ILP appeared to be moving towards a syndicalist position, and the Spanish experience was bound to strengthen this trend.

Yet, the Spanish example also seemed to show the ILP that anarcho-syndicalism was not the complete answer to modern political problems. Brockway noted that the Spanish anarchists had been forced by circumstances to join the Republican government,[33] and although many ILPers accepted that their socialist utopia might closely resemble that of the anarchists, and were hostile to state socialism,[34] they still believed that the state, once it was controlled by the workers, would have an important part to play in the development of a wholly socialist country. Therefore many of the ILP's leading thinkers seemed to be attempting to create a synthesis between libertarian socialist or anarchist beliefs and communist thought which would combine all that they found noble in anarchism with all that they considered to be practical and realistic from Marxism.[35]

However, it would be wrong to suggest that all ILPers were following quite the same path at quite the same speed (or that they all remained constant in their beliefs[36]). The ILP, like most political parties, was effectively a coalition (sometimes, it would appear, held together as much by social activities and friendships as by political beliefs[37]) and contained within it several different strands of socialist thought. John Aplin, a former ILP Industrial Organiser and London NAC representative, left the Party in 1941. Six years later, in a letter to *Tribune*,[38] he claimed that the ILP was composed of '(a) Pacifists, varying from those with a Leftish tinge to those who are primarily socialists with a pacifist background, (b) Trotskyists, varying from a strongly organised cell to its fringe supporters; (c) Left socialists who feel the need for a party not tied to the policies and actions of the Labour Party and (d) Socialist purists who long for the return of the pioneering days'. Aplin did not indicate the relative proportions of these various groups, but his letter does suggest the political complexity existing within the ILP. There seem, though, to have been few socialist 'purists' in the ILP at this time.

One or two of the Party's pioneers, including Fred Jowett and Willie Stewart, stayed with it when it disaffiliated, and the Party seems to have attracted a small number of 'socialist "cranks"'.[39] But generally the ILP's policies were considered anything but pure by other socialist parties,[40] and purists were more likely to be attracted by the Socialist Party of Great Britain or the Socialist Labour Party[41] than they were by the ILP.

There has also been a tendency amongst some ex-ILPers to over-emphasise the importance of the Trotskyist elements in the ILP, given that the Trotskyists only ever dominated a handful of ILP branches, seem to have consisted of no more than 100 or so individuals, and were politically divided amongst themselves.[42] The evidence suggests that the ILP was feeling its way towards a new revolutionary philosophy during the years following disaffiliation and, having rejected the RPC's Stalinist approach, it found itself developing in some similar directions to those being taken by Trotskyists. But the Party's Trotskyists were never able to persuade the ILP to affiliate to the Fourth International or to adopt any of their other policies, and were forced to accept that even the ILP's left-wing members differed from them on a number of questions 'both fundamental and tactical'.[43] However, the Trotskyists in the Marxist Group, which operated within the ILP from 1934 to 1936, and the much smaller number of Trotskyists who remained in the Party after 1936, were subsequently blamed by some former ILPers for the ILP's revolutionary line during this period, in the same way that many ILPers later blamed the machinations of the Communist Party of Great Britain (working through the RPC) for the Party's decision to disaffiliate from the Labour Party in 1932.[44]

The influence of the pacifist elements within the ILP during this period has also been exaggerated by its opponents and by some observers.[45] The Party was consistently anti-militarist and generally anti-war,[46] and there was, it is true, a large pacifist minority in the ILP, but no pacifist resolutions were passed at any ILP annual conference during the period from 1932 to 1950, and the ILP's opposition to the Second World War was based on socialist principles which were shared by other parties who could never be described as pacifist.[47] A few ILPers did advocate peace at any price during the Second World War,[48] but that was never the Party's official policy and the majority of ILPers were committed to fighting to defend a socialist Britain.[49] Indeed, the Party had a thriving armed forces branch from early 1943 and the ILP never attempted to dissuade ILPers or other socialists from joining the armed forces.[50] Some ILP slogans may have sounded pacifist,[51] and the Party's leadership was willing to work with other anti-war and peace organisations, including the Peace Pledge Union, on specific issues such as the defence of conscientious objectors and the protection of civil liberties, as long as those organisations did not advocate peace at any price and allowed the ILP to proclaim its socialist interpretation of the war.[52] But that is no reason to assume that pacifism dominated the Party at that time, nor does the evidence support such an assumption. It is only in the 1950s, when, perhaps indicatively, the ILP was led by a succession of pacifist Party Chairmen, that the Party adopted and espoused a clearly pacifist line.[53]

Most ILPers seem to have come within the group that Aplin called Left socialists. However, these definitions are of little use when considering the alignment of forces in the major ILP controversies during this period. Pacifists and Trotskyists could be found, for example, on both sides of the debate concerning reaffiliation to the Labour Party in 1945, and revolutionary socialists in the ILP might be found either in uniform during the war or working on the land as conscientious objectors as their individual consciences dictated.

It should also be noted that there was a group of Christian ILPers. Despite the Party's formal attachment to Marxism (which is generally hostile to religion, which its sees as a conservative force), the ILP still contained a number of men and women who were active church members. Campbell Stephen was a Congregationalist (and former priest), and John McGovern a practising Catholic. Maxton has been described by a close friend as 'a religious socialist – his religion being humanism' and Maxton often talked of the need of awakening within people 'faith as a religious conception, an ethical conception'.[54] The ILP also had a number of lay preachers amongst its most active members, and a few branches were dominated by Quakers.[55] Many other ILPers had attended socialist Sunday schools in their youth and they still carried with them the strong moral sense that they had acquired there.[56] There was, however, no easy correlation between the religious beliefs and the political views of ILPers; some religious ILPers were reformist, some were revolutionaries.[57] But there does seem to have been a strong moral or ethical strain running through the ILP's propaganda and in its activities which would seem to owe more to a religious influence, or at least to the ethical teachings contained in Robert Blatchford's *Merrie England*,[58] and in the writings of William Morris,[59] R. H. Tawney[60] and John Middleton Murry,[61] than it does to a narrow interpretation of the teachings of Karl Marx.[62]

The ILP contained, therefore, a variety of different types of socialists who identified to a greater or lesser extent with the Party's drift towards revolutionary libertarian socialism. However, despite all their differences the vast majority of ILPers seem to have accepted what Ian Bullock has called the 'ideological bedrock of the ILP', which was 'a fundamental commitment to socialism, democracy and the spirit of egalitarianism'.[63] Moreover, most ILPers agreed on the kind of society they wished to see resulting from their political activity. This common ideal was summoned up in the ILP constitution's definition of a socialist commonwealth[64] as:

A classless society in which all economic resources are commonly owned and controlled, the power to live by rent, interest and profit is ended, all forms of monarchical or hereditary government is abolished, and all perform work of social value according to their ability and share in the common resources according to their need, and in which the willingness to perform work of social value is the basis of citizenship.

4

The ILP's Propaganda Work

———————

A mongst the membership's responsibilities enshrined in the ILP's constitution is the injunction that 'in all its works the ILP will disseminate as widely as possible a knowledge of socialist principles'.[1] The ILP, and others on the Labour Left, had since the earliest days of the Labour Party carried out the bulk of the socialist propaganda work in the Labour Movement,[2] and the ILP still believed after 1932 that it was particularly suited, because of its experience and the purity of its socialism, to remain the major force in this field.[3] It looked on electoral contests as a key vehicle for its propaganda work and often fought them just to gain publicity for its socialist message. Yet these fights could not, and did not, constitute the bulk of the ILP's proselytising. General elections, for example, occurred usually only once every five years, and by-elections, although taking place fairly frequently were not always in areas where the ILP felt strong enough to mount a campaign. It was also apparent that the Party's message did not always get across distinctly in election campaigns. During parliamentary elections, independent observers and the ILP itself noted that constituents were not always clear about the differences between the ILP and the Labour Party, even after several weeks of campaigning,[4] and at local government level, experienced ILPers claimed that people voted more often for the individual than for the party or programme he or she espoused.[5]

Moreover, electoral campaigns were very expensive, and this limited the number the ILP could fight. Most branches, therefore, rarely if ever became directly involved in these contests[6] and so had to find other ways of fulfilling their propaganda duties. Some individuals could use their trade union activities as a way of spreading the ILP's message,[7] but the ILP Head Office suggested that for others the most effective way they could carry out this work was through their personal contacts, including by offering the use of their branch's hall or providing other assistance to organisations that might provide fertile ground for ILP propaganda;[8] and indeed local branches did assist the National Unemployed Workers' Movement (NUWM),[9] the Old Age Pensioners Association,[10] and the Glasgow Homeless League.[11] However, where there might have been an opportunity to make political capital out of one of these bodies, as for example in the case of the NUWM, the ILP often found that the CPGB had beaten them to it and were firmly established in the organisation![12]

Public meetings were therefore the main propaganda outlet for most branches. Some of the larger branches which had their own halls were able to hold such meetings every week, or at least once a fortnight.[13] However, the majority of branches were not lucky enough to have such good facilities and many had to hold their branch meetings in a member's home. Their proselytising work was usually, therefore, carried out through open-air meetings on street corners or in public parks, with an occasional indoor meeting in a hired hall.[14] In this way the ILP managed to broadcast its message in areas considered by the Labour Party to be unfruitful.[15]

Some large branches and many Divisional Councils ran classes in public speaking for ILP members,[16] and Head Office occasionally issued speakers' notes on topics of current interest.[17] Often, however, branches asked the local Divisional Council or ILP Head Office to send them a speaker.[18] The ILP had a panel of 'star' speakers comprising the Parliamentary Group, the Party's full-time officers, and a small number of other ILPers who had shown themselves to be good orators[19] and were willing to give up their weekends for the ILP. The members of this panel would normally travel to a branch and address one or two meetings over the weekend in return for their meals, a night's accommodation at a comrade's home, and the cost of their return fare.[20] But during the war, John McNair, the Party's General Secretary, frequently complained to branches that they were relying too much on the services of this overstretched panel, and in particular on Maxton and McGovern, and pleaded with them to use their own home-grown speakers for ordinary local propaganda meetings.[21] Moreover, some branches were considered too remote[22] to receive such weekend visits, but they would still occasionally have a guest speaker when McNair, or the local Divisional

Organiser, reached them during one of their regular tours of inspection.[23]

Occasionally the ILP would conduct a nationwide revivalist-style campaign, such as the one 'For a Socialist Britain Now' in 1942.[24] The campaigns themselves seem to have had only limited success, but they did encourage ILPers to take the Party's message into areas where its organisation was weak. Usually for these campaigns the ILP's star speakers were used in pairs, with each pair allocated a particular area to proselytise. Maxton, McGovern and Brockway were usually the main speakers, and would be accompanied by a 'junior' comrade, such as Will Ballantine, John McNair or Walter Padley, who were expected to begin the meeting by outlining the major points of the campaign. The main speaker would then present the ILP's more general case against the injustices of the capitalist system or against the war. Maxton was particularly good in this kind of situation, and his effect on an audience was said to be electric.[25]

Campaign meetings, branch meetings and election rallies were advertised by the branches through the local press and via posters and pavement or wall chalking.[26] Occasionally loudspeaker vans and poster parades were also used to advertise meetings or publicise ILP candidates, but the Party had few loudspeaker units at its disposal and, without a large local branch, parades were difficult to organise.[27] However, once the ILP had obtained an audience for a meeting it did its best to impress them. A reporter from the social research organisation Mass Observation noted that the ILP took more trouble to make its meetings look interesting than did the other major parties. The stage and hall were decorated with posters, and there were leaflets on all the chairs.[28] Branches also displayed their banners which normally bore the initials of the Party and the branch name,[29] and the ILP's own banner which consisted of a white flag with a circle in the middle containing the letter S intertwined with the initials ILP. After the war the ILP's Organisation Committee, in an attempt to make the Party's public meetings more attractive to the young, recommended that the Party affiliate to the Workers' Musicians Association so that bands could be made available at such gatherings.[30]

Yet no matter how interesting the Party made its meetings, it could not hope to reach many people that way. Maxton and McGovern could attract audiences of one or two thousand at public meetings in Glasgow, and a couple of hundred to similar events in England, but few ILPers had their drawing power, and local branch public meetings rarely drew more than a score of non-party members.[31] Then during the war some branches found it impossible to hold public meetings at all because of the blackout and bombing.[32] The Party's literature, therefore, had to carry the ILP's message to the masses. Party leaflets were distributed for free by the branches at public meetings and during election campaigns. They generally carried the bare outlines of the ILP's policies and were purchased from Head Office at 1/6d for 500 or 2/6d per 1,000.[33] Pamphlets, which carried fuller explanations of the ILP's policies, cost the branches 9d for 12, but they were expected to sell them at 1d each.[34] Branches in a Division often combined together to buy and distribute ILP literature to share the costs,[35] and Head Office would sometimes offer to exchange a quantity of new pamphlets for an equal number of unsold older pamphlets so that branches could obtain copies of the latest publications without losing a great deal of money in the process.[36] The pamphlets were usually well produced, on good paper with attractive cover designs and layout, and interesting (if sometimes misleading[37]) titles. Their range was also quite impressive for such a small party. Head Office aimed at issuing a new pamphlet every eight to ten weeks,[38] and was generally successful,[39] although some pamphlets were just reprints of ILP MPs' speeches from Hansard, or articles from the *New Leader*. But the majority were specially written pieces on topical questions, or more general expositions of the ILP's policies and programme.[40] There were also a number of works written by the Party's 'experts' on topics that concerned them and which Head Office believed would be of general interest.[41] Not surprisingly, the quality of the content of the pamphlets varied considerably. Some were well written; others seem pedantic and repetitive. They normally avoided the Marxist jargon so beloved of the CPGB at that time,[42] though some still talked in terms of the class war and a few were bogged down in tables and statistics.[43] But generally they expressed their points in simple language without talking down to their readers. They seem to have been aimed largely at the educated working man, though, as one critic of the Party has noted, when the ILP began to talk, as it sometimes did, of 'the revolutionary Marxism of Rosa Luxemburg or of the POUM, it might have been talking of the Athanasian Creed for all such terms meant even to the politically conscious in Britain'.[44]

However, sales of these pamphlets were never huge[45] and they did not constitute the bulk of the ILP's printed propaganda, which was supplied instead by the Party's newspapers. Some branches issued their own which contained local news as well as a socialist analysis of national and international events. The Bradford ILP paper, for example, edited by Fred Jowett,[46] ran for several years, but most branch newspapers were short-lived and copies have not survived.[47] A few branches sold their local news-sheets separately, but most included them within copies of the *New Leader*, and thus, they claimed, boosted the sales of that paper.[48] The Party's newspaper had been founded in 1889 as the *Labour Leader* by James Keir Hardie and was originally the organ of the Scottish Labour Party, though in 1893 it became the newspaper of the ILP. It was reorganised in 1922, when it changed its name to the *New Leader*, and again in 1934 when it attempted to boost its sales by becoming less parochial. By 1939 this weekly paper was selling between 20,000 and 30,000 copies a week, which compared well with the sales of the left-wing paper *Tribune* at the same time, but was a long way behind those of the CPGB's *Daily Worker*.[49]

The *New Leader* suffered the disadvantage of not consistently being sold by newsagents. Before the war they were reluctant to handle the paper because it sold for only 1d, which did not allow them to make a reasonable profit out of it. To try to overcome this problem, the ILP raised the price of the paper to 2d in January 1940 and compensated its readers by making it twice as long.[50] However, in May 1940 the National Association of Wholesale Newsagents decided to stop handling the *New Leader* and other anti-war newspapers, and so it completely disappeared from the newsagents.[51] It reappeared on some newsstands after the war, but sales through that avenue were never large.[52] Most *New Leader* copies were sold by ILPers calling door-to-door (which sometimes formed part of a local ILP Cycle Club's activities[53]) or by an ILPer with his or her street corner pitch, or by postal subscriptions, though postal sales rarely exceeded 1,000 copies a week. To encourage its members, Head Office

ran competitions to find out who was selling the most copies of the
paper. It seems some individuals were distributing as many as 300 copies
a week,[54] and their diligence was usually rewarded with a free place at
that year's ILP summer school. But despite such incentives, sales suffered
during the war, partly because of paper shortages but mainly through the
domestic disruption that could afflict both sellers and customers.[55] Sales
dropped to 11,000 copies per week in 1940, and, although there was a
brief revival at the end of the war when circulation reached 16,000, by
1948 it had fallen to 8,000 and as ILP membership in the post-war period
declined, the circulation of the *Socialist Leader*, as the newspaper was
called after 1946, fell to just a few thousand and it was eventually reduced
to being a fortnightly paper.[56]

The newspaper's primary target audience seems to have been the
manual worker, or at least those who identified with the working class.
The newspaper's content was primarily concerned with domestic
industrial disputes[57] and the inequities of capitalism both at home and
abroad. It carried little general news and, between 1939 and 1945, almost
completely ignored the military progress of the war. During Fenner
Brockway's time as editor, the *New Leader* carried a fairly full exposition
of the ILP's own case on most major issues through its articles and
editorials. But after he resigned as editor in June 1946, the newspaper
gradually adopted a less partisan position and featured a number of
articles by non-party members, and reports on foreign industrial and
political disputes.[58] This tended to weaken the value of the newspaper as
a propaganda tool for the ILP for, as one independent observer noted, it
became increasingly difficult for a reader of the *Socialist Leader* to
determine the ILP's stand on any particular issue.[59] Many articles now
carried an editorial footnote explaining that the writer was expressing
his or her own opinion and not that of the paper or of the ILP, but the
Party's official position on the particular issue was frequently not given
for comparison.[60] Yet no matter what the various editors did during
these years, they could not either satisfy the Party's rank and file or
increase circulation figures. Both the *New Leader* and the *Socialist Leader*
constantly lost money and had to be subsidised by donations from
readers and from ILP funds,[61] and at the same time ILPers had various
and often conflicting ideas about how sales could be improved. Some

complained that the newspaper's articles were too narrow and sectarian,[62] while at the same time others argued that the paper had become too highbrow, and was devoting too much space to non-socialist subjects such as film reviews and articles on Greek history.[63]

ILPers also, however, saw the power of other media as propaganda weapons, including film, and one of the ILP's main social activities had been the formation of branch film clubs. In 1938 the ILP acquired a film called *Blow, Bugles Blow* which had originally been made for the Labour Party by the Socialist Film Council. The hour-long film depicted a fictional and highly successful attempt by the workers of the world to stop a world war by calling general strikes in every country. The Labour Party had refused to accept the film in 1934 because it had changed its mind about the use of the strike weapon for this kind of purpose, but it still fitted in with the ILP's philosophy and, after the film's producer joined the ILP in 1938,[64] the Party showed *Blow, Bugles Blow* widely, until the outbreak of war, when it disappeared from view. Moreover, in 1938 Fenner Brockway, who saw the wider potential of this medium, asked the London Division to approach the Norwegian Labour Party, which had some experience in this field, for advice concerning the possibility of developing film propaganda, though nothing seems to have come of this.[65]

It was, however, the potential of radio which gripped the imagination of the ILP's propagandists. They realised that 'street corner methods' of propaganda could not compete successfully against the wireless,[66] and they were very angry when the BBC refused to allow them to state ILP policies over the air during the war and at subsequent elections.[67] In fact the ILP appears to have had a rather exaggerated faith in the power of radio propaganda. Both Maxton and Brockway, for instance, seemed to believe that a socialist government would be able to destroy Hitler merely by broadcasting over the radio its socialist peace offers to the German people who, on hearing them, would rise in revolt against Nazi tyranny and overthrow it.[68]

Perhaps paradoxically, in view of the importance attached by the ILP to its propaganda work, it is impossible to judge how successful the Party was in that field of endeavour, because by its very nature propaganda is a subtle weapon the effects of which are not easy to chart. The ILP's rise in membership during the war might be taken as an indicator of its success in spreading its message. However, a survey conducted by the ILP in the middle of 1945, when its membership was at its highest level for several years, indicated that the majority of the sample of ILPers questioned had become socialists and members of the Party because of their family backgrounds, their personal contacts with other socialists, or their own everyday experience of life. The reading of books and pamphlets had converted only a few, and public meetings had only won over about five per cent.[69] The sample was small and so possibly unrepresentative, but it must cast serious doubts on the claims made by some ex-ILPers that the ILP was an important and effective propaganda body which could have been of invaluable assistance to the Labour Party if it had been allowed to reaffiliate.[70]

5

The ILP's Social and Economic Policies

After disaffiliation the ILP was vulnerable to criticism that its social and economic policies were merely Labour Party policies plus the small amount necessary to make them more electorally attractive. This was a particular problem at local government level where ILPers had often worked in close harmony with their Labour Party colleagues, despite differences in outlook on some questions, right up to the time of disaffiliation. Immediately after disaffiliation this alliance broke down and ILP councillors found themselves in opposition to both the Conservative and the Labour parties. Labour Party councillors were quick to point out that the ILP was now opposing Labour Party proposals that it had apparently supported only a short time before.[1] Yet the ILP could not refrain from pitching its demands higher than those of the Labour Party. If it formulated a programme that was less radical than that proposed by the Labour Party it would have been accused, both by its critics and by the advanced sections of its own party, of being reactionary. If on the other hand it advanced proposals which closely resembled those of the Labour Party it could hardly claim at municipal or other elections to be an alternative to that party. Therefore, it had always to be more radical than its larger rival.

It would be unfair, however, to give the impression that the ILP merely tried to outbid the Labour Party. It realised the electoral value of having an advanced social policy,[2] but it genuinely did seem to have a more radical outlook on social questions than the majority of Labour Party members. After all, the break between the two parties stemmed from the ILP's belief that the Labour Party was adopting a timid approach to the social and economic problems caused by the Great Depression. The basic difference between the parties was a vital one. Despite its libertarian socialist tendencies, the ILP firmly believed that the state owed its citizens a living. In return for the useful work that each citizen was expected to perform the ILP believed that the state, even the capitalist state if it could be forced to accept its responsibilities, had a duty to provide the individual with the opportunity to enjoy a happy, healthy and productive life from the cradle to the grave.

At its most utopian this view led the ILP to call for the state to supply every citizen with food, clothing and shelter free of charge.[3] But generally its demands were more practical. For instance, the ILP proposed a free integrated national health service as early as 1930.[4] And the Party at local and national level carried on an unceasing battle to try to force central government to provide free milk for working-class children and the opportunity for them to obtain school meals so that they should grow up healthy as well as educated. In the field of education during the 1930s the ILP was calling for a unified system for all children from nursery school to university.[5] Apparently the ILP did not show the same interest in the question of the selection of children on the basis of intellectual ability that was beginning to concern some members of the Left.[6] But the Party was very anxious to end the encouragement of class differences which it believed was inherent in the retention of fee-paying schools.[7] The ILP did, however, have a problem over the question of who supplied non-fee-paying schools. Maxton said that he supported secular education as the ideal solution, but he did not wish to divide the working class 'by religious antagonisms'.[8] The existence of church schools, and in particular Roman Catholic schools, was a thorny problem for the ILP, because some ILPers were Christians and, perhaps more importantly, many of its supporters in its Glasgow heartland were Roman Catholic and so it had to tread carefully on this issue for fear of losing their support.[9]

The ILP, along with many others of the Left, wanted the school-leaving age raised to 16 years.[10] The Party argued that in the short term this should ease the unemployment problem and would also improve the children's education, which would be a long-term gain for them and for the community. Maxton, as a former schoolteacher, was more concerned, however, with obtaining a good all-round education for children than with any immediate benefits to the community that raising the leaving age might bring. He therefore proposed that education should be dominated by cultural rather than industrial needs. He also claimed that the quality of teaching should be the primary concern of any educational plan. This meant attracting well-qualified people into the profession by paying good wages and cutting class sizes, even if that implied that in the short term the raising of the school-leaving age would have to be delayed.[11] Maxton also had a particular interest in adult education, which was shared by many of his colleagues in the Party.[12] But the ILP was primarily concerned with trying to obtain maintenance grants for working-class children for the time that they were at school or university so that they could take full advantage of the available educational facilities (and remove the burden of their financial support from their parents) while they were young rather than having to catch up on their education later in adult life.[13]

Once the child had finally finished its education the ILP expected the state to provide it with a job,[14] or full maintenance, at a living wage. Under the ILP's proposals this living wage was to be established by a commission with input from trade unions, consumers and producers and would 'represent the minimum standard of civilised existence which should be tolerated'.[15] Here, as in all ILP policies, there was no discrimination between the sexes. The Party expected the state to provide a job for every woman who wanted one, and free nurseries to enable mothers with young children to work if they wished.[16] Moreover the ILP believed in equal pay and equal unemployment and sickness benefits for men and women.[17] During the Second World War the ILP urged trade unionists to give women brought into industry full union rights so that the unions could be strengthened and the women would not be treated as second class citizens.[18] Moreover, Campbell Stephen attacked the disparity in the level of compensation paid to men and women (and in particular housewives) disabled by enemy action.[19] The ILP had, indeed, despite the under representation of women in its own decision-making bodies,[20] a long tradition of supporting equal rights for women, though it was less vocal in its championship of issues like abortion on demand and birth control – probably, again, because it was anxious not to offend its Roman Catholic supporters.[21]

The ILP campaigned vigorously for increases in the pensions of those retired through old age or ill health. The ILP was pressing for an old-age pension of £1 per week in the mid–1930s[22] at a time when the Labour Party's National Executive Committee was telling its rank and file that a pension of that size on a non-contributory basis, which was what the ILP was suggesting, was unlikely to be achieved because money for it could not be raised by 'feasible or acceptable taxation'.[23] Yet within a few years the country was spending vast sums on armaments, a fact that the ILP was not slow to point out.[24]

To complete its package of proposed social reforms the ILP called for a national plan to provide sound, healthy houses for all workers at affordable rents. The Party suggested that this could be done by building the houses under public control and with direct labour which it insisted would cut costs. The ILP also wanted central government to give local authorities interest-free loans so that existing council houses could be maintained and new homes built without having to charge the current tenants higher rents.[25] This housing policy was always a key feature of the ILP's social programme but after the Second World War, when unemployment was much less of a problem, housing became the most important item in this programme and the subject of much Party propaganda.[26]

However, clearly the most unusual feature of the ILP's social programme was the provision for financing it. The Party claimed that it was unjust to expect the workers to pay anything from their wages towards the amelioration of the social conditions caused by the capitalist system.[27] The ILP therefore opposed either contributory systems to cover sickness and unemployment benefit or insurance schemes for retirement and disability pensions.[28] Moreover, the Party would not accept the need for any means tests. Any worker or worker's dependent, therefore, would obtain full benefits under the ILP's programme. The ILP also wanted to end the collection of rates from all but the rich and to provide all municipal services free of charge.[29] Instead the rich were expected to bear the full cost of these services in the short term through a capital levy.[30] The ILP also proposed that all wealth, including land, should be conscripted and turned over to public use. Then once all capital had been conscripted it intended to introduce a 100 per cent tax on personal incomes over a certain amount (fixed at £500 per annum in 1939).[31] In this way, the ILP believed, the money would be found to pay for its policies and at the same time the current financial inequalities in society would be eradicated.

The ILP realised that this expropriation of wealth could only be a short-term method of funding its schemes. Even if all the country's wealth was in public hands, and there was the greater flow of spending money in circulation that the Party expected would result from paying a living wage and higher pensions and from taking less from the workers' pay packets in rents and insurance contributions, it accepted that there would still not be enough money in the economic system to keep the social services going indefinitely. The ILP's solution to this problem was to insist that the nation should 'plan for plenty'.[32] This entailed immediately 'socialising the commanding heights of the economic system', which included, in addition to land, all banking and finance (especially the Bank of England), transport, and the production of iron and steel, coal, power, plastics, rayon and chemicals. With these assets, financial institutions and industries under public ownership – the non-socialised industries subject to production controls, and investments being regulated through a National Investment Bank[33] – government could plan a budget which balanced production, investment, infrastructure costs and consumption at the highest possible level and allow it to distribute the remaining industrial profits equitably through the social services. The ILP believed, therefore, that by equal distribution the economic and social basis of socialism would be established. The ILP did not believe that this plan would face any economic difficulties because it thought that Marx had proved that all so-called wealth in a capitalist system came from exploiting labour. Therefore, the ILP argued, it should be a simple matter for a socialist government to issue money to the same value as the total real wealth produced by the country, although quite how this was to be done was never clarified.[34]

Fred Jowett, ILP veteran and post-disaffiliation ILP National Treasurer until his death in February 1944, was accepted by the ILP as its financial expert. He was convinced, and the Party apparently agreed with him,[35] that inflation and all other monetary problems were caused primarily by the banks, who made their profits by producing vast sums of money in the form of loans for capitalist concerns. He told the Party that banks were allowed to lend up to the value of nine times the security they held. This they did, thus flooding the world's economic system with huge amounts of money which had no real backing. As for the 'gold standard', Jowett dismissed that as a swindle.[36] In fact the ILP showed little concern for the possible effects of its social and economic policies on the strength of the country's currency. The Party dismissed the orthodox economic theories of the day, including Keynesian economics, because they all seemed to suggest that it was possible to make capitalism work.[37] ILPers preferred to believe the ex-Liberal economist J. A. Hobson, when he seemed to suggest that British unemployment and other economic difficulties were caused by over-saving and underconsumption *in Britain*.[38] Therefore, argued the ILP, the export trade was relatively unimportant and so the value of Britain's currency on the world's market was irrelevant. Maxton pointed out, for example, that British exports in 1939 accounted for only 16 per cent of its national production, and that therefore it was ridiculous to give the export market any special attention.[39] The ILP proposed that there should be a state monopoly of foreign trade under which import and export boards would be set up which could ensure that all imported goods were necessities for the people and not just luxuries for the rich.[40] British industry could then concentrate on satisfying the needs of the home market first, and when this was done it would produce enough goods to exchange for the essentials that would have to be imported through the 'old Empire trade network' and newer alignments with other socialist states.[41] The ILP accepted that there might still be a trade gap, but it believed that, if defence and other unproductive government spending was drastically reduced, the resulting financial deficit would be small and easily absorbed by the country as a whole.[42]

A social policy, therefore, which contained some measures which were radical for the time but ultimately practical, was underpinned by an economic programme which was both revolutionary in intent and simplistic in outlook. The ILP had not solved the problem of formulating a reformist programme for a revolutionary party. It demanded social and economic reforms from a capitalist government the cost of which would have meant the destruction of the capitalist system.[43] Moreover, the ILP never gave the impression that it had a clear view of the economic system it would use to replace capitalism. It appears to have viewed capitalism as a system of private ownership which was evil because it resulted in maldistribution of goods and services. Therefore if the private owners of capital were expropriated and distribution was equalised the country's social and economic problems would disappear. It was an outlook hardly appropriate to the complexities of modern society.

6

The ILP's Industrial Policies

The ILP had always placed great store by industrial activity. All ILPers were expected to be members of an appropriate union,[1] and the ILP's programme called for 100 per cent union membership amongst the workers. Moreover, as the Party's faith in conventional political action began to wane, it put more and more emphasis on industrial activity, until by 1935 it declared that it should be 'the "spearhead" of the ILP's work when and where practicable'.[2] As a consequence, it attempted to build up its own industrial organisation. In 1938 it set up Industrial Organisation Committees in Glasgow and Manchester and formed an Industrial Sub-Committee of the NAC. Throughout the period under consideration it also tried to have Industrial Organisers in all its Divisions (paid or volunteer) to co-ordinate and report on ILPers' industrial activities in their regions, and this reached a peak in 1942 when all but one Division had a full-time paid Industrial Organiser.[3]

From a low point in 1932, by 1939 the Party had managed to build up its industrial strength until it had members on the executives of 12 unions, as well as at least one member on a number of district union committees and representatives on 52 trades councils, and during the war it boasted several delegates to the TUC.[4] The ILP's main footholds were in the National Union of Distributive and Allied Workers (NUDAW) (which later merged to form the Union of Shop, Distributive and Allied Workers (USDAW)); the National Union of Railwaymen (NUR); the Miners' Federation of Great Britain (MFGB), and the Chemical Workers' Union (CWU). It also had representation in the leadership of some of the white collar unions including the Post Office Workers' Union. The ILP could never compete in terms of union membership with the Labour Party or the CPGB, and its overall industrial position remained weak, but it did exert some influence due to the dedicated work of men like Walter Padley of USDAW, Will Ballantine of the NUR, Bob Edwards of CWU and Tom Stephenson of MFGB. Their loss to the Party in the late 1940s and early 1950s was to spell the end of the ILP's industrial strength.[5]

It was axiomatic in the ILP that all its members should work within the existing unions and not attempt to form breakaway unions as members of the CPGB sometimes did. The ILP considered these breakaway unions divisive because it believed that the majority of the workers could not be won away from the unions they had learned to accept as their own.[6] On the other hand the Party was far from happy with the existing leadership and structure of the unions. It believed that the unions were being led by reformists who were always ready to collaborate with the bosses even if it meant sacrificing the interests of the workers. The ILP rejected the kind of long-term wage settlements that it claimed union leaders were trying to make with the employers because the Party believed that such agreements prevented speedy and effective class action by the workers.[7] The ILP also supported all strikes, except demarcation disputes, even if they were declared unofficial by the union officials. The ILP argued that the workers did not suffer the hardship of a strike unless they had a genuine grievance and that if they did not get union support that must be because the union leaders were reactionary and out of touch with their rank and file.[8]

The ILP therefore waged intermittent war on the leadership of some unions, often lecturing them on how they should run their unions, and criticising their handling of industrial negotiations;[9] and the Party also tried to encourage the growth of a Shop Stewards' Movement built on small, factory-based Shop Stewards' Committees. Such organisations would obviously be easier to infiltrate and control than the executive councils of the unions, and some ILPers were alive to the possibilities that this offered the ILP.[10] But the ILP's philosophy generally and genuinely favoured the independence of small units, and the Party continued to favour the idea of a Shop Stewards' Movement even though it could never match the influence that the CPGB exerted amongst shop stewards.[11] The ILP wanted to see the creation of a national system of shop stewards and workshop committees, directly answerable to the workers on the shop floor, which would be responsible for negotiating *all* local conditions of work.[12] The ILP saw this as a step in the direction of industrial democracy, but only a small step, for the Party believed that with the growth of monopoly capitalism workers could no longer adequately protect their rights, let alone improve their status, while they relied on the old craft unions.

Most unions had grown from national amalgamations of local craft unions. Even the 'new' unions, which had been formed at the end of the 19th Century to cater for the unskilled or semi-skilled workers, tended to be dominated by groups of workers who were linked by a common work function.[13] This meant that most industrial factories contained men organised into a variety of unions jealously guarding their own rights and privileges, which often led to demarcation disputes and allowed employers to play the unions off against each other during wage negotiations. All these difficulties, the ILP argued, could be avoided if the men were organised into one union for each industry rather than one union for each craft, but the Party did not take the next logical step and advocate one huge union for all workers as it argued that such a union would be too unwieldy to be effective.[14] The ILP also recognised that although craft unions were obsolete the 'crafts' themselves were not dead and that 'workers in any craft have not only their own traditions and pride of workmanship, of which they are justly jealous, but also problems of management and conditions distinct from those of other crafts in the same industry'.[15] The Party seemed to believe, however, that the autonomy of the crafts could be protected within a system of industrial unions though it never explained how. Nor did the ILP give any lead on the problem of how the difficult transition from craft to industrial unions was to be accomplished. The ILP appeared to believe that the rank and file could be relied upon to effect the change once it fully grasped the need for the creation of a new structure.

The ILP was partly interested in industrial unions as defensive weapons, arguing that individual employers (whether companies or the state) often had virtual monopolies in particular industries and so the workers needed to be organised in a monopoly union to challenge them effectively. But it was much more deeply invested in the idea of their long-term value as mechanisms the workers could use to obtain the complete control of industry, for it saw the potential of industrial unions as the bodies through which the workers would run industry after a socialist revolution. The ILP envisaged the creation of a parliament of industrial unions which could manage the whole of industry and would be a vital part of the socialist economy.

In such an economy, the ILP claimed, Britain's industries, now under what the Party envisaged as workers' control, would produce goods according to the national assessment of human needs and at fixed prices. They would buy their machinery and raw materials through state industrial departments and distribute their goods through state agencies in collaboration with the Co-operative Movement. This, the ILP argued, would allow the people total control over the industrial system. The ILP was clearly influenced by its brush with Spanish anarcho-syndicalism, but the Party came to accept that an industrial system based on the free association of self-contained industrial unions would be difficult to realise in an industrially complex country like Britain. It called, therefore, in 1949 for the setting up of a Planning Commission as part of its industrial plan for a socialist Britain.[16] This Planning Commission, elected by the people, would survey all the country's resources and make decisions concerning the use of raw materials, the setting of production targets and the planning for future production. The details of how this Planning Commission would work and how clashes could be avoided between this bureaucratic body and the parliament of the industrial unions, each under what the Party described as workers' control, were never spelt out.

The ILP had used the appealing but largely unarticulated slogan 'workers' control' for a number of years, but it was not until the Party was coming to grips with its new revolutionary socialist stance in the mid–1930s that it finally began to formulate its ideas on industrial democracy. The NAC statement presented to the 1935 annual conference, for example, talked of workers' control, but this apparently meant little more than an insistence on the workers' rights to select their own foremen and to control dismissals.[17] This programme was not expanded over the next four years, and the ILP directed most of its industrial propaganda towards securing the maximum participation by the workers in their unions. At this time the Party seemed divided as to whether the ill-defined workers' councils or the Shop Stewards'

Committees might be the right revolutionary tool for the overthrow of capitalism, and indeed whether workers' control would follow the revolution or precede it.[18]

With the outbreak of the Second World War the ILP concentrated its propaganda on the problem of maintaining existing union rights in the face of the government's emergency measures. However, a demand for the immediate introduction of workers' control of industry appeared in an ILP policy statement in August 1940.[19] Then Fenner Brockway articulated this demand in the course of his election address for the Lancaster constituency by-election in October 1941. Brockway claimed that the management of industry should be responsible not to private owners, but to central government and to the workers represented by works' committees.[20] The policy was further developed by the 1943 ILP annual conference, which passed a resolution demanding that all managers and administrators should be elected by the workers in a particular industry and subject to the overall control of a worker-elected central committee for each industry.[21]

For the next two years the ILP made no apparent attempt to develop this policy into a fully fledged programme. Most of its interest was centred on its anti-war activities and on day-to-day industrial problems. But in July 1945 a Labour government was returned to power with a mandate to nationalise many of the 'commanding heights' of the capitalist system. The ill-defined 'socialisation' of these same industries had long been at the core of the ILP's social and economic policies, and it now became a matter of some urgency for the Party to produce at least an outline of its proposals for how these industries should be run before the coming of the socialist revolution, if it were to show that it had a programme that was distinct from that of the Labour Party.[22]

However, it did not prove very easy to articulate an agreed ILP programme of socialisation to oppose the Labour government's nationalisation policy.[23] Most ILPers saw socialisation as differing from nationalisation over the question of control. Nationalised industries were normally run by boards of professional managers, while ILPers believed that socialised industries should be run by the workers themselves. But the details of how this was to be achieved were the subject of much debate. James Carmichael, for example, in his maiden

THE ILP'S INDUSTRIAL POLICIES

speech as an ILP MP in November 1946, called for more workers' control, but it was clear from what he said that he only meant more workers' participation on the nationalised industry boards.[24] This was obviously out of line with the thinking of the militants in the ILP who had moved on from that position ten years before, and Carmichael seemed unaware of the controversy which was raging in the ILP on this question at that moment. Will Ballantine had opened this debate in the *Socialist Leader* on 17 August 1946. He advocated a complicated system of control from the shop floor upwards with Shop Committees and Area Councils, drawn largely from the trade unions, and a complementary system of control from above with ministers chosen by Parliament acting as watch dogs on the industries and supervising various advisory councils and industrial boards which were intended to protect the interests of the consumers.

Some ILPers attacked Ballantine's reliance on the unions to provide the people for the committees. They argued that management was a different function from wage negotiation and so different men would have to be elected as managers from those whom the workers were used to choosing as union officials.[25] Moreover, it was not obvious to all ILPers that unions would be necessary after the socialisation of industry. Others seized on the question of parliamentary control. Some reiterated the argument that it would be necessary to have a separate industrial parliament, while others claimed that Parliament itself would be obsolete once industrial democracy was introduced and an industrial parliament set up through which the workers could settle all problems.[26] The debate continued irregularly in the columns of the *Socialist Leader* and in *Between Ourselves,* but little real progress was made. The ILP's official pamphlets and its published conference decisions on workers' control were all still couched in very general terms.[27] In 1948 the NAC was forced to admit that it seemed that 'workers' control cannot be attained inside a capitalist system, and that at the moment no blue print for it could be drawn and only time and experience would perfect the method'.[28] And F. A. Ridley, a former editor of the *Socialist Leader*, concluded that 'a good deal of the attractiveness of the slogan (workers' control) currently derives from its vagueness. If those who are continually extolling its importance were occasionally to define "workers' control" in exact terms, not *why*, which we all agree with, but *how* and *what* the workers should "Control", the slogan might acquire an actuality which it, at present, lacks'.[29] However, the ILP continued to use the slogan in an ill-defined way, trusting in the creative talents of the workers to find the right answers when the time for the introduction of workers' control arrived.[30] But once again it meant that the ILP was restricted to waiting on events rather than providing a clear lead which might have given it more impact in the Labour Movement.

7

The ILP's International
Contacts and Foreign Policies

From its inception, the ILP declared that it was an international socialist party dedicated to striving for the emancipation of the workers of all countries and for the establishment, initially, of a United (Socialist) States of Europe, leading eventually to the creation of a United Socialist States of the World. It claimed to recognise no barriers to co-operation in differences of race, colour or creed. The ILP accepted that there were cultural differences between peoples, but it considered these to be of small importance compared with the vast strength of the bonds which held them together. The Party always believed that there were only two nations, the rich and the poor, and that it was the ILP's job to make one nation of all mankind by overthrowing the rich and raising up the poor. This necessitated the ILP working on two fronts. It had to achieve the emancipation of its own exploited masses and those of Britain's empire, and at the same time join with its fellow socialists abroad in the worldwide struggle against capitalism and imperialism.

Co-operation with foreign socialists was difficult without some kind of organisation and so initially the ILP affiliated to the Second International, which was formed in 1889 and composed of socialist and labour parties. The ILP worked within this International until the outbreak of the First World War, when many of the constituent parties decided that their loyalty to their country came before their loyalty to their class. The International broke up, therefore, in some confusion in 1916 with only a small number of socialist parties, including the bulk of the ILP, continuing to call for united working-class opposition to the imperialist war, while the majority encouraged their members to join the armed forces or produce munitions for their fatherland.[1]

When the Second International reformed in 1920 it was a pale shadow of its former self. It consisted of the delegates from the social democratic parties of a small number of European countries, whilst the revolutionary socialist parties had nearly all joined the Third International (the Comintern) set up by the Russian communists in 1919. In August 1920 the ILP disaffiliated from the Second International because of that body's condemnation of both the German socialists (for supporting Germany's war effort) and the Russian Bolsheviks, and also over its support for reparations. The ILP then considered affiliating to the Third International. But this move failed due to both the opposition of some ILP leaders, including MacDonald, and the Third International's insistence on the need for an armed uprising to achieve socialism which was anathema to many ILPers: and so the ILP voted against joining the Third International at its 1921 annual conference. The ILP decided instead to join the small group of socialist parties meeting in Vienna which was attempting to form a bridge between the two Internationals. The International Working Union of Socialist Parties, or Two-and-a-half International as it was rather derogatorily called, struggled on with this impossible task until May 1923 when it dissolved and the majority of its constituent parties, including the ILP, merged with the Second International to form the Labour and Socialist International (LSI).[2]

Many ILPers, however, were not happy in the LSI. They believed that this organisation was not radical enough in its policies, or truly an International because so many countries were not represented. The Party's dissatisfaction with the LSI was widely known and in 1927 the ILP received a letter from the tiny International Bureau of Revolutionary Socialist Parties asking for a representative to consult with its permanent secretariat in Paris. The NAC asked Brockway to go and maintain a watching brief.[3] Three years later the ILP drew up a 'Basis for International Activity and Organisation' with four of the Bureau's small revolutionary parties,[4] and after the ILP disaffiliated from the Labour Party it left the LSI and joined with members of the Bureau in the (temporarily) renamed International Committee of Independent Revolutionary Socialist Parties.[5] However, despite a multiplicity of impressive titles that the Bureau adopted over the next few years, this so-called International was mainly a 'paper body' with few members and little real organisation. At the same time the ILP was flirting with revolutionary socialism which resembled in some ways Russian-style communism and the Party's rank and file, led by the RPC, pressed the reluctant NAC in 1933 into approaching the Third International again to discover how the Party could 'assist' in the work of that body. Negotiations dragged on for some time, but it eventually became obvious that the Third International would only consider co-operation on its own terms. It wished the ILP to become an affiliated party and to accept the strict discipline and party orthodoxy expected of the communists. The majority of ILPers were not ready to abide by these conditions and the talks broke down in a welter of mutual accusations and recriminations.[6] The RPC's attempt to get the ILP to affiliate to the Third International was soundly defeated at both the 1934 and 1935 annual conferences, and the majority of the RPC left the ILP.

The ILP now fell back on its contacts with the small group of disillusioned communists and revolutionary socialist splinter groups which made up the International Bureau of Revolutionary Socialist Parties. The Bureau's headquarters moved to London and were then dominated by the ILP, while Brockway became the Bureau's chairman. In February 1933 the Bureau sent a telegram to both the Second and Third Internationals calling on them to take united action against the Nazis in Germany, and in 1936 it organised an International Congress against War and Fascism in Brussels to which 156 delegates, claiming to represent 14 countries, came and discussed revolutionary socialist solutions to the world's international problems.[7] But this group of parties did not claim to constitute a true International, although its members agreed that the Second and Third Internationals had failed and that at 'the proper moment of historical development they may be prepared to unite in an International'.[8] In the meantime they preached class war and called for the revolutionary overthrow of the capitalist system. Like the Trotskyist Fourth International, which was formed in 1938 (and which the ILP refused to join), this organisation, including the ILP, pledged support for the Soviet Union, because it was the first workers' state, and called upon the workers of the world to resist any attempts by their capitalist rulers to wage war on it. Nevertheless the

Bureau criticised the bureaucratic leadership of the ruling Communist Party which it believed had robbed the Russian people of their full democratic rights, and over time it became, like the ILP, disillusioned with the Soviet Union's foreign policy.[9] The Bureau was anti-capitalist, anti-imperialist, anti-fascist and anti-war, but its specific aims were vague. It did not believe that it was possible to form an International simply by issuing a manifesto to which the workers were invited to subscribe, and it attacked as unrealistic the Trotskyists' attempt to do just that. However, this perspective left the Bureau's affiliated parties with little to do but hold meetings amongst themselves, exchange information, and carry out some propaganda work. In the long term the members were just waiting for the workers to start the revolution.

The ILP and some of the other affiliated parties sent aid and fighting contingents to assist the Bureau's Spanish representative, the POUM, during the Spanish Civil War. And for the next three years the constituent parties used the simple organisation they had set up to arrange the escape from fascist hands of a few socialists from Germany, Austria and Czechoslovakia. But the march of the forces of fascism and reaction across Europe during the late 1930s relentlessly destroyed the flimsy structure of the Bureau. By 1938 the Bureau, and its offshoot the International Workers Front Against War, claimed to have affiliated parties from Sweden, Holland, Germany, Italy, Spain, Poland, Palestine, Rumania, Bulgaria, and Britain. Moreover fraternal delegates attended its meeting from parties in America, Czechoslovakia, Greece and France.[10] However, many of these parties had a shadowy existence by 1938 and their presence amongst the list of affiliated parties must cast doubts on the Bureau's strength. By 1938, for instance, the socialist parties in Germany and Italy had been suppressed, POUM was under attack from the Republican government in Spain, and the Archio-Marxist Communist Party of Greece, which was apparently sending fraternal delegates to these meetings, had been persecuted for two years with notable success by the Greek dictator General Metaxas.[11] It seems likely that some of these parties were being represented at Bureau meetings by members living in exile. All the other parties were very small except for the French Socialist Party of Workers and Peasants (PSOP), which finally joined the Bureau in 1938, and the Independent

Labor League of America (ILL) which took an interest in the Bureau's affairs until 1941 when the ILL broke up.[12]

Once the PSOP had become a full member of the Bureau it was decided to transfer the Bureau's headquarters back to Paris.[13] Brockway remained the Bureau's chairman but the ILP's influence was weakened. In the face of Hitler's advance into Western Europe in 1940 the Bureau transferred its headquarters to New York and then, after the break-up of the ILL in January 1941, to Mexico. There two organisations were set up: the International Marxist Centre (also called the Revolutionary Marxist Centre), with Marceau Pivert of PSOP acting as its secretary, and the International Workers Front Against War (also called the International Bureau for Revolutionary Socialist Unity) which had Julian Gorkin of POUM as its secretary. These two men worked closely together sending out words of advice, encouragement and occasionally criticism to their colleagues in America and Britain.[14] There was initially some confusion within the ILP as to which of these two organisations the ILP now belonged,[15] but this was clarified by the NAC in 1942 when it told the annual conference that the Party was in fact affiliated to both.

Then in May 1943 the Russians dissolved the Third International, and the ILP reacted to what it saw as a betrayal of the workers by declaring that it would take steps to form a new International dedicated to international working-class unity.[16] Three months later the *New Leader* announced that the NAC had asked its Political Sub-Committee to prepare a report on this subject and to begin contacting revolutionary socialist parties in other countries. However, true to the ILP's libertarian socialist philosophy, the NAC declared that any new International could only arise from 'a mass upsurge of the workers', though it claimed that the ILP could help to lay the foundations, and in the event nothing came of this initiative.[17] After the war the ILP renewed its international connections with some like-minded socialist parties and with individual foreign socialists,[18] primarily in an attempt through socialist unity to prevent the outbreak of another world war. But the Bureau was not reconstituted, because after 1945 many of its constituent parties, including elements of POUM, had merged with their countries' larger labour or social democratic parties.[19] The Bureau had been strong in its condemnation of fascism and capitalism. Its members had fought in

Spain because they believed that they were fighting to protect a socialist revolution in Catalonia against the forces of fascism. But they could not take part in the Second World War and fight to save their comrades in Poland, Czechoslovakia, Romania and Greece because they believed that this was an imperialist war fought to protect capitalist interests.

The ILP felt particularly strongly about this question of the imperialist nature of any war in which capitalist Britain would be willing to fight. It was one of the ILP's deepest held beliefs that the British Empire was the most sinful institution of the modern world. Many ILPers were convinced that all the worst features of Nazi rule in Europe could be found duplicated in the British administration of the empire, and that it was pure hypocrisy on the part of the British Government to claim that it was fighting for democracy against tyranny.[20] Maxton called, for example, on the government to give total independence to Britain's African colonies,[21] and he spoke out in defence of Newfoundland after that colony's constitution had been suppressed in 1943.[22] But it was the plight of India which symbolised for the disaffiliated ILP the tyranny of British rule.[23] This was probably because India contained a huge population existing at near starvation level while Britain was apparently obtaining great riches from that country. Moreover it had a large and very vocal nationalist movement, led by the Congress Party, which claimed that it was ready and able to run India without British interference. The ILP had become involved in demands for Indian independence before the First World War,[24] and in 1924 the ILP presented a resolution at the Labour Party conference calling for the drawing-up of plans for self-government for India.[25] Two years' later its own conference passed a resolution demanding total independence for that country,[26] which was 12 years before the Labour Party made even an unofficial commitment to Indian independence.[27] After 1932 the ILP continued to place demands for freedom and self-government for India in the forefront of its propaganda,[28] and to treat this issue as a test case for Britain's claim to be a democratic country.

However, this support for Indian self-determination lays the ILP open to charges of inconsistency. In the first place the Congress Party, which the ILP supported, was not a socialist party in any sense that the ILP would normally have accepted. The ILP was therefore supporting a capitalist group in its struggles against a rival capitalist power, a thing which it refused to do either in 1935 when the Italians invaded Abyssinia or during the Second World War when the Axis Powers attacked a number of countries in both Europe and the Far East.[29] Moreover, many revolutionary socialists, including Rosa Luxemburg, rejected as a bourgeois idea the notion of national self-determination. Yet although Maxton once claimed that he could not understand loyalty to 'geographical areas',[30] here was the ILP supporting a movement which was fighting primarily for this bourgeois idea. The ILP defended itself by stating that it was prepared to give 'qualified support to movements of national liberation, not because this is an end in itself, but because it represents a step towards the achievement of complete working class emancipation in colonial countries'. 'For', the ILP stated, 'only when a nation is free from foreign domination can it develop its struggle for its own social and economic freedom'.[31]

The ILP was ready to support self-government as the 'inherent right of every people'[32] but it struggled with the problem of self-determination for the countries within Great Britain. The Scottish Division of the ILP had called for immediate Home Rule for Scotland in 1922 and in 1924 Maxton said that he could ask for no greater job in life than to make Scotland into a socialist commonwealth free from its present ties with England.[33] Yet in 1943, under pressure from the Scottish Nationalists to make his position on this question clear, Maxton stated that he had never envisaged a free Scotland standing alone against the world, but had only thought of it as part of an international socialist commonwealth.[34] Campbell Stephen, on the other hand, was an unreserved supporter of Scottish Home Rule[35] and in February 1947 the Scottish Divisional Council reiterated its support for the principle of self-government for Scotland.[36] Moreover F. A. Ridley, a leading ILPer, said in 1946 that the ILP should work first for a United States of Britain before it suggested the formation of a Socialist Europe or a Socialist World.[37] But the position of Wales was not apparently mentioned in ILP discussions after disaffiliation[38] and officially the Party had no policy regarding the 'English colonies' in the British Isles except for Ireland. The ILP's attitude towards Ireland had always been very clear. The Party had called for the withdrawal of British troops from that country and the granting of 'full rights of self-determination' for it in 1920.[39] It had hailed the birth of Eire[40] and the disaffiliated ILP continued to support it even though it was not a socialist state. The Party also opposed partition and called for the setting up of a united Ireland under one parliament.[41] The ILP continually attacked the Northern Ireland government, which it claimed was in some ways as repressive as the Nazis, but appeared to forget that a majority of the electorate in Northern Ireland at that time did not wish to join Eire.

The ILP had a similar blind spot about the problem of Palestine. The ILP supported the Jewish demand for a national home, but it was obvious that there were going to be serious clashes between the Arabs and Jews. Some ILPers originally thought that a partial solution would be to give the Jews a home outside Palestine,[42] and during the war, when the full horror of the Holocaust became known, the ILP suggested that the Jews should be settled in the USA, though, when it became clear that the Jews did not want this, the Party dropped the idea.[43] The ILP was convinced that the cause of the difficulties between the Jews and Arabs was to be found in the machinations of native and foreign capitalists, and 'in the ambiguous and vacillating policy pursued by previous British governments in their relations with both Jews and Arabs'.[44] The only solution, the ILP stated, was for the workers and peasants of both nations to combine together in a socialist state and drive out all capitalist forces.[45] To this end the ILP had helped in 1937 to set up a British Committee for Jewish Arab Socialist Unity.[46] The problem was not, however, that simple, and the ILP was still calling for a United Socialist State of Palestine as the war broke out between the Jews and the Arabs in 1948.[47]

The ILP's weakness (and what often appeared to be a lack of interest[48]) in the field of foreign affairs seems to have been caused by a combination of: its conviction that all problems, domestic and foreign, were caused by capitalism and could not be solved until capitalism was overthrown; by its judgement that foreign policy was of no interest to British workers;[49] by its lack of concern for foreign trade; and by its apparent belief that socialism could be built in one country at a time.[50] This meant that it saw its primary task as the creation of a socialist Britain, while leaving foreign socialists with the responsibility of establishing socialism in their own countries. Moreover, whenever the ILP did try to take a foreign policy stance, as it did for example over the invasion of Abyssinia in 1935,[51] it ran the risk of dividing the Party over the correct interpretation of the underlying economic factors and the proper socialist response to them. Small wonder, then, that the ILP tended to take the longer-term view and to concentrate on working towards the creation of a world federation of socialist states rather than trying to formulate an agreed foreign policy for the capitalist era.

SECTION 2

A History of the ILP 1938 to 1950

———

8

The End of The Dream

By the time the ILP's annual conference met in 1938 it was obvious that the Party had reached a critical moment in its history. Party numbers had dropped dramatically from 16,500 individual members in 1932 to less than 3,000; only 124 out of its putative 220 branches were paying fees to the ILP's Head Office and the Party's finances showed a deficit of £900.[1] Moreover, its local government representation had fallen from the several hundred wards it previously held across the country to less than 30 councillors concentrated mainly in Glasgow, Merthyr, Norwich and Great Yarmouth. And the Party's poor showing in the 1935 general election,[2] when its parliamentary representation was reduced to four seats in Glasgow's East End, was a clear indication that it was failing to gain the support of the working class as it had hoped it would when it had disaffiliated in 1932.[3] Moreover, its political strength was soon to be further weakened by the impending defection of George Buchanan,[4] one of its last four MPs.

Fenner Brockway, the Party's Political Secretary, remained publicly optimistic, pointing out that the Bolshevik Party in Russia had been comparatively tiny until the very eve of the revolution in October 1917. He claimed that the ILP was now in many ways stronger than in 1932 because it had been cleansed by its revolutionary programme.[5] However, Britain was not yet in a revolutionary situation and many ILPers admitted privately that the Party was in a very difficult position.[6] Moreover, it was clear that the ILP was becoming increasingly isolated from the mass of the working class during what the Party believed to be a critical time. In the early 1930s the ILP had expected capitalism to collapse quickly in Britain and to be followed by the establishment of a socialist society, though in the event the ILP had to accept that capitalism had proved resilient and that the workers had been possibly too

65

demoralised by the ravages of mass unemployment to become a revolutionary force. Now the ILP began to fear that the collapse of capitalism might take an international rather than a domestic form and result in the triumph of fascism not socialism.[7] Therefore the Party felt that it was its duty to strengthen its contacts with the mass of the workers in order to do what it could to prevent political reaction from succeeding in Britain. But the ILP could no longer work with the CPGB, and the Labour Party had made it clear that it would not allow factions within it to work with either the ILP or the CPGB and so, if the ILP was to retain any political contact with the mass of the working class, it had to try and reach some kind of arrangement with the Labour Party as a whole.

Brockway had attempted such an approach to the Labour Party NEC in February 1935 in connection with a public demonstration that the ILP was planning to mark the anniversary of the Austrian Civil War.[8] However the NEC was suspicious of the ILP's motives at that time and the overture was rejected.[9] Later that year the NEC gave voice to these suspicions at the Labour Party conference. It declared that it had decided that membership of the ILP was incompatible with membership of the Labour Party; although it assured the conference that the door was still open for the ILP to reaffiliate on the same conditions that had applied in 1932. But it was determined that individual ILPers should not be allowed to 'come in merely for the purpose of changing (Labour Party) policy'.[10]

Yet the hostility was not all one-sided. Brockway had been one of the keenest advocates of disaffiliation in 1932, and despite his approach to the Labour Party he rejected all talk of reaffiliation in November 1936 because he believed that party was reformist, bureaucratic and undemocratic.[11] A year later he was still claiming that the ILP must triumph in the end because the Labour Party was 'spiritually dead'.[12] At the same time James Carmichael,[13] full-time Secretary of the Scottish ILP and leader of the ILP group on the Glasgow Council, was arguing that if the ILP reaffiliated unconditionally to the Labour Party, as he had heard some ILPers suggest, it would be disastrous not only for the ILP but for the working class as a whole. He insisted that the Labour Party had a reformist policy which was bound 'to lead to a crisis, with the terrible prospect of the working class movement being smashed',[14] and at this time, apparently, the majority of ILPers agreed with his view. But the fact that reaffiliation was being discussed seriously at all was an indication that the Party was beginning to have doubts about its position as an independent body. These doubts must have been increasing rapidly for by Easter 1938 Carmichael, while still attacking unconditional affiliation, was criticising the Party's 'splendid isolationists' who were not prepared to consider conditional affiliation.[15] Brockway had also come to believe (after carrying out a review of the ILP's position in 1937) that, despite the block vote of the trade unions, which he had always in the past described as a brake on radical change within the Labour Party, it might now be possible for a tight disciplined unit like the ILP to enter that party and achieve fruitful results.[16]

Brockway and Carmichael were slowly beginning to accept that the ILP must rejoin the Labour Party if it was to survive, although at this time they still believed that the Party might be able to join on better terms than those under which it had functioned within the Labour Party up to 1932.[17] Tom Taylor,[18] a Glasgow ILP councillor and an ex-leader of the ILP's Guild of Youth,[19] had already decided that reaffiliation was the only solution for the ILP, and he urged the Party to consider it at the 1938 ILP annual conference. But the opposition to this move was very strong. It was led by Fred Jowett, the Party's National Treasurer; Dr Charles Smith, a leading London ILPer and one of the Party's 'theorists'; and Jennie Lee,[20] the darling of the Scottish ILP. The NAC, for its part, after agreeing at a preconference meeting that it was in favour of common action and an electoral agreement with the Labour Party, supported a mild composite resolution which called for talks with the Labour Party 'for the purpose of securing the maximum common action against the National Government'[21]. Even this puny resolution was only just passed by the conference with fifty-five votes to forty-nine.

Following this decision Brockway held an unofficial meeting with James Middleton, the Labour Party General Secretary, and then, with the agreement of the NAC, wrote to the NEC requesting a meeting between representatives of the two parties, to which the NEC agreed.[22] On 14 June the ILP's Inner Executive of James Maxton, Campbell Stephen, John McGovern,[23] Fenner Brockway and John Aplin[24] met with George Dallas,[25] Mrs Ayrton Gould,[26] George Latham,[27] Hugh Dalton,[28] Harold Laski,[29] James Middleton[30] and James Walker[31] of the NEC. Maxton opened the discussion by stating that the isolation of the ILP was 'no longer defensible',[32] and that there were many Labour Party MPs who were at greater variance with Labour Party policies than were the ILP MPs. Both Maxton and Brockway then made it clear that they were seeking a closer co-operation with the Labour Party because of the frightening international scene. The ILPers informed the NEC representatives that the ILP was willing to offer the Labour Party its assistance in propaganda campaigns and election contests and to guarantee that it would not unilaterally increase the number of its own parliamentary candidates. Maxton also conceded that the question of the PLP's standing orders, which had been the final breaking point between the two parties in 1932, was now of small importance. In return the ILP asked for electoral adjustments to favour ILP parliamentary candidates in Bradford East, North Lanark, and Norwich, but when pressed Maxton admitted that a failure to come to terms on this issue was not likely to prevent an accord between the two parties.

The ILP was apparently willing to pay a high price for the chance to work with the Labour Party, and Maxton concluded by stating that the Party was now primarily interested in propaganda work. Even so the NEC representatives were not very encouraging. They pointed out that relations between the Labour and Co-operative parties, (which were formalised under the Co-operative Party's constitution in 1938), were not easy because of clashes of function and that the Labour Party had already been damaged on occasion by ad hoc committees which had taken it upon themselves to conduct propaganda which should have been left to the Labour Party itself. Nevertheless, after a short discussion following the departure of the ILP representatives, the Labour Party negotiators decided to recommend to the NEC that the most satisfactory way to heal the breach between the two parties was for the ILP to reaffiliate. This recommendation was accepted at the next NEC meeting[33] and then conveyed to the NAC. The NAC was in a difficult position, however, because the 1938 conference had specifically instructed the council to ask for co-operation and not affiliation. The NAC decided that it must have more information before it could make a recommendation to the Party,[34] and Brockway wrote to Middleton asking for confirmation that the ILP would have the same rights as it had enjoyed in 1931 and that its MPs would be allowed the same latitude with regard to the standing orders as that given to George Lansbury over the question of rearmament. Middleton replied after some delay that the conditions for affiliation had remained unchanged since 1932.[35]

Meanwhile McGovern had now come out strongly in favour of reaffiliation. In July 1938 he informed the *Daily Herald* that he was going to present a motion to the NAC meeting in August supporting affiliation and requesting the NAC to call a special conference to obtain permission to proceed with negotiations to that end.[36] When the NAC refused to accept his recommendation he announced his resignation from the ILP's group negotiating with the Labour Party because, he claimed, he and the majority of his fellow members of the Glasgow ILP were in favour of unconditional affiliation, and that the international situation was too serious to allow for any further dissension in the ranks of the working class.[37]

Then just over a month later the ILP was suddenly paralysed by internal dissension, with John McGovern at its centre, caused by this international situation. The storm blew up over an issue on which in fact the ILP was basically agreed. Hitler was seemingly prepared to make war on Czechoslovakia in order to seize the Sudetenland, which he claimed should belong to the German Reich. Because of an interlocking system of treaties it appeared that the whole of Europe would be drawn into the conflict.[38] The NAC met on 25 September and issued a statement, based on a draft by Fred Jowett, claiming that if war broke out it would not be a fight to defend democracy but simply a conflict between rival imperialists 'for economic power in the Balkans, the Near East, and the colonial territories'.[39] The Party pledged itself, the statement continued, to stand for peace as it had done in 1914, and to do all it could to unite the workers of the world to work for the overthrow of capitalism, which was the cause of all wars. It was a pronouncement very much in accord with the ILPs basic beliefs.

However, on 30 September the British prime minister, Neville Chamberlain,[40] reached agreement with Hitler in Munich on the terms that would be acceptable to Germany to settle the crisis over the Sudetenland without war. This agreement gave Hitler nearly all that he had wanted and left the Czechs virtually defenceless. Brockway issued a statement to the press calling it a bad peace which was meant to lay the ground for a four-power pact aimed at isolating the Soviet Union and strengthening the forces of reaction.[41] This press release was in line with ILP policy and might have been the last word spoken by the Party on this issue. But on 4 October, during the second day of the Commons debate on the Munich Agreement, Maxton rose to speak. His speech was like many others he had given in the House. He began by stressing the humanitarian aspect of the question, pointing out the horrors of war and the untold suffering it caused to the common people on both sides of any conflict, continued with an indictment of the capitalist system which had brought the world to the edge of the abyss yet again, and ended with a claim that true world peace required a socialist revolution and the end of capitalism and imperialism. But in a moment of apparent thoughtlessness[42] he stated that the prime minister had done what the common people had wanted by securing peace and congratulated him for the work he had accomplished in the last three weeks.

Unfortunately, the newspapers pounced on these few words of congratulation and featured them in their reports of the debate, practically ignoring the rest of what Maxton had said.[43] The *New Leader*, the ILP's weekly newspaper, did not carry a report of the debate until 14 October, and so until then ILPers were left with the impression that Maxton had delivered a speech full of praise for Chamberlain and nothing else. McGovern, aware of the hostility that Maxton's words had aroused in some sections of the Party, decided to show his loyalty to his parliamentary colleague with typical bravado by delivering a speech in the Commons on 6 October filled with praise for Chamberlain and ending with the words 'well done thou good and faithful servant'.[44] This was really too much for some ILPers to take. Both the London and the Manchester Federations of the ILP issued public statements disassociating themselves from the speeches of their MPs and claiming that these were contrary to ILP policy.[45] A few ILPers reputedly resigned from the Party straight away,[46] and a serious breach occurred within the Party's leadership when, following a meeting of the Party's Inner Executive during which the Munich debate was discussed, Brockway and Aplin announced to the press that they opposed the Munich Agreement and disapproved of those parts of their MP's speeches which praised Chamberlain.[47]

When the NAC next convened it rejected by nine votes to five a resolution calling on it to repudiate the MP's speeches, and while the divisional conferences, which met in January 1939, were generally critical of Maxton and McGovern they would not censure them.[48] However, resolutions had been proposed by the Croydon and Clapham branches calling for the expulsion of the two MPs, and similar resolutions were being sent into the NAC for inclusion on the agenda of the annual conference. It was obvious that there was still a great deal of disquiet in the Party. Meanwhile the chief protagonists were ensuring that the dispute would not die a natural death. In November McGovern, speaking in the Commons, struck back at the critics of his Munich debate speech.[49] Then in December he announced that he would not address meetings of those London branches which had criticised Maxton's speech.[50] Brockway meanwhile was continuing his attacks through the *New Leader*[51] and in the Party's discussion magazine *Controversy*.[52] In the April edition of *Left/Controversy* (as the magazine was now called) the two sides of the argument were again restated even though by then other questions – including affiliation; the Party's attitude towards the government's plan to reintroduce a National Register (which might be used to aid wartime conscription), and the vexed question of how far ILPers should co-operate with the government's scheme for Air Raid Precautions – would seem to have been more deserving of this kind of detailed examination.

As it was, even important issues raised by this controversy were lost in the debate at the annual conference which took place on a motion to refer back the Parliamentary Group's Report (which amounted to a censure motion). McGovern bitterly attacked Brockway, Aplin and the rest of the London Division, calling them 'double-crossers' and 'fireside theoreticians and middle class dilettantes'. Maxton also criticised Brockway, who had apparently gone back on a promise he had given that he would not issue any statement after the October meeting of the Inner Executive until he had given the whole matter 24 hours' thought. Brockway and Aplin made reasoned replies and tried to bring the discussion back to the question of how a revolutionary socialist should have reacted to the Munich Agreement. However, the Parliamentary Group had succeeded in turning the debate into a test of the Party's confidence in Maxton, and in the light of the ILP's great love for him there could be no doubt of the result. The reference back of the Parliamentary Group's Report was defeated by 65 votes to 43.[53] The deeper question which this argument had raised concerning the correct party line to be taken when faced with a situation in which the choice was simply between capitalist peace and capitalist war was not resolved. It was to haunt the ILP for the next two years.

This controversy had also threatened the loose alliance of affiliationists within the Party. Brockway was now in favour of affiliation but his most vocal allies in his dispute with Maxton were from the ranks of the anti-affiliationists, including Charles Smith and Hugo Dewar,[54] while the other leading affiliationists – McGovern, Stephen and Carmichael – were Maxton's main champions and Maxton himself was now reputedly firmly against affiliation.[55] The bitterness within the NAC caused by the Munich debate dispute was so acute that neither Stephen nor Brockway would agree to serve on the NAC for the next year if the other was elected Chairman, and so they both withdrew their names as nominees. Brockway telephoned Charles Smith and asked him to put forward his own name for the post. Smith, who had not been on the NAC for three years, was most surprised to find himself returned unopposed.[56]

Little progress had been made in the Party's negotiations with the Labour Party. The divisional conferences in February had voted on the whole against unconditional affiliation, but they seemed more inclined than ever before to support the idea of conditional affiliation although it was not clear what obligations they would accept.[57] The NEC had made it obvious that it was only offering the same terms that the ILP had had in 1932. Yet the ILP seemed impervious to this. Even the NAC appeared out of touch with reality. It set up a sub-committee of James Carmichael, John Aplin, Percy Williams (the Yorkshire representative), Emrys Thomas (the Welsh representative), and Bob Edwards (the Lancashire representative) to consider the question of the Party's relationship to the Labour Party. This committee eventually reported that it was against reaffiliation but in favour of allowing individual ILPers to become members of the Labour Party as well, apparently unaware that this was specifically prohibited by the Labour Party's conference decision of 1935.[58]

The NAC declared in April 1939 that it was evenly divided on the question of affiliation and so was unable to make a recommendation to the 1939 annual conference.[59] The delegates to that conference were also apparently not sure what they wanted. They rejected unconditional affiliation by 63 votes to 45, and the sub-committee's proposal by 68 votes to 42, but they carried a resolution calling for conditional affiliation by 69 votes to 40 votes. Faced with this confusing result, and with no indication from the Party what conditions it wanted before it would support affiliation, Maxton told the conference that he took the vote to mean that the Party was instructing the NAC to carry on negotiating with the Labour Party.[60] Brockway therefore wrote another letter to James Middleton asking for further clarification of the terms of affiliation,[61] but the Labour Party Secretary merely reaffirmed that the conditions were the same as they had always been, and that the NEC would not make special arrangements to meet special cases.[62]

It was now pointless for the NAC to carry on attempting to negotiate with the NEC, and at its August meeting a majority voted in favour of recommending affiliation. The council's statement made it clear that the ILP still differed from the Labour Party on many important issues, but it said that the NAC was willing to concede that there were many members of the Labour Party who shared the ILP's views on key issues, and that the Labour Party was 'the political expression of the working class'. The ILP's duty, the statement continued, was to co-operate loyally with the Labour Party, seeking to strengthen it organisationally, and ideologically, for the task of overthrowing capitalism, winning workers' power, and establishing socialism.[63] The NAC was therefore calling a special conference to meet on 17 September 1939 to consider its recommendation to affiliate. In view of the confused nature of the decisions reached by the 1939 conference it is impossible to be certain what this special conference would have decided.[64] A special edition of *Between Ourselves* was produced in August in which Brockway, Edwards and (somewhat reluctantly) Maxton argued for affiliation, while Jowett, Smith and Fred Berriman argued against. As it was, the special conference never met because Britain declared war on 3 September, and the NAC decided that, as the Labour Party was supporting this war and the ILP was bitterly opposed to it, affiliation was now out of the question.[65]

The indecisive nature of the 1939 annual conference discussions and decisions meant that the ILP entered the Second World War still separated from the Labour Party and with only limited contacts with the wider Labour Movement. It had also allowed the debate on the Munich Agreement speeches to centre on personalities and not policies; and so, although the ILP was in agreement on its opposition to what it considered to be the second major imperialist war of the century, it had thought out none of the implications of its anti-war stand. It was ill-prepared for the future it faced.

9

The Imperialist War

The ILP established its position as an anti-war party early in its history. Keir Hardie, the Party's first leader, declared in 1900 that the Boer War was 'a war of aggression and an outrage on the moral sense of a civilised community' and went on to give his analysis a socialist bent by declaring that the origins of this war lay in a capitalist conspiracy to exploit cheap labour in South Africa.[1] The ILP shared with the Liberal Party the opprobrium of opposing this popular war and suffered at the polls in the general election of 1900 as a result. This did not stop it, however, from accepting the widespread unpopularity which inevitably resulted from opposing the First World War as well. Its manifesto on the outbreak of that war declared that 'Out of the darkness and the depths we hail our working class comrades of every land. Across the roar of the guns we send sympathy and greetings to the German socialists ... They are no enemies of ours, but faithful friends'.[2]

The ILP manifesto was drawing on the older of the two different but not incompatible strands of thought on the origins of war which influenced socialists at this critical time.[3] This strand was based on the belief that there was a common bond between humans which transcended national barriers and was greater than parochial interests. It could be argued, therefore, that it was unnatural for men to kill each other in war and if they did so it was because they were being manipulated by evil forces to act against their own interests. Originally the devil was seen as the malign force at work here but from the 17th century onwards there were people who argued that it was instead economic interests which actually lay at the heart of these conflicts, and that such interests used wars to extend the area they could exploit by subjugating weaker powers or by destroying trade rivals.[4] This analysis was easily appropriated later by socialists who simply cast the capitalists in the role of the evil economic interests and the workers as the misguided cannon fodder who actually fought the wars. The ILP's manifesto reflects this strand of argument by emphasising the comradeship and lack of enmity between the workers of the warring lands.

This position had been given a theoretical basis by the Liberal economist J. A. Hobson in the aftermath of the Boer War. He argued that capitalism had reached a stage in its development when it needed to obtain cheaper raw materials and new markets if it was to avoid a collapse caused through overproduction and underconsumption at home. This, he said, led to wars because all the advanced capitalist countries had reached a similar state and were forced to fight to gain new colonies where they could obtain their raw materials and open up new markets.[5] Lenin later expanded on this argument. He claimed that all wars fought between modern capitalist powers were imperialist wars of the type described by Hobson. They were, therefore, of no concern to the workers and should not be supported even if that led to the defeat of the workers' own country. This became enshrined in a tactic known as revolutionary defeatism. And he urged the workers to turn these imperialist wars into civil wars during which the workers would overthrow the capitalists and introduce a socialist state.[6]

Lenin was also aware of the other strand of socialist thought on the origins and nature of modern wars which had strongly influenced the thinking of Marx and Engels. This strand roughly divided wars into two categories: wars fought for oppressive powers, which all socialists should oppose, and wars fought against oppressive powers which socialists were duty bound to support. From this idea came the concept of 'progressive wars' in which socialists were expected to support the side which was more democratic against the side which was more reactionary, even if the socialists lived in the country which was deemed to be reactionary, as loyalty to class should come before loyalty to country. This idea enabled Lenin to justify the subversive activities of the Bolsheviks during the First World War, for undermining Russia, the most reactionary country in Europe, must advance the lot of the workers if it meant victory for the more progressive Germany. But this concept also helped to undermine international working-class solidarity. Before the outbreak of the war, the Second International[7] had passed several resolutions calling on the workers of the world to oppose capitalist or imperialist wars. However, once the war had started the International was split because many of the delegates decided that they had to support their own nation's war effort as they felt their country was the more progressive of the combatants.[8]

The ILP's underlying anti-war stance actually contained elements of both these strands of thought on the nature of war but it would be wrong to suggest that the Party spoke with one voice in its opposition to the First World War. At least three clearly defined messages could be heard.[9] One group, centred on George Lansbury[10] and Dr Alfred Salter,[11] combined Christianity with their socialism. They argued that for Christians the taking of life under any circumstances was impermissible. The ILP worked closely with the No-Conscription Fellowship (NCF) in supporting conscientious objectors, whether party members or non-party members, and helping them to present their cases to the tribunals set up to assess the validity of claims for exemption from military service. This work with the NCF drew to the ILP many conscientious objectors, of whom a large number were Quakers and other Christian pacifists. Indeed in 1916 the ILP annual conference adopted a resolution committing the Party to a pacifist stand on the war. After 1918 the pacifist element within the ILP was weakened by the defection of many of the Quakers and other Christian pacifists who had joined during the war. But that element was never to disappear completely.

Others in the ILP, although perhaps personally committed to pacifism, did not take this pacifist Christian position but argued along socialist lines that the First World War was an extension of the capitalist market economy and that both sides were equally to blame. The advocates of this line, including Fenner Brockway, Thomas Johnston[12] and Clifford Allen, did not, however, follow Lenin by calling on socialists to turn the imperialist war into a civil war, preferring instead to demand an immediate end to the war and a negotiated peace. In this call they had the support of the ILP's leader, Ramsay MacDonald, who believed that the war engendered international hatred and that the only solution was a negotiated peace, though he was willing to give lukewarm support to the government's war effort. A third strain, centring on the Scottish ILP and its leading figures David Kirkwood, James Maxton and Emanuel Shinwell, insisted that they would be willing to fight but only to defend a socialist Britain, and were happy to accept prison terms as conscientious objectors rather than support this imperialist war. On the other hand many ILPers did feel that there was a difference between the two sides in the First World War, or believed simply in the need for national defence, and so joined the armed forces along with millions of their fellow workers.[13] During the Second World War some ILPers continued to base their anti-war stand on a personal pacifism rooted either in their Christianity or in humanism and the Party was to fall under the influence of pacifists in the 1950s. But in the interwar period, and particularly after the break with the Labour Party in 1932, the ILP adopted a more clearly revolutionary socialist outlook on all social and political issues and this included accepting as party doctrine (the ILP's understanding of) the Marxist analysis of the causes of war.

This did not itself, however, help to make it any easier for the Party to agree on its attitude to specific wars. After Italian forces invaded Abyssinia in October 1935, for example, the League of Nations called for the imposition of sanctions on Italy. In the Commons Maxton and the other ILP MPs refused to support sanctions or the threat of them because, they claimed, that would be tantamount to a declaration that there was a real difference between the Italian dictatorship of Benito Mussolini and the Abyssinian 'dictatorship' of Emperor Haile Selassie 1, something which as socialists they refused to accept. Another ILP faction, led by Brockway and the Marxist Group, while refusing to support the 'capitalist' League of Nations,[14] nevertheless felt that Italy was the more reactionary country and so had to be opposed by the workers, and they supported a call for 'workers' sanctions' against Italy. Maxton managed, however, to carry the Party with him by threatening to resign as Party Chairman if the members did not support his stand.[15]

On the other hand the Party did agree to send aid and a contingent of fighting men to support the Republican side in the Spanish Civil War. At first the Party had declared that, although it sympathised with the Spanish workers, it accepted Karl Liebknecht's[16] thesis that the workers' main enemy was their own ruling class and that their primary responsibility was to defeat the class enemy in their own country, leaving the destruction of foreign capitalist or fascist rulers to the indigenous working class. The ILP's real duty, therefore, was to overthrow the British Government. If that was achieved, it argued, a workers' government sympathetic to the Spanish workers would be set up in Britain which should be able to supply arms and food to the Republican side to help defeat the Nationalists and their fascist allies. But within a short time Bob Edwards[17] and other supporters of the Spanish workers' cause were able to persuade the Party that in fact in Spain a different situation existed in which the ILP had to take sides. They argued that this was not just a clash between rival capitalists but a war in which rampant capitalism was attacking a Republican government which, although predominantly capitalist (in the ILP's estimation), had as its ally a nascent socialist state in Catalonia. They could claim, therefore, that the Republican side, or at least the Catalonian element within it, represented the progressive side which Marxists believed should be defended against the forces of reaction represented by the Nationalists and fascists.[18] The majority of the ILP accepted this analysis (though some pacifists promptly left the Party[19]) and even Maxton claimed in the Commons that if called upon he would go and fight in Spain.[20]

But this resort to military action by the ILP, while showing that it was not a pacifist party, did not mean that it had become pro-war. The very men who seemed to be leading the call to send fighting men and supplies to Spain – Edwards, Brockway and Maxton – were to be at the forefront in opposing Britain's participation in the Second World War. This was largely because the ILP refused to accept that the British, French and American governments represented the more progressive side in this struggle with fascist Italy and Germany.[21] The Party argued, along with Hobson, that capitalism had developed into imperialism to avoid collapse and extended this argument to fascism, declaring that fascism was merely the form capitalism took when it was not allowed to expand into the colonial field. It was pointless, therefore, fighting fascism by military means because that would do nothing to solve the underlying social and economic problems of capitalist society.[22] Once again, many ILPers became political (or pacifist) conscientious objectors, and the ILP tried to protect the rights of all conscientious objectors whether party members or not in the House of Commons or by supporting the work of the Central Board for Conscientious Objectors.[23] Not all members of the Party, however, accepted this analysis in its entirety and as in the First World War some ILPers did join the armed forces. Indeed the ILP maintained an armed forces branch from 1943 onwards, and was careful not to try to dissuade ILPers from joining the military.[24] Other ILPers simply left the Party in protest at its anti-war stand.[25]

The ILP pointed to British actions in India to prove that British imperialism was every bit as evil as fascism, and it argued that the British ruling class would resort to fascist methods in Britain as soon as it was threatened by outside attack or internal disturbance.[26] It did not, however, as Lenin had done in the First World War, call on the workers actively to work for the defeat of their own country. It claimed that that tactic merely aided the foreign capitalist power, and the ILP had no interest in helping any capitalists or fascists.[27] But the ILP did argue that if the British workers overthrew their capitalist masters and set up a socialist state, the German and Italian workers would be bound to follow suit and the war could then be ended with a socialist peace; though, if those foreign workers did not revolt, it might then be necessary to fight Hitler and Mussolini to defend socialism.[28]

No matter how far-fetched and naive this analysis may appear with hindsight, it had a considerable attraction for many British socialists at the time. George Orwell had fought with the ILP contingent in Spain and joined the Party in June 1938. In 1937 he wrote to a friend that he could foresee fascism being imposed by the British Government on the British people at the beginning of the next war, and said it was futile to be an anti-fascist while attempting to preserve capitalism.[29] In October 1938 he signed a manifesto which declared that a war over Czechoslovakia would not be a fight for democracy but merely a struggle for imperialist interests and that it was the workers' duty to resist such a war.[30] In fact when war was declared he abandoned this position, left the ILP, and became a vocal supporter of the war effort. But right up until the eleventh hour he had held a very similar position to that of the ILP.

Yet it was not only people associated with the ILP who advanced this kind of analysis. The Labour Party had officially supported Britain's war effort in the First World War but the Versailles Treaty which ended the war seemed to many Labour Party members to show that the ILP had been correct in its analysis of the Allied governments' aims in fighting this war. The Labour Party now adopted the same position as the ILP on the causes of modern wars and declared that it would not be tricked into supporting an imperialist war again.[31] It voted together with the ILP against the Conservative government's military estimates and demanded that Britain's expenditure on armaments should be cut. With the rise of the fascist regimes in Europe, the Labour Party initially swung its support behind the League of Nations while still opposing the National Government's military estimates, because it argued that the government did not need a large military force to fulfil its obligations under the Covenant of the League. If, therefore, the government still asked for a large military establishment, the Labour Party argued, it must be to use these forces against the workers in the empire or at home. But by 1935 the Labour Party's faith in the League of Nations as a way of settling international disputes and of halting the threat of fascism had drained away. The pacifist George Lansbury was replaced as leader by Clement Attlee[32] and the PLP, unlike the ILP MPs, ceased to vote against the military estimates and indeed demanded that the National Government should rearm at a faster rate.[33]

The majority of the Labour Party may have decided in 1935 that British capitalism was a lesser evil than Italian and German fascism but that did not hold for all sections of the party. The Socialist League, which had been formed in part from those radical ILPers who chose to stay in the Labour Party after disaffiliation, remained suspicious of the motives of the National Government. The Socialist League leader Stafford Cripps[34] argued at the 1935 Labour Party conference that the government could not be trusted with extra armaments or powers because it would fight not to safeguard democracy but merely to preserve and extend its own imperialist possessions.[35] Cripps and Aneurin Bevan[36] declared that only a socialist government could be trusted to use its armed forces to fight the fascist powers and not to use them either for imperialist adventures or to keep the British workers subjugated.[37] Bevan claimed as late as 1937 that to support rearmament under a Conservative-led government was to put a sword in the hands of the workers' enemy which might be used to cut off the workers' own heads.[38]

The Socialist League worked with the ILP and CPGB in 1937 in the Unity Campaign to try to form a United Front which would overthrow the National Government and replace it with a socialist administration before there was a war. Meanwhile the *Tribune* newspaper, which acted as the unofficial organ of the Socialist League, carried articles which echoed those which were appearing in the ILP's *New Leader* by claiming that capitalism and fascism were only different in degree and that British rule in India was just as bad as fascist rule in Europe. The *Tribune* also argued, as the ILP was doing, that the British Government would adopt fascist methods in Britain if faced with a domestic crisis or foreign invasion. Every preparation the government made for war, particularly its moves to introduce conscription, were denounced by the *Tribune* as an attempt to strengthen its regime against the potential threat of a revolt by British workers while its attempts to appease Hitler were seen as proof that it had no serious intention of opposing fascism.[39]

On the outbreak of the Second World War, however, unlike the ILP, the former members of the Socialist League did not maintain their position and carry it to its logical conclusion by opposing the war. Instead Cripps and Bevan declared in the *Tribune* that, while they believed that there was an element of fascism present in every country which had to be opposed, the present war was at least in part a genuine attempt to stop fascist aggression and as such should be supported by every socialist.[40] This only left the pacifists within the Labour Party opposing the war, though the party's distrust of the Conservative dominated government's motives for fighting the war took a while to die away. Moreover there remained throughout the war a belief amongst some elements of the Labour Party's intelligentsia that to defeat fascism would take more than just military force. What was needed, they argued, was a change in Britain's moral position brought about by the adoption of socialism at home and the end of imperialism abroad.[41] In that way, of course, the imperialist war would become a war in defence of the progressive side which all socialists could happily support.

The other major party on the British political left, and the one which claimed to carry the torch of Marxism and Leninism, the Communist Party of Great Britain, also argued that wars were the result of imperialism and that the British capitalists were every bit as bad as the

European fascists. Yet the CPGB also believed that the main duty of the communist parties of all countries was to protect the Soviet Union, which was the first workers' state and as such had to be defended against the forces of reaction no matter what the cost. The CPGB was anxious to overthrow the British capitalist government, and so it formed the 'United Front' with the ILP and the Socialist League, but when that failed, it was willing to support the military rearmament introduced by the National Government as that would make Britain a more effective ally of Russia against the fascist powers. It gave this a theoretical gloss by arguing that although the capitalists were the main enemy of the British workers, their position was being strengthened by the success of reaction in Europe. If, therefore, fascism could be defeated that would be a tremendous blow against the workers' enemy in Britain.[42]

The logic of this argument forced the CPGB to call on the workers to fight a war on two fronts; on the one hand a military campaign against the Nazis, and on the other a political campaign to overthrow the British Government and to set up a socialist government which would ensure that the war was really against fascism and not just to protect imperialism.[43] Unfortunately for the leaders of the CPGB, the Soviet Union signed a non-aggression pact with Germany on 23 August 1939 and the official Soviet line changed in late September and now claimed that the struggle of Britain and France against Germany (and from June 1940 Italy as well) was merely another imperialist war. The CPGB, despite having already asked the workers to support the war for democracy, now had to denounce it and to call on the British workers to oppose this imperialist war.[44] The CPGB maintained this official line, which resembled that adopted by the ILP, until June 1941 when the Soviet Union was invaded by German forces. Overnight the Second World War, which the CPGB had declared was an imperialist struggle and of no concern to the workers, became for Communists a war for democracy and the liberation of the peoples of Europe from fascism which all workers should support wholeheartedly.[45] The CPGB now bitterly attacked the ILP (and carried on these attacks throughout the rest of the war) for maintaining that this was an imperialist war and for failing to support the one existing socialist state, the Soviet Union, in its struggle against the forces of fascism.[46] The CPGB organ *Labour Monthly*

defended this second change of line by quoting from Lenin's letters to
Boris Souvarine[47] and Rosa Luxemburg[48] during the First World War in
which he claimed that it was un-Marxist to condemn all wars out of
hand because a change in the political circumstances could alter the
whole nature of a war.[49]

The small groups of British Trotskyists also accepted Lenin's analysis
of modern wars, and some factions, including the Revolutionary
Socialist League which operated within the Labour Party, approved the
tactic of revolutionary defeatism, though they were too small to do much
about it.[50] The Workers' International League (WIL), however, followed
the lead of American Trotskyists, who in turn were acting on the advice
of Trotsky. They called on the Allied governments to arm the workers
under trade union supervision so that they could defend their homes
against foreign invasion. At the same time the WIL argued that this was
an imperialist war and that the workers should do nothing to aid the war
effort.[51] When the Soviet Union entered the war the WIL began to
demand that all arms should be sent to the Soviet Union to enable the
workers to defend the gains of the Russian Revolution but the party still
refused to support the war.[52]

The smaller British socialist parties tended to stand aloof from the
Second World War while adopting variations of the basic socialist
analysis of its causes. The Socialist Party of Great Britain (SPGB) was
formed in 1904 from a disaffected faction of the Social Democratic
Federation.[53] The SPGB was not pacifist, because it believed that armed
force would be needed to support a socialist revolution, but it opposed
the First World War declaring that 'the capitalists of Europe have
quarrelled over the question of the control of trade routes and the
world's markets, and are endeavouring to exploit the political ignorance
and blind passions of the working class of their respective countries in
order to induce the said workers to take up arms in what is solely their
masters' quarrel'.[54] And the party axiom that it did not matter to the
workers which side won the war was maintained throughout that
conflict. The SPGB took an identical stand during the Second World
War. It argued that this war was just another phase of a constant struggle
between the various rival capitalist groups and that the workers should
not become involved in the fighting because the party believed that in

the long run Britain would be no worse off under fascist rule than it was under capitalism.[55] The entry of the Soviet Union into the war was to have no effect on the SPGB's position because it denied that the Soviet Union was a socialist state.[56] The party also refrained from advocating revolutionary defeatism because it insisted that socialism could only be introduced when the vast majority of people in the country wanted it. The SPGB dedicated itself, therefore, to the task of turning the workers into socialists through propaganda and education so that they would be ready to overthrow capitalism and so end both this war and the cause of all wars.[57]

The tiny Socialist Labour Party (SLP) had left the Social Democratic Federation in 1903 and now followed the teachings of the American Socialist Daniel De Leon. It had opposed the First World War, stating that all wars had their origins in the economic conditions which produce conflicts over markets. It repeated this claim when faced with the Second World War and argued that the workers had nothing to gain by fighting their masters' battles and that the only way to combat fascism, capitalism and militarism was to join together into an industrial union which could act as a weapon in the workers' struggle to take control of the state from the capitalists. In the meantime the party did not advocate any form of revolutionary action, believing instead, like the SPGB, that socialism could only come when the vast majority of people were socialists.[58] The SLP's position only really differed from the analysis put forward by the other left-wing groups in its insistence that as the Second World War was not being fought for colonies it could not be described as an imperialist war but merely a capitalist one,[59] though this question of definition was of little importance.

It was not only avowedly socialist groups, however, which seemed to accept some part at least of the socialists' analysis of the Second World War. The Peace Pledge Union (PPU), the most important pacifist organisation of the period, which had been formed in 1934, issued a manifesto in March 1938 which argued that capitalist democracy would have to surrender itself to totalitarian regimentation if it tried to contend with fascism by military means, and also declared that the maintenance of the British Empire was not conducive to fighting a war to defend democracy.[60] The PPU's newspaper, *Peace News*, also declared that Hitler and all that he stood for could only be destroyed by the German people's own efforts.[61] Even W. O. Brown, an ardent Scottish nationalist who did not believe that Scotland should become involved in 'English' wars, based much of his argument against the Second World War on its imperialist nature.[62]

Clearly, therefore, the ILP was drawing on a set of widely held beliefs to justify its anti-war stand in 1939. Its analysis of the war was neither unique nor particularly incisive. The Party could claim, however, that it was consistent and was not being deflected by either political expediency or by the needs of the Soviet Union. It had its position which it believed it could justify from its political beliefs and from the practical experience of the previous four decades. Now in September 1939 it only needed to find a way of putting its anti-war policies into effect.

10

The Phoney War

———————

B ritain declared war on Germany on 3 September 1939 and Odhams Press, who normally handled the *New Leader*, refused to print the paper for that week even though the material in it had been passed by the censor. The ILP hurriedly found a firm willing to print an anti-war paper but the disruption caused by Odhams' decision meant that the *New Leader* which appeared in the first week of the war consisted of a single sheet of paper carrying little more than a straightforward denunciation of this new 'imperialist war'.[1] The following week the *New Leader* was published in full carrying a message of goodwill to the workers of all other lands, and a pledge that the ILP would keep alive the spirit of international socialism and work for a socialist peace. There was also an announcement of the Party's wartime programme. This was largely a restatement of current ILP social, political and industrial policies, with the addition of a few specific demands for a greater equality of sacrifice, including the conscription of all wealth and a call for increases in the wages of soldiers and in the pensions of people disabled as a result of the war.[2] The Party also warned the workers that their trade union rights were being endangered by the concessions which their union leaders were making to the government to help the war effort,[3] and that their civil rights were being attacked by the emergency powers granted to the government by Parliament.[4]

But although the *New Leader* stated that the ILP would work for a socialist Britain and a socialist peace and listed these demands, it did not state what the Party was going to do to achieve these objectives. In view of the revolutionary resolutions which had been passed at ILP conferences since 1935 dealing with the Party's response to an outbreak of war this was a surprising omission. In 1935, for example, the ILP had agreed that the workers should resist war with every weapon they possessed including the general strike.[5] This call for a general strike against war was repeated by the two following annual conferences and then it disappeared from the ILP's stated agenda, although the 1938 conference decision on the Party's attitude to war was said to be in addition to the resolutions passed in previous years.[6] There was no contradictory statement made at the 1939 conference and so the ILP was officially committed to calling for a general strike as soon as war broke out. Yet there was no such call made in this copy of the *New Leader* or in any subsequent edition.

Apparently the young trade unionists on the NAC (Will Ballantine, Bob Edwards and Tom Stephenson) had managed to convince their council colleagues, before the war broke out, that the workers would only strike over industrial issues not political ones, and that therefore it was pointless to call for a general strike against the war.[7] This unwelcome news was repeated to the 1940 ILP annual conference by Ballantine when he informed his fellow delegates that a resolution which had been put down calling for a general strike to end profiteering was meaningless in view of the simple fact that the workers would only strike over wages and working conditions.[8] It was also painfully apparent to some leading members of the ILP that, even if the workers had been inclined to strike, the ILP did not have enough influence in the Labour Movement to lead them.[9] Therefore, although the ILP did not abandon industrial activity during the war, and indeed it continued to support strike action, it narrowed its horizons and struggled for limited gains and did not attempt to ferment a revolution by industrial means.

There was also a growing feeling within the Party that it had been wrong to expect a spontaneous uprising against Hitler by the socialists in Germany and by those in the countries already under Nazi occupation as soon as war was declared. A few ILPers had been involved with the German, Austrian and Czech socialist underground organisations in the months before the outbreak of the Second World War helping to arrange the escape of their comrades from Nazi hands. The Party also received a number of messages just before and just after the war started, purporting to come from German socialists and declaring that there was widespread unrest inside the Reich which would soon result in a general uprising. The Party members, who had seen the socialist resistance at work, and other ILPers who wanted to believe that it was true, accepted these messages as genuine.[10] McGovern was equally certain, however, based on the first-hand experience that he had acquired during Continental trips in 1938 and 1939, that the vast bulk of the German people were either supporting Hitler or at least acquiescing in what he was doing and that these messages were actually being sent by refugees living in Paris who wanted to encourage the Allies.[11]

The ILP officially treated these messages as genuine and talked as though it expected a revolution to break out on the Continent at any moment, but in fact the NAC appears to have accepted McGovern's interpretation of the evidence and to have acted accordingly. It had become axiomatic in the ILP's revolutionary socialist philosophy that any revolution of the working class in a major European country would result in similar revolutions breaking out in all the other capitalist countries on the Continent and in the British Isles. It was also part of the Party's dogma that a British capitalist government, when faced with a defeat in war or a social revolution at home, would drop its democratic mask and adopt totalitarian measures.[12] In other words, the ILP expected a revolution in Germany to produce a revolution in Britain and subsequently an attempt at counter-revolution by the British Government. Both these things would have to be met by a revolutionary party prepared for action. Yet the ILP was not prepared and did not now begin making preparations despite receiving these encouraging messages from Nazi-occupied territories.

In fact as early as September 1938 the London Division of the Party had issued a circular in which it declared that the ILP was not organised in a way that would enable it to continue as an underground group if it should be declared illegal by the government. The circular went on to suggest that the ILP should consider forming factions within the Labour Party and arranging for a small central leadership to be set up with general powers to act on all issues so that it could take over the running of the Party when it was forced underground.[13] A few months later Brockway and Edwards obtained parts for a radio transmitter in Belgium and smuggled them back into this country. They assembled the transmitter and acquired a van which could be used to transport it from one secret hiding place to another.[14] Brockway also drew up a contingency plan which included provisions for printing propaganda illegally and arranging meetings through a system of coded messages sent over the radio. However, the NAC rejected both the London Division's circular and Brockway's plans,[15] and the radio was sent to Perth where it spent the war under the stage of the ILP hall.[16] Indeed the NAC had resolved in August 1938 that the ILP should refrain from going underground or from carrying out any illegal acts in the event of war, while the ILP Parliamentary Group had given unsolicited assurances just before the outbreak of the war that it would not disrupt 'or unnecessarily prolong the work of the House.'[17] Apparently there was a certain amount of panic at ILP Head Office on the declaration of war which resulted in orders being sent to some Divisions to destroy their papers,[18] but generally the NAC acted as though it still did not think that there was any need for it to contemplate preparing for underground activity. That would suggest that leading ILPers did not really believe in the imminence of revolution in either Germany or Britain.

Events were to prove that the NAC and the Parliamentary Group[19] were correct in their assessment of the situation. There was no revolution in Germany or in Britain on the outbreak of war, and the British Government made no attempt to suppress the ILP. It seems the police carried out surveillance on some ILPers for a while,[20] and apparently the Party's telephones were tapped for about six weeks.[21] Notes were also taken by policemen at ILP meetings[22] and Special Branch evidently had information about the Party and its leading members.[23] But, apart from one or two local police stations which appear to have been rather overzealous in their attempts to keep the peace during ILP public meetings,[24] the authorities did not interfere with the ILP. This seems to have been the deliberate policy of the wartime government. In the first few days after war was declared the government did introduce proposals for defence regulations which included a clause making it an offence 'to influence public opinion in a manner likely to be prejudicial to the defence of the realm or the efficient prosecution of the war',[25] but many MPs believed this clause was too harsh, because in that form it could be used against any anti-war propaganda including statements of religious objections to war. The government was urged in the Commons to amend this regulation, and it did so, altering it to read that it was an offence knowingly to use false information as anti-war propaganda.[26] Yet even before this regulation was changed the Cabinet had decided that action should only be taken against anti-war groups if it could be shown that they were having an effect on public morale.[27]

The Cabinet continued to keep an eye on such groups through reports prepared by the Home Secretary,[28] but although the coalition government took action against the BUF in the summer of 1940,[29] and in January 1941 suppressed the *Daily Worker* which was taking a violent anti-war line, it does not seem to have considered the threat to the war effort posed by any anti-war groups to have been particularly serious. It rarely even discussed the ILP![30] Indeed the ILP's revolutionary socialist pronouncements of the previous seven years also seem to have been forgotten by the Party itself. There was no call for a general strike against the war, no demand that the workers refuse to fight for their bosses, no clarion cry for revolution. Instead the ILP merely announced that it would not abide by the electoral pact,[31] which had been arranged by the three major parties for the duration of the war to allow each other a clear run in the seats they had won in 1935; and it called on the workers to 'stop the war', although it did not presume to tell them how.[32]

However, within a few weeks of the outbreak of the war, Poland was defeated by Germany and it appeared to some people in Britain, including David Lloyd George[33] and the right-wing pacifist the Marquis of Tavistock,[34] to be pointless to continue with a war which had been started with the sole aim of defending that country. Germany began to put out peace feelers to the Allies, and talk of a negotiated peace was in the air, though as yet it seems to have had little popular support.[35] On 6 October the ILP announced that it was going to press for a socialist peace.[36] It made it clear that this did not mean that it was endorsing Hitler's peace terms, because it claimed that an imperialist peace would only be a truce which would soon be broken by another imperialist war. The Party was suggesting instead a socialist peace which would 'serve as a challenge to Soviet Russia to use its influence on behalf of such a peace', and would 'reach the working class in Germany and ... give the courageous socialist opposition new hope'. Yet the Soviet Union was now backing the German call for peace as it had shared with that country in the division of Poland and there was no indication in the ILP's announcement why it believed the Soviet Union would automatically support a plan which was bound to be opposed by Hitler.

On 27 October 1939 John McNair wrote an article in the *New Leader* demanding the calling of an international conference of workers, to be held at the same time as any negotiations which might take place between the warring governments, so that the working class could obtain a socialist peace. Yet how this proposed conference was to do this was not specified. The ILP was now suffering from the same kind of confusion in its thinking that had occurred over the Munich Agreement and which should have been resolved by the 1939 conference. For nearly a year the Party seemed to be speaking with several voices. The ILP, in conjunction with other anti-war groups in London, Norwich and Glasgow, held a series of meetings throughout the winter of 1939–1940 calling for an immediate armistice and peace negotiations while at the same time insisting that it would only accept a socialist peace and would not negotiate with Hitler.[37] Meanwhile the ILP Parliamentary Group associated itself with George Lansbury's Parliamentary Peace Aims Group which said that it wanted an armistice even if that meant negotiating with Hitler.[38] Maxton was attacked at the 1940 ILP annual conference by Jennie Lee for putting his interpretation on ILP policy, but the resolution on the war adopted by that conference did not clarify what was official party policy. The formula it used was similar to the one advanced by McNair in October. It called for a working-class conference to meet at the same time as the armistice conference, but it did not specify whether or not it would consider beginning negotiations while the Nazis were still in power in Germany.[39]

The ILP's by-election activity only added to the confusion. The Party declared that it would fight contests during the electoral 'truce' in order to maintain democracy by providing an opportunity for the general public to express their views on the war.[40] But the ILP's less altruistic reason for joining in the fray stemmed from its desire to obtain the maximum publicity for its own views.[41] As it happened, there was a contest pending when the ILP declared its intention to fight suitable by-elections. However, it was in a Labour Party seat and the ILP had decided from the start that it would not 'strain the loyalties of Labour voters' by contesting by-elections against official Labour Party candidates no matter how pro-war that candidate might be.[42] But there was already an anti-war candidate in the field at this by-election in Clackmannan and East Stirlingshire: Andrew Stewart, who was an ex-ILPer and was now the Assistant Editor of the Peace Pledge Union's paper *Peace News*. The ILP had contested this seat in 1935 with little success, but Maxton and McGovern, who were well known throughout Scotland, decided that they would speak on Stewart's behalf. The ILP gave him a small amount of help with his campaign in addition to the services of these two speakers, but there was little on which Stewart now agreed with his old party (except on the need to end the war), and the ILP was not downcast when he polled rather badly.[43]

Stewart had been a socialist pacifist; the next candidate that the ILP supported was one of its own members and a man who had fought for the Republican side against Franco in Spain. Bob Edwards was chosen by the Lancashire Division of the ILP to contest the vacant Conservative seat of Stretford on the outskirts of Manchester. The Party did not have a strong branch in the constituency but in 1935 the Labour Party candidate had polled 35 per cent of the votes and so there was a large potential Labour vote to draw on. Edwards stressed the ILP's social policies when he came to drawing up his election propaganda, and he received support early on in his campaign from local Labour Party members and from Alex Sloan, a pacifist Labour Party MP.[44] Edwards made little contribution to the clarification of the ILP's peace proposals. He called for an immediate armistice and 'international socialist peace'.[45] He was adamant that he did not want a 'Hitler peace', but he did not explain how an international socialist peace could be achieved, although he assured the voters of Stretford that if they demanded such a peace by supporting him their message would reach the German people over the heads of the Nazis and give them a lead in their fight to overthrow Hitler.[46]

However, the contest soon went off on a tangent from the issues that Edwards had been trying to raise. Eric Gower, who had been the prospective Labour Party candidate for the constituency from 1938 until just before the outbreak of war,[47] announced that he was going to contest the seat on behalf of the CPGB. The CPGB had originally supported the war against Hitler, but the signing of the pact between Germany and the Soviet Union in August 1939 and the division between them of Poland had caused a rapid volte-face within the party, and the Communists now apparently believed that this conflict was just another imperialist war. Gower, therefore, also stood for a negotiated peace but, before his campaign really got under way, Russia invaded Finland on 30 November in an attempt to secure its northern flank against possible attack from either side in the European war. Ralph Etherton, the Conservative Party candidate, immediately seized on the rape of Finland as a stick with which to beat his two opponents, accusing both of them of supporting this act. The local press and the national newspapers, which had given little coverage up to now to the campaigns of the two left-wing candidates, took, however, a great interest in the Russo-Finnish war. Edwards was anxious, apparently, to avoid being injured by a wave of anti-communist feeling and he rose to the bait by roundly attacking the Russians.[48] Gower was forced to defend the Russian action, and both men spent a great deal of campaigning time on something which was almost certainly not an issue with the voters.[49]

The by-election campaign also suffered because of the blackout. The Conservative candidate, for example, stated that he was only holding a limited number of meetings because of it.[50] Moreover, as the blackout in December started at 4.30 pm, it meant that most people had to go to the polling booth in the dark after work. Understandably the turnout was low. Also, despite the Party priding itself on its propaganda skills, Reg Reynolds, one of the ILP's literary figures, complained that he had only seen one diminutive poster emanating from the ILP in the whole of the constituency.[51] Nevertheless Edwards polled 4,424 votes (15.1 per cent of the poll), beating his Communist opponent into a poor third place. The ILP claimed that this result showed that the ILP was leading the anti-war elements in the working class movement.[52] The CPGB replied by drawing attention to newspaper reports that members of the BUF had been active in Stretford urging people to vote for Edwards.[53] But even if true, it is unlikely that this unasked for help would have been of much assistance to the ILP candidate in view of the BUF's own unpopularity and appalling electoral record at that time.[54]

The ILP declared that it had taken heart because of this result and would now be considering fighting the government's candidates again in the near future.[55] In March 1940 it did indeed join with representatives of the reconstituted No-Conscription Fellowship and the PPU to form a by-election committee with the object of organising contests in which opposition to the war could be expressed.[56] But, between the Stretford contest in December and this move in March, the ILP had considered and rejected four other contests. In two of these, Southwark and Kettering, there were anti-war candidates already prepared to take the field and so the ILP decided not to enter the contest, but at the other two, Leeds East and Southampton, there was no other anti-war candidate and the Party gave no adequate reason for its decision not to stand.[57] It was apparent, however, that the ILP was not finding it easy to raise the money needed to fight these contests. The National Treasurer wrote to the *New Leader* at the end of December complaining that a number of ILPers were failing to pay their dues, and at that time the Party was still appealing for funds to cover the cost of the Stretford contest.[58] The *New Leader* was also in financial difficulties, due to falling sales, and was asking for more donations from party members.[59]

Meanwhile in early February 1940 the *Daily Express* noted in its 'Opinion' column that the ILP had decided not to contest the Southampton seat and remarked that perhaps it might be better if the ILP did embark on a number of contests against government candidates in by-elections as 'then it would be shown how determined (was) the country's support for the government's present policy'. The paper claimed to believe that the ILP would not get many votes, but the article had a sting in its tale for it declared that 'the electors are deprived of their rights by a deal made in Westminster, a political rig, a party game'.[60] The paper's owner, Lord Beaverbrook,[61] appears to have decided to give the ILP even more encouragement to fight by-elections. He approached Maxton, whom he knew slightly and admired greatly,[62] through W. J. Brown, a leading trade unionist and ex-ILPer, and invited the ILP Parliamentary Group to dine with him at his London home, Stornoway House. At this time, one of his biographers claims, Beaverbrook was 'not convinced of the wisdom or necessity of the war itself, it still seemed to him folly to have given a guarantee to Poland that could not be implemented'.[63] But what was discussed at the meeting which took place at Stornoway House on 5 March 1940 is a matter of dispute.[64] McGovern, later claimed that Beaverbrook wanted the government to negotiate a peace settlement straightaway and withdraw behind the empire's defences. Then, he believed, it could build up Britain's arms so that it would be ready to meet Hitler's next attack. At this time a Gallup poll was reporting that 29 per cent of the people it questioned were in favour of discussing peace terms with Germany,[65] and Beaverbrook may have believed that public opinion was moving steadily in that direction. McGovern argued that Beaverbrook wanted the ILP to step up its by-election campaigns so that the government would be placed under some pressure to negotiate a peace treaty with Germany. In return McGovern said Beaverbrook promised the ILP full publicity for its campaigns in his newspapers, and even offered some financial assistance with its election expenses if the ILPers showed that they were conducting their election fights seriously.[66]

Three weeks later the NAC decided to nominate Annie Maxton[67] as the ILP's candidate for the by-election which was pending in East Renfrewshire.[68] The ILP had held this seat on two occasions in the 1920s, and Annie Maxton was a local councillor in Barrhead, a small town within the constituency, and was well known and well respected locally.[69] She was also promised the assistance of W. O. Brown of the Scottish National Party, who had a large local electoral following,[70] although a similar offer of help from the CPGB was rejected by the ILP because it claimed that the Communists' support for the Russian attack on Finland showed that the CPGB could not be considered to be a genuine anti-war party.[71] And, as she made very plain from the beginning, the anti-war policy of the ILP was to be the main plank of Annie Maxton's campaign.[72] She interpreted this policy in a very simple way. She wanted the war stopped right away and a peace negotiated, although she insisted that there could not be a *lasting* peace while capitalism remained and so she also called at the same time for social changes to bring about socialism.[73] Her peace programme may have been electorally attractive in a constituency where a Mass Observation reporter found the highest percentage of voters (11 per cent) in favour of an immediate end to the war in any contest that MO had covered up to that time.[74] Moreover, this Mass Observation researcher noted that the ILP's posters were both more numerous and more imaginative than those of the government's candidate.[75]

The ILP was apparently very happy with the way the contest in East Renfrewshire was progressing,[76] and during the last week of the campaign it announced that Dan Carradice, a Lancashire ILPer, had been chosen to contest the Middleton and Prestwich constituency in a coming by-election, even though, as the *Manchester Guardian* noted, any support that the ILP had once enjoyed in that constituency had long since dwindled away.[77] However, the ILP was not to have the chance of testing its support in this constituency. The East Renfrewshire by-election had been fought against the background of the abortive attempt by the British and French to stop the Germans capturing Norway. On 10 May, the day the result of this by-election was announced, Chamberlain was forced to resign as prime minister and was replaced by Winston Churchill. McGovern had written to Beaverbrook on 9 May asking whether, in view of the fine show that Annie Maxton had put up (despite losing by a considerable margin[78]), he was still willing to assist the ILP. But, before Beaverbrook could have had a chance to read this letter, he was already considering the offer of the post of Minister of Aircraft Production in the new coalition government. He finally wrote to McGovern pointing out that things had changed since they had spoken in March and could never be the same again.[79]

The ILP had apparently already seen this for itself. On 10 May Carradice announced that he was withdrawing his candidature in the Middleton by-election 'in view of the present tension'.[80] On the very day his decision was reported in *The Times*, the Germans captured the Netherlands and began sweeping through Belgium and into France. It was to be 15 months before the ILP considered that the 'present tension' had eased enough for it to begin contesting by-elections again.[81] The Phoney War was indeed over.

11

The Spitfire Summer

A s the military situation in France worsened and it appeared that Britain would soon be invaded, the government strengthened the Defence Regulations to enable it to take steps against potential members of Hitler's so-called Fifth Column in this country. The new Regulation 18B empowered the Secretary of State to detain without trial people connected with organisations 'subject to foreign influence or control or in sympathy with the governments or systems of government of enemy countries where these organisations may be used to damage the war effort'. The day after this regulation was introduced Sir Oswald Mosley[1] was arrested and between the end of May and August 1940 almost the entire active membership of the BUF followed him into prison.[2]

However, the Attorney General doubted whether it would be legal to detain persons under this regulation who carried out anti-war or anti-government propaganda if they were not supporting the enemy's cause; and, as the government had no intention of introducing regulations against anyone who could not clearly be shown to be a potential traitor, few non-fascists went to prison under Regulation 18B.[3] But the government did introduce new regulations covering the publication of anti-war literature. Regulation 2D empowered the Home Secretary to prohibit the publication of any newspaper if he was satisfied that it systematically published matter 'calculated to ferment opposition to the successful prosecution of the war'. This regulation was given further teeth by the introduction of Regulation 94B which allowed the Home Secretary to seize any printing presses used for the production of such a newspaper.[4]

This regulation was never used against the *New Leader* even though the paper often carried attacks on the war and the government that were every bit as bitter as those in the *Daily Worker* which caused that paper to be suppressed in January 1941.[5] But the regulation did affect the ILP. The firm Buck Bros. and Harding, which had taken over printing the *New Leader* in September 1939 when the Odhams' subsidiary Victoria House Printing Co. Ltd. refused to continue doing so, decided in May 1940 that it could no longer print the *New Leader* or the PPU's *Peace News*, because it feared that the police might seize its presses if those papers were banned.[6] It may be that this new regulation was used as an excuse by Buck Bros. and Harding to enable it to cease working on publications whose anti-war slant the firm now found distasteful,[7] for, at the same time as the printers decided not to print these papers, the National Association of Wholesale Newsagents announced that it would no longer distribute the *New Leader* and *Peace News*. No reason was given but it seems likely that it was because of the anti-war line carried in these two publications.[8] This meant that the *New Leader* was not sold by newsagents again until 1946.

These two decisions had a damaging effect on the *New Leader*. The ILP had its own printing firm, the Blackfriars Press, and so it was able to continue printing the paper without a break, though the wartime restriction imposed on paper supply was a constant problem. But the press was in Leicester and the *New Leader* editorial office was in London which meant that copy had to travel backwards and forwards between these two places by train during the middle of the Blitz.[9] Yet, while this was inconvenient, the problem of distribution was more serious. The Party had traditionally relied on ILPers to sell the bulk of the newspapers door to door, but now the Blitz and other wartime exigencies meant that many party members could not keep their paper rounds going. If the newsagents had continued to sell the paper, the situation might have been somewhat eased. As it was, by the end of the summer of 1940 sales of the *New Leader* had dropped to half their pre-war level.[10]

Party propaganda was also affected because it was difficult to hold large public meetings in those areas in the front line of the Blitz. Political marches had already been banned,[11] and the Metropolitan Police began to take a tougher line with anti-war speakers in an attempt to prevent breaches of the peace.[12] But people were also less inclined to attend a political meeting if it meant that they were likely to be caught away from home when an air raid started. Branch meetings (and the lives of individual ILPers[13]) in some places were frequently disrupted by visits from the Luftwaffe, and local activities were also seriously curtailed because of the demands made by civilian war service on branch members.[14] Moreover, in many areas ILPers found that the public were far less tolerant of the Party's anti-war message than they had been during the Phoney War period, and so some ILPers decided it was best to 'keep their heads down' for the time being.[15]

However, it was not only a sense of discretion which reduced the volume of ILP propaganda at this time. There was also the very real problem of deciding what the Party was going to campaign about. Maxton admitted in September 1940 that no matter what the people might feel in their hearts, it had been obvious from the time of the East Renfrewshire by-election that they were not ready to do anything yet other than give the government a mandate to carry on the war.[16] Fortunately, however, although the Speaker would not acknowledge Maxton as the Leader of His Majesty's Opposition after the Labour Party joined the wartime coalition government in May 1940,[17] he did recognise the ILP as a separate party.[18] He and his successors, therefore, were always careful to ensure that at least one member of the ILP Group had a chance to speak, if they wanted to, during the course of every debate. And the ILP MPs used this opportunity whenever the chance arose to attack the capitalist system and imperialism; to put down questions concerning the liberty of the subject under wartime legislation and the government's treatment of minorities, and to propose ILP alternatives to practically every social and economic measure brought by the government before the House.[19] They also took advantage of the fact that the Labour Party was not acting as an opposition party and tabling amendments to the Loyal Address by trying to table their own amendments framed along socialist lines attacking the war and British capitalism and imperialism.[20] The ILP Parliamentary Group, therefore, made one last attempt to resurrect its demand for a negotiated peace by proposing an amendment to the Loyal Address on 5 December 1940 which called on the government to state the terms on which it would be willing to make peace. The debate had an unreal quality because the ILP MPs, while calling for a negotiated peace now, were insistent that they were not suggesting that Hitler's terms should be accepted but that a socialist peace should be made. Maxton was finally made to look foolish by Attlee during an exchange in which the Labour Party leader asked what the ILP would do if Hitler rejected its socialist peace proposals. Maxton replied that 'I and my friends will not be found wanting' which suggested that the ILP would then support the war even though, of course, the economic forces on each side would not have changed, and by the ILP's own definition it would still be an imperialist war.[21]

The *New Leader* argued that this had been a glorious performance[22] and apparently the Scottish ILP received 100 applications for membership during the following week as a direct result of these speeches, while Maxton claimed to have received hundreds of letters of support for his position.[23] But it was obvious that this debate had sounded the death knell of the ILP's negotiated peace policy. McGovern continued for some time to speak on platforms with various pacifist groups and to repeat the call for a peace by negotiation, but Maxton declared in Glasgow in February 1941, somewhat disingenuously perhaps, that the British workers had made a move and it was now up to the German workers to show their opposition to the Nazis in a public way. Only then, he said, could the British workers go on to give further signs of their antagonism to British imperialism.[24] Maxton seemed to be proposing a kind of leapfrog revolution which was a long way from traditional ILP policy. He never repeated his call for a negotiated peace.

If, however, it was ridiculous during the Blitz to call for a negotiated peace, what else could the Party campaign about? In May 1940 the NAC issued a statement reaffirming that the ILP would resist the imposition of any form of Nazism on the people of the UK (though it did not specify how), but it claimed that under war conditions the capitalist countries would 'inevitably move towards dictatorial totalitarianism.' It called, therefore, on the workers to press for real social equality based on a national wage scale and the abolition of luxury incomes; the conscription of wealth; the liberation of all colonial peoples and a declaration of socialist peace terms aimed at the German people. It also called on the British workers to prepare to establish a government (presumably led by the ILP) which would boldly put this programme into operation.[25] At the same time, it attacked the Labour Party for joining the coalition government led by Winston Churchill, and the TUC for agreeing to further government encroachments on trade union rights, though it was forced to admit that these moves had the people's support.[26] It also criticised the government's internment of political prisoners under Regulation 18B, but it was not an issue on which to mount a nationwide campaign in view of the animosity that the BUF had brought upon itself; even Maxton was said to be relatively unconcerned about the arrest of fascists as he believed that they had courted trouble.[27]

The ILP was debarred, by its anti-war stance, from taking part in the main political disputes of the period because they generally centred on the way that the war was being fought. It did attempt to mount campaigns against the British blockade of Europe and the use by Britain of bombing planes against civilians,[28] but, although neither of these weapons were universally popular at the time, it does seem that most people believed that they were the only means by which the war could be carried to the Germans.[29] On the other hand, the Blitz had exposed terrible weaknesses in the government's Air Raid Precaution schemes, particularly, though not exclusively, in East London. Shelters were often badly built[30] and insanitary, and re-housing arrangements completely inadequate.[31] Walter Padley[32] and Fenner Brockway saw this as an issue which they could use to educate the workers in the reality of the class struggle. They wrote a series of letters to the responsible ministers demanding more adequate shelters, a proper plan for re-housing, and additional medical facilities to guard against the outbreak of epidemics amongst people in the shelters. Meanwhile, the New Leader called on the government to take over the shelters and unoccupied houses of the rich for the benefit of bombed-out families.[33] However, the CPGB had already grasped the significance of these issues and was making them the cornerstone of its campaign for a People's Convention which would demand the formation of a people's government.[34] The Communist Party was very active in the areas where the shelter situation was particularly bad, and, despite the ILP's attempts to attack both the Convention and the CPGB,[35] it could not displace the CPGB as the champion of the workers on these issues.

During this lull in party activity some ILPers began to re-examine their anti-war beliefs. George Orwell was an early defector from the anti-war camp for as soon as the Second World War broke out he left the ILP and threw himself wholeheartedly into the war effort.[36] Jennie Lee, however, was less sure about the nature of this war in September 1939,[37] and she took a government post which assisted the running of the war while remaining a member of the anti-war ILP. But as France staggered towards defeat she apparently resolved her doubts and wrote to the *New Leader* stating that the British had no alternative now but to fight for their lives.[38] Lee remained nominally a member of the ILP for another 18 months and then resigned.[39]

There were other defections at this time by lesser-known ILPers who were no longer certain that the Party's anti-war stand was logical or right under the present circumstances. But their loss was felt only at local level and their small numbers were easily replaced by the influx of anti-war socialists and left-wing pacifists that was swelling the ranks of the ILP.[40] But, as the 'Spitfire Summer' of 1940 drew on, Dr Charles Smith, the Party Chairman since April 1939, began openly expressing his own doubts about the Party's position on the war. This led to the only real attempt within the ILP during this period to consider the implications of its opposition to the war. Smith, a decorated First World War veteran, had reacted to the horrors he had seen by becoming a pacifist and member of the ILP.[41] But he slowly moved away from his pacifist position and shocked the 1936 ILP annual conference by proclaiming that if he had been in Abyssinia, he would have taken up arms against the Italian invaders without regard to the economic forces which lay behind the conflict. Later that year he became an ardent supporter of the ILP's armed intervention in Spain. Smith advocated non-involvement during the Munich crisis,[42] however, and in September 1939 he wrote articles in the *New Leader* and in *Left* defending the ILP's opposition to the war.[43] Yet two months later he was talking of offering his services as a soldier to the Finns against the Russians,[44] and in June 1940 after the fall of the Low Countries and France he started to question the ILP's anti-war position.[45] At this time he was writing a series of articles on socialist morality for the *New Leader* under the pen-name Philo, and on 27 June he departed from his usual themes to attack the vagueness of revolutionary socialist parties' slogans on peace. In a scarcely veiled reference to the ILP, he wrote that 'some of them say "Peace by

Socialism", without making it clear which they put first, i.e. whether they mean "To socialism through Peace", "To peace through Socialism" ... a vital difference ... Some of them claim that their comrades in Germany have resisted Hitler even unto death, and then favour capitulation to Hitler now".[46] In the July edition of *Left* he wrote that, as it was impossible to fight for socialism at the moment, socialists should give serious consideration to the question of national defence if they believed that the Nazis provided a greater immediate threat to the working class movement than did British imperialism. Later that month he completed his transition from the ILP's accepted position by claiming that workers who served tyranny, including the German workers and soldiers who were now aiding Hitler, had no right to expect other workers to take their attack lying down, and the sooner they were 'bumped off the better'.[47]

The ILP had always accepted as an article of faith that their fellow workers in other lands might be misguided, but they only needed enlightenment and they would then see that all their domestic and international problems were the result of capitalism. Indeed in July 1940 the ILP helped persuade the BBC to broadcast a call from the International Workers' Front Against War to the German workers warning them against being misled by their Nazi leaders and asking them to join in the fight for socialism and for liberty.[48] Only if members of the working class attacked a worker's state should they be killed as a necessary sacrifice, but to talk of 'bumping them off' under the present circumstances was heresy. John McNair replied to Smith's article by stating that the ILP's duty was to establish a socialist state in Britain and then the Party would try to persuade the German and Italian workers and soldiers to join in a socialist peace and only if that appeal failed would the ILP be ready to defend a socialist Britain by force of arms.[49] He also reminded Smith that the German workers had only the same degree of responsibility for Nazi aggression as the British worker had for British imperialist aggression. But Smith retaliated by asking what the difference was between defending a socialist Britain against attack by foreign workers fighting for a capitalist master, which all socialists, except the pure pacifists, agreed would be a class duty, and defending a capitalist Britain, where the people enjoyed a large measure of personal and political freedom, against workers fighting for a reactionary power which, if victorious, would destroy all semblance of freedom for the working class.[50] And he added later that 'any man who says that Hitlerism is no worse than British capitalism of 1939 (or 1940) is either a fool or a fascist.'[51]

These arguments continued for nearly a year in the columns of the *New Leader*, in the pages of *Left* and on the typescript sheets of *Between Ourselves*. Most contributors opposed Smith's position and he was belaboured with quotations from his earlier articles in which he had defended the orthodox ILP line; and he was assailed from afar by missives from Marceau Pivert and Julian Gorkin of the International Marxist Centre in Mexico.[52] But all that this discussion proved was that the ILP did not have an answer to the simple question 'what would you do if the Germans invaded tomorrow?'. Indeed, Maxton again found himself wrong footed by Attlee on this issue. Attlee asked him what he would do if Hitler invaded Britain, to which Maxton replied that he would resist fascism by force if necessary. Attlee then asked him under these circumstances 'is it not better to tie [the Nazis] down across the Channel and thereby prevent them from invading the country?', to which Maxton had no reply.[53]

This internal discussion also revealed that some ILPers held quite different opinions on what the Party's policy was, or should be, on the war. A few still believed that the ILP was committed to calling for a negotiated peace (as its MPs had done in December 1940), even though Maxton, speaking for the platform, rejected a resolution framed in those terms moved at the 1941 annual conference because it would, he said, 'pin the ILP down to a purely pacifist approach'.[54] The Party's pacifists would indeed not accept that there was any difference between pacifism and socialism on this issue. They argued that invasion should be met with non-violent resistance, for they claimed that socialism was nothing if it was not humane, and that the way to conquer an idea was with a superior idea and not with violence.[55] Therefore socialists should negotiate to end the war, or suffer an invasion and defeat and then work to win over the enemy to the socialist point of view. It was a counsel of perfection which the majority of ILPers could not accept, and it had certainly not been the Party's attitude towards the conflict in Spain. This dispute highlights what has been described as an apparently growing incompatibility between the 'pacifist sentiment' within the Party and the ILP's revolutionary socialist policy. Indeed, it has been claimed that this incompatibility had only been patched over before the war by a compromise favoured by the ILP majority claiming that revolutionary violence might be necessary under certain circumstances, but then denying that these circumstances currently existed (except in Spain).[56]

There were also a minority of ILPers who supported Lenin's favoured tactic of revolutionary defeatism even though it was against ILP official policy. They argued that as it was a socialist's duty to defeat the capitalists in his or her own country first, it was only sensible that he or she should take advantage of every difficult situation in which the capitalist government found itself to undermine its position. That meant that the socialist should be ready to hinder the capitalists' war effort to such an extent that the combined pressure of the foreign attack and the internal disruption would produce a crisis from which the government could not recover. The resulting crash would enable the workers to seize power.[57] There was, of course, the very real danger that these tactics would result in the military defeat and perhaps occupation of your own country, but Lenin had insisted during the First World War that socialists should accept this result if necessary because it would mean the end of their own capitalists. He was certain that a combination of the workers of the invading country and of the conquered country fighting against the victorious capitalists would soon ensure that capitalist power was destroyed in both places.[58] F. A. Ridley, one of the leading advocates of this tactic in the ILP in 1940, argued that in view of the evils that the British were perpetuating in the empire it was by no means clear that a victory for the fascists would be any worse for the world as a whole than would be a victory for British imperialism.[59] This argument was in fact quite close to what had been accepted as the ILP's official policy for the past decade. The Party had often claimed that there was little to choose between fascism and imperialism, and both Smith in November 1939 and Padley in October 1940 had declared that socialists should be ready to take advantage of the misfortunes of their capitalist rulers, and that the military fortunes of capitalist Britain were of no concern to ILPers.[60]

However, in December 1940, despite many years of the ILP claiming that fascism and imperialism were merely two sides of the same capitalist coin, the NAC adopted a resolution in which it 'recognised fully that a Nazi victory would be a disaster for mankind involving the further enslavement of peoples, the suppression of liberty of thought and speech and person, and the crushing of an independent working class movement'[61] and clearly Smith and Padley, like the majority of ILPers, balked at the full implications of the revolutionary defeatist policy which they had so nearly accepted.[62] Few were altruistic enough to stand by happily for the sake of their class brothers in the colonies and watch the Germans invade their country, kill their family and friends, destroy their institutions and enslave them.[63] And so they refused to encourage sabotage of the war effort,[64] and rejected revolutionary defeatism as an ILP tactic. Brockway wrote two articles, during the controversy over Dr Smith's pronouncements, attacking revolutionary defeatism because he claimed that Lenin had only intended the tactic to be used when the country being attacked was more reactionary than the aggressor country, as it had been in 1914 when Russia was being attacked by Germany. He also claimed that 'no socialist wants to see a Nazi victory over Britain – despite the tyrannies of the Empire'.[65] Brockway seemed to be close to claiming that British imperialism was the lesser evil, in which case it is difficult to see why the ILP could not give the war critical support as Smith was suggesting. But perhaps, after all, Brockway was merely arguing that Nazism and British imperialism were equal evils, and as such neither should be assisted by the socialist. But whatever he meant, his contribution did not clarify what the ILP's policy was to be if Britain was actually invaded by Nazi troops before it had become a socialist state. Luckily for the ILP it was never faced with the reality of a German invasion and so never had to decide what to do when confronted by unenlightened foreign workers with rifles in their hands.

This internal party dispute gradually petered out without a satisfactory conclusion having been reached. Dr Smith resigned as ILP Chairman at the 1941 conference and during 1942 gradually drifted out of the ILP. He said at the time that his work commitments were now too great to allow him to remain active in the Party, but in 1944, when he joined the new left-wing party Common Wealth, he admitted that he had left the ILP because he disagreed with its attitude to the war.[66] Meanwhile the Party as a whole appeared to be stagnating,[67]and suffered a serious blow when its London Head Office was destroyed on 10 May 1941 during the Blitz.[68] Then in June 1941 the war took another dramatic turn and the ILP reacted by taking fresh heart and accepting new challenges.

12

Socialist Britain Now!

On 22 June 1941 the Germans invaded Russia. The British Government thought that this new development in the war would only give this country a brief respite from the major German assault that it still faced,[1] but apparently for many members of the working class this marked a watershed moment. After a brief period of uncertainty, the CPGB changed its party line again and became a fierce supporter of the war and of Churchill's government,[2] and Emanuel Shinwell later wrote that with the entry of Russia into the war the country's morale changed overnight and there was a new spirit in the factories.[3]

The ILP did not share in this general wave of enthusiasm. The Party had welcomed the Russian Revolution of October 1917 as the dawn of a new era, and nearly a quarter of a century later it was still proclaiming that the Soviet Union was the first workers' state and as such was owed a special allegiance by the workers in other countries.[4] But, after the rise of Stalin to supreme power in Russia, the ILP became increasingly at odds with that country's domestic and foreign policies. The ILP suffered continuous verbal attacks from the Comintern, and it had been appalled by the Moscow Trials of old Bolsheviks, the communists' actions against the POUM in Spain, and the Russo-German pact.[5] These events, followed quickly after the outbreak of war in Europe by the Russian invasions of Poland and then Finland, had convinced the majority of ILPers that the Soviet Union had drifted a long way from the ideal workers' state. The ILP line on the Soviet Union now was that it was a country where capitalism had been destroyed and so it was basically a workers' state, but one that was being led astray by a bureaucratic leadership which would have to be removed and workers' democracy reintroduced before the Soviet Union could be put back on the road to true communism.[6]

In the meantime the ILP did not believe that the entry of Russia into the war had altered the conflict's imperialist nature. The ILP condemned the 'Nazi aggression' and extended fraternal greetings to the workers and peasants of the Soviet Union. It also declared that it would give all possible (non-military) aid to the Russian workers, and it would do all in its power to prevent the capitalist states from making an alliance against the Soviet Union, but it claimed that the only way it could actually help its Russian colleagues was by overthrowing British capitalism. It argued that only a socialist government could be trusted to give the Soviet Union unselfish assistance (as it believed that Churchill was only interested in protecting British interests and would turn against Russia when the time was right), while at the same time acting as an example to the Russian workers that would encourage them to throw off their bureaucratic leaders.[7]

Not all ILPers accepted this party line. Both Tom Taylor and Tom Stephenson tried to persuade their NAC colleagues to demand that the government give military aid to Russia, and the ILP's Trotskyist elements, based mainly in London and the North East, attempted to commit the Party to agreeing to the supply of all the arms produced in Britain to the Soviet Union to enable it to defend the gains of the October Revolution. But the NAC refused to entertain the idea that it should encourage the capitalist government in any of its war-making ventures under any pretext. Bob Edwards, for example, argued that if 'we go one step in the direction of supporting the war, we must go the whole way', while James Maxton claimed that 'we could not send military aid to Russia without assisting imperialist and Stalinist purposes'. Instead the NAC argued that, once the working class was powerful enough to force the capitalist government to send the arms it produced exclusively to the Soviet Union, it would automatically be in a position to overthrow that government and introduce socialism. Until then the workers would have no way of controlling what the government did with the war materials it produced.[8] John Aplin, although he had not been an active party member since the outbreak of war, tried to persuade his ILP colleagues that the invasion of Russia had indeed altered the nature of the war and that the time had now come to give it critical support. But his appeal had little effect on the Party and he left the ILP in protest.[9]

Nevertheless the invasion of Russia did appear to have a profound impact on the ILP. After months of inactivity the Party began to stir. The NAC announced in the *New Leader* of 23 August 1941 that it had decided that the ILP should again fight by-elections 'whenever the circumstances promise a representative vote for the party policy of Peace by Socialism'. It immediately established a by-election committee[10] to reach prompt decisions on suitable contests and authorised the setting up of an election fund. The council gave as one of its main reasons for adopting this course that the ILP was now the only party with parliamentary representation that had not committed itself to supporting the war, and so was still defending the workers' rights against government encroachment.[11] It also seems likely that the council expected that the ILP would gain recruits from those who had previously supported the CPGB's anti-war line.[12]

As a result of this decision the Lancashire Division of the ILP decided to nominate Brockway as its candidate in the forthcoming by-election in the Conservative stronghold of Lancaster, which he had contested previously in the 1922 general election, even though four other candidates had already declared their intention to stand.[13] Brockway accepted the challenge, though his campaign differed in many details from those fought by the ILP earlier in the war. Abandoning the ILP slogan 'Stop the War by Socialism' which the Party had used since October 1939, Brockway now assured the voters that the war could be *shortened* by socialism. He stated that a socialist Britain would be an example to the German people, and they would respond by overthrowing Hitler. There was no call for a negotiated peace in his address, and his literature gives the impression that he envisaged that Britain, after the socialist revolution, would continue the military struggle against Hitler until victory or a German socialist revolution brought the Nazis down. As if to mark his break with the older party line on the war, Brockway did not refer to himself as an ILPer, but said he was the 'socialist candidate'.[14] Apparently Maxton was not happy about these developments,[15] but he joined Brockway on his hustings. Brockway laid great stress on the social aspects of the ILP's programme and seemed to be aiming at the constituency's Labour Party voters.[16] Maxton, on the other hand, was already looking beyond this war, and claiming that the time had now come to lay the foundations of a new social order which would prevent a third world war from breaking out.[17]

The Lancaster by-election proved to be a difficult contest for the ILP to fight. It was a large constituency which included the county town of Lancaster; Morecombe a seaside resort, and a vast rural area where the ILP, despite the demand for a £3 per week minimum wage for farm workers which appeared in Brockway's programme, was not likely to pick up many votes. After nomination day Brockway found himself faced with just a Conservative and an Independent Liberal as opponents, and the CPGB threw its support behind the Conservative.[18] Brockway, with 5,418 votes got 19.5 per cent of the poll to take third place. But he had received almost the same percentage of the votes as the official Labour Party candidate had in 1935 and Brockway believed that this meant that the ILP could now win a seat in an industrial constituency. The ILP Chairman, Bob Edwards, argued that the result was entirely satisfactory and that Brockway had suffered because of absentee voters, who, Edwards claimed, were mainly workers and would have voted for the ILP.[19]

Ten days after the Lancaster result was declared the ILP Executive Committee announced that it had decided to launch a new propaganda campaign 'For a Socialist Britain'. This was to take the form of a series of regional conferences made up of delegates from any working-class organisation which wished to be represented, and supported by the publication of a pamphlet setting out the campaign's programme. In addition the Party planned to organise large demonstrations, although it was stressed that the ILP was only intending to give a lead in what it hoped would soon develop into a mass working-class campaign. In November the NAC approved the proposal, although it added the word 'Now' to the original title and sections on fire-watching and female conscription to the programme.[20] The programme of the Socialist Britain Now campaign closely resembled that used by Brockway as the basis of his election address in Lancaster.[21] It contained the ILP's usual demands for social and economic change in Britain and in the colonies and promised that the war could be shortened if a socialist Britain was established because, the programme continued, it could use all the propaganda weapons at its disposal to convince the German people that the socialist new order was superior to the New Order of Europe ('Neuordnung') proposed by the Nazis, and to call on the German workers to overthrow Hitler.[22]

Later in November the ILP Parliamentary Group introduced an amendment to the Loyal Address in the Commons based on the programme of the Socialist Britain Now campaign.[23] The debate on this amendment did not go well for the ILP. MPs pointed out that only just over a year before McGovern had been saying that it was very unlikely that the German people would be willing or able to rise against Hitler, and yet the ILP was now proposing a policy based on that assumption.[24] Moreover, Labour Party MPs claimed that this amendment was merely an attempt to embarrass the Labour Party because it contained much that its MPs would normally support jumbled up with a view of the war which they could not accept. Only Sir Richard Acland, a Liberal MP who had recently become sympathetic to socialist ideals, voted with the ILPers.[25] This debate in many ways epitomised the problems the ILP MPs faced during the war. The ILP Group could not hope to bring down the coalition government on its own and the ILP's anti-war stand largely antagonised members of the Labour Party's left wing. It could only normally rely, therefore, on the support of a handful of pacifist Labour Party MPs, some of whom had been ILPers not long before. It is true that very occasionally some members of the non-pacifist left wing of the Labour Party, including Bevan and Sydney Silverman, would vote with the ILP Group on one of its motions,[26] but generally they were suspicious of the ILP's motives,[27] and, while sometimes willing to speak for the ILP's case, they would not usually follow this through with a vote, so that at no time could the ILP Group count on obtaining more than a dozen votes for any motion or amendment it proposed. On a few occasions the ILP MPs did find themselves in the division lobbies with backbench Labour Party MPs rebelling against their party whip, but this was invariably on issues which had stirred the Labour Party left wing into action quite independently of any prompting from the ILPers.[28]

However, despite the poor performance on this particular amendment, the ILP was confident that its new campaign would gain working-class support. In the first week of December the NAC's by-election committee agreed to a request from the Scottish Division that the Party should contest the vacant parliamentary seat of Edinburgh Central, even though the ILP's organisation in that city was weak.[29] Tom Taylor, the Scottish representative on the NAC, was chosen as the candidate, and given help from the Glasgow ILP and from members of the North of England branches. Taylor was described by a neutral observer as a good candidate,[30] and he threw himself into the campaign with enthusiasm. While ILPers normally limited themselves to chalking campaign slogans from the New Leader on constituency pavements, Tom Taylor was only just stopped in time by the authorities from painting his slogans on the Edinburgh pavements in red paint![31] He based his campaign on the Socialist Britain Now programme, with the addition of a demand that the conscription regulations forcing Scottish girls to work in English munitions factories should be altered. There were many jobs vacant in Scotland and the transfer of girls from their Scottish homes to work in the south was generally disliked north of the border.[32]

Maxton spoke for Taylor and attracted large crowds. The ILP was also very active in attempting to mobilise the potential Labour vote in this working-class area of Edinburgh,[33] but once again the Party was to suffer as a result of a change in the fortunes of war. On 7 December the Japanese launched a surprise attack on the American fleet at Pearl Harbour. Three days later, on what has been described as the blackest day of the war for Britain,[34] two British battleships, HMS Prince of Wales and HMS Repulse, were sunk by Japanese aircraft as they steamed to protect the British base at Singapore. The loss of these two ships had a dramatic effect on the Edinburgh by-election campaign, turning the attention of the people away from female conscription and back to the issue of winning the war. The ILP had reacted to the attack on Pearl Harbour by expressing its solidarity with Japanese socialists, and the ILP speakers had a very difficult time with their audiences for the last few days of the contest.[35] The result of the election was of little use to the ILP in gauging the effectiveness of its new campaign.[36] Taylor obtained 1,950 votes, which was 29 per cent of the poll, and that was the highest percentage achieved by an ILPer so far, but he had still fallen far short of the support received by the Labour Party candidate in 1935 (41 per cent), and the turnout had been a derisory 20 per cent.

In the meantime, however, the Socialist Britain Now campaign was progressing in other ways. In January 1942 the Party invited working-class organisations to send delegates to regional conferences which the ILP had arranged for that March in nine major cities in Britain, with an additional series of meetings in some of the smaller Scottish towns. The first meeting was held in Glasgow, and was apparently a great success. It was followed by meetings in Liverpool, London, Norwich and Huddersfield, which also lived up to the ILP's expectations. The cost of all these meetings was only the equivalent of one election contest, and the 1942 ILP annual conference gave the project a large vote of confidence.[37] Indeed a number of recruits, including two prospective Labour Party parliamentary candidates, Tom Colyer and Will Morris, were won over to the Party, 12 new branches were formed and the sales of the New Leader rose as a direct result, the ILP claimed, of the campaign.[38]

Apparently this increase in strength emboldened the NAC and the Divisional Councils, for the Party began to employ more full-time Organisers. Walter Padley had been the full-time Organiser for the London and Southern Counties Division since 1940, but it had been several years since any other Division had had one.[39] Now full-time Organisers were appointed in Scotland, Lancashire and the North East, and part-time Organisers in Yorkshire, the Midlands, and in South Wales. These men were paid by their Divisions but the NAC had to donate some money because Divisional income was insufficient to meet this kind of extra expense.[40] It was, therefore, a gamble for the Party both locally and nationally when it employed these extra officers.

The fall of Singapore on 15 February 1942 caused a hostile public reaction in Britain against Churchill's government, and George Orwell believed that a revolutionary situation could be at hand.[41] Faced with this unrest the ILP's response was far from revolutionary, but the NAC did decide to contest two by-elections in the same month, both of which were bound to attract public attention as they were against government ministers. At the beginning of April 1942 Brockway fought a campaign against Sir James Grigg, the newly appointed Secretary of State for War, in the Cardiff East constituency. Brockway used the Socialist Britain Now programme, and stressed that the ILP was not advocating any deal with Hitler, and was indeed calling on the German people to overthrow him.[42]

However, Brockway was bitterly attacked by the CPGB which accused the ILPers of being agents of Nazism,[43] and by both the local and national newspapers.[44] The ILP's difficulties in this contest were exacerbated by a lack of large halls in which its star speakers could perform. The Cardiff Police Commissioner agreed to lift an earlier ban on all outdoor meetings, but small street corner meetings were not as effective as large indoor meetings might have been for getting the ILP's message across to the largest number of people in the shortest possible time. Moreover the voters showed little interest in the contest. The turnout was only 33.1 per cent though Brockway received 3,311 votes, which was a respectable 24.8 per cent of the votes cast, and the ILP considered that very satisfactory in a seat it had never believed it could win.[45]

Meanwhile the other contest had begun. When the ILP had nominated James Carmichael to fight the Glasgow Cathcart seat it had expected him to be standing against Sir T. D. King Murray, Solicitor General for Scotland. However, Murray withdrew and the Conservative candidate was now Francis Beattie. There was also a Scottish Nationalist in the contest, and William Douglas Home, author and younger son of The Earl of Home and at this time a serving Army officer, was standing as an independent progressive candidate. The CPGB again campaigned for the government candidate and declared that a vote for the ILP was a vote for the betrayal of the Soviet Union.[46] The newspaper, *Forward*, also carried a series of attacks on the ILP written by Patrick Dollan, the Labour Lord Provost of Glasgow, who had himself been anti-war during the First World War and a leading member of the ILP until disaffiliation.[47] However, most of the newspapers ignored the ILP's candidate and concentrated instead on Douglas Home. He obtained the publicity and 21 per cent of the votes. Although Beattie easily won the seat, Douglas Home beat the ILP candidate, who with 2,493 votes, and 13.8 per cent of the poll, only just saved his deposit. The *New Leader* claimed that this result showed that within the present body of anti-government opinion there was a solid core of people who accepted the ILP's international socialist philosophy.[48] Yet it was clear that, despite its early successes, the Socialist Britain Now campaign for which Carmichael had stood was not gathering momentum. The ILP was still gaining some recruits, but was forced to admit that it had not been able to interest the wider Labour

Movement in the programme.[49] The speakers at the conferences and meetings called to support the campaign had all been ILPers, and the meetings were abandoned after the first series had been completed. In October 1942 an American Trotskyist living in Britain, Marc Loris, asked in what other ways the ILP planned to carry on this campaign 'now that it had clearly given up the conference method'.[50] He received no reply.

But, even as Loris was criticising the Socialist Britain Now campaign, the major British Trotskyist party, the Workers' International League (WIL), was noting in its internal bulletin that the ILP was 'beginning to penetrate the fringes of the trade union movement'.[51] This was a notable achievement in view of the Party's abysmal record in this field. The ILP had attempted to strengthen its industrial organisation and contacts at the beginning of the war, and had offered space in the *New Leader* to contributors of any party who wanted to send in details of industrial disputes.[52] But by September 1940 the paper had to admit that it was in fact receiving less industrial news than it usually did.[53] The Scottish Division attempted to strengthen the ILP's industrial organisation in Scotland in November 1940 by setting up a committee to co-ordinate its industrial work and provide a mechanism for co-operation with English ILP trade unionists. It was not a success.[54] Rank-and-file ILPers tended to blame ILP Head Office for what they considered were the Party's weaknesses in this field, but the ILP was suffering under the double handicap of having an anti-war policy at a time when the country seemed in danger of immediate invasion, and of being faced with competition from the CPGB which had had a strong foothold in the trade unions for a number of years.[55] Then after Russia was invaded by the Germans the CPGB switched from supporting practically every strike to opposing nearly all of them. This gave the ILP a chance to take over the CPGB's mantle of leadership of the militant section of the industrial workers. In September 1941 the NAC set up an Industrial Committee,[56] which announced a national campaign to promote its industrial programme, although it stressed that it was doing so 'for the good of the workers and not for the benefit of the ILP; the (party) policy was merely a basis for discussion amongst unionists'.[57]

The first conference in a planned series to promote the campaign was held in Bradford on 6 September 1941. Walter Padley and Will Ballantine addressed the delegates and attacked both the harshness of the government's trade union legislation and the feebleness of the TUC which had allowed it to go unchallenged.[58] Two months later Padley repeated a similar sermon to 125 union delegates in Birmingham.[59] However, both Padley and Ballantine were needed for the Socialist Britain Now campaign and the series of industrial conferences had failed to attract the support of leading non-ILP unionists. It could not, therefore, gather momentum on its own. Without the active participation of Padley and Ballantine the conference method of carrying on the campaign had to be abandoned.[60] But the Industrial Committee issued a short series of pamphlets on industrial matters, and Padley encouraged Divisions and large branches to appoint an industrial officer who would communicate with local unionists and put forward the ILP's case.[61]

Meanwhile the ILP was giving at least vocal support to a number of unofficial strikes and it was gaining a foothold in some new areas as a result. This was particularly true in the mining districts where a legacy of hostility and distrust bred during the interwar years was combining with a series of grievances caused by under-manning and low wages to produce what James Griffiths[62] of the Labour Party's NEC described as 'a poisonous atmosphere in the (mining) industry'.[63] A wave of unofficial strikes followed. In January 1942 the miners in the Betteshanger Pit in Kent struck over a wage dispute. The ILP supported their claim and issued appeals in the *New Leader* for a strike fund.[64] A few months later Tom Stephenson, a member of both the NAC and the Miners' Federation Executive, and Hugh Brannan, a young Lanarkshire miner and ILPer, wrote a pamphlet on conditions in the mining industry in which they attacked both the government and the union leaders and advocated the nationalisation of the pits under workers' control.[65] Their arguments and proposed solutions were similar to those being advocated by Trotskyists who also apparently had members active in the mining areas assisting in strikes and distributing literature.[66] In December 1942 the CPGB claimed that the ILP had combined with Trotskyists to persuade miners at the Cortonwood Colliery to prolong their strike, although the *Daily Worker* could provide no proof for this assertion.[67]

However, a month later, Stephenson and Brannan began to

contribute to *The Militant Scottish Miner* which was a newspaper that had grown out of an organ of the Militant Group of Trotskyists who were members of the Labour Party. Brannan seemed to believe that he could use this new paper to increase his influence amongst the miners. He wrote a series of articles defending the miners' right to strike, which came close to incitement, and he and other contributors attacked the existing miners' leaders who were nearly all CPGB members or sympathisers. In the summer of 1943 Brannan stood for election as President of the Lanarkshire Miners Union and used the newspaper to publicise his campaign.[68] The Militant Miners Group, as the men behind the newspaper were now called, were active in strikes in the area, though the paper was quick to deny that its members were in any way responsible for their outbreak.[69] Abe Moffat, the communist Chairman of the National Union of Scottish Miners, and one of the paper's prime targets, saw the influence of the Group behind every dispute,[70] but neither the Ministry of Labour,[71] nor the police,[72] could find any evidence that this ILP–Trotskyist group had any real influence on industrial conflicts.[73]

Just as the Militant Miners Group was coming into existence, a similar organisation was growing up in the engineering industry, where the abandonment of long cherished so-called restrictive practices, and the stresses of working in an industry heavily involved in war work, had also led to a wave of unofficial strikes during the period after the invasion of Russia. In February 1943 the Militant Trade Unionist Group was formed in London with Don McGregor, a member of both the Amalgamated Engineering Union and the Wood Green ILP, as its Secretary. This Group advanced a programme very similar to that of the ILP, as did the Clyde Workers' Committee which was formed in Glasgow in June 1943.[74]

In autumn 1943 Roy Tearse, who had been in the ILP a short time before and was now the Industrial Organiser of the WIL, set up the Militant Workers Federation. This body was intended to co-ordinate the activities of Militant Workers Groups in Glasgow and London, and to encourage the creation of similar groups in Sheffield, Huddersfield, Barrow and Rugby. The police and MI5 were both keeping a close eye on Tearse but neither could find any evidence that he was in any way responsible for aggravating the current industrial unrest.[75] That was until the Tyneside and Clydeside engineering apprentices struck during the early months of 1944 because they believed they would be conscripted into the mines, before they had finished their apprenticeships, as Bevin Boys under the new scheme[76] introduced by the Minister of Labour and National Service, Ernest Bevin.[77] Tearse already knew J. W. Davy, the Secretary of the Tyneside Apprentices Guild, and through him the Trotskyists were able to help in the organisation of the strike.

Just at this moment a wave of strikes had broken out in the mining industry over a dispute concerning piece rates.[78] The CPGB claimed that the ILP and the Trotskyists were behind all these stoppages,[79] and, although most observers thought these suspicions groundless,[80] Bevin agreed with the CPGB that political agitators were at the bottom of these strikes.[81] Tearse and three Trotskyists colleagues were arrested and tried under the Trades Dispute Act of 1927 for their part in the apprentices' strike,[82] and Bevin introduced Defence Regulation 1AA which made it an offence to incite anyone to strike who was working in an essential industry except during the course of a properly convened union branch meeting. Many ILPers thought that party members would be arrested as soon as this regulation came into effect, and both the ILP and the Trotskyist Revolutionary Communist Party (RCP) (into which the WIL had merged) believed that this new regulation tolled the death knell of the Militant Workers Federation and its Groups.[83] In fact no one was ever arrested under that regulation.

This industrial activity had an unfortunate sequel for the ILP. During the course of this work members of the Trotskyist parties had apparently managed to win some ILPers over to the policies of the Fourth International.[84] T. Dan Smith, who was Organiser and NAC member for the North East Division from 1943, had become a secret member of the RCP,[85] and within a short time, it was later claimed, a majority of the members of the North East Divisional Council were sympathetic to the Trotskyist cause. Allegedly this council then rigged the next divisional conference, and Smith's election to the NAC, by allowing branches believed to be controlled by Trotskyist sympathisers,[86] to be over-represented, while non-Trotskyist-dominated branches were deprived of their true representation. This divisional conference then passed a number of what some local branches perceived as Trotskyist resolutions. Four North East branches immediately complained to the NAC which subsequently declared the North East divisional conference unconstitutional and suspended the Divisional Council.[87] An enquiry was carried out in the area by Bob Edwards, Percy Williams and John McNair and found some evidence of malpractice. After a stormy meeting the NAC dissolved the North East Divisional Council and suspended Smith.[88] At the 1945 ILP annual conference the revelation that an RCP Internal Bulletin boasted of having factions working within the ILP convinced the majority of ILP delegates that the NAC had taken the right action.[89] As the Party's constitution prohibited ILPers from belonging to organised factions of another party, Smith and four other members of the North East Divisional Council were expelled from the ILP and openly joined the RCP.[90] Several more Trotskyist sympathisers in the North East walked out of the ILP leaving the Party seriously weakened in that area.[91]

However, three years' earlier, in the autumn of 1942, a political party had been formed under the name Common Wealth, which was to prove a greater threat to the ILP's position as the main left-wing opposition party to the coalition government than the RCP ever could.

13

Common Wealth

In March 1941 Tom Taylor wrote in *Between Ourselves* that the 'issue for or against the war becomes largely academic as the war proceeds'. Brockway's address for the Lancaster by-election, which talked of *shortening* the war by socialism, seemed to indicate that the ILP was indeed beginning to accept that the war would have to be fought out until either Hitler was defeated militarily or overthrown.[1] McGovern confirmed this at the 1942 Scottish Divisional annual conference, and James Carmichael claimed that if Britain became socialist during the war it would proclaim *this* war at an end, only to immediately declare its own war on Hitler which would continue until victory had been achieved or a social revolution had occurred *in Germany.*[2] But Maxton made it very clear that the ILP would not attempt to make its programme more electorally attractive by dropping its opposition to this imperialist war.[3] Yet a move to soften the ILP's position on the war must, however, have been politically tempting. The electoral truce had worked well for the government until March 1942. But since the beginning of the year Britain had endured a series of military defeats in both the Far East and Near East, and was suffering serious shortages because of the German U-boat campaign in the Atlantic. During March and April three government seats fell to independent candidates who stood for greater efficiency in the prosecution of the war and for more equality of sacrifice.[4]

There were other straws in the wind indicating that there was increasing support in the country for a progressive policy for fighting the war and winning the peace. In 1940 the Liberal MP Sir Richard Acland had written a book called *Unser Kampf* in which he advocated a reassessment of British values to include a greater degree of community spirit and social responsibility in all layers of society to provide the country with a new faith for which to fight. The book was an immediate bestseller. Just over a year later he wrote another book in which he further developed these themes, and called for greater common ownership of Britain's resources to give everyone a stake in the country and remove the gross inequalities in the economic structure of society. He called on people who agreed with these sentiments to write to him. The response was so good that he decided to form a movement called, like the second book, Forward March, dedicated to the concept of common ownership.

The by-election successes in 1942 of independent candidates made Acland think very seriously about putting forward candidates from his own movement. Then in July 1942 Acland's group merged with the 1941 Committee, which was a loosely organised band of intellectuals who believed that a new philosophy was needed to enable politics to become more humanitarian and more efficient. The new party formed by this merger, called Common Wealth (CW), supported common ownership but rejected the concept of the class struggle and initially at least did not consider itself to be a socialist party. Its main adherents were members of the middle class, but its socialistic philosophy and its call for a more efficient prosecution of the war made it potentially attractive to Labour voters at a time when the electoral truce was preventing them from identifying themselves in Conservative- or Liberal-held seats.[5]

Brockway gave this new party a guarded welcome. He said he was pleased to see that there was now a party which seemed to be awakening a response to socialist measures in the breasts of the middle class because he did not believe that a socialist revolution could succeed in Britain without the assistance of technicians and other members of that class. However, he said he was worried by the fact that the party rejected the name socialist, had no roots in the working-class movement and, in his opinion, had no clear political philosophy. He was afraid that it might drift towards fascism. But he believed that the party did contain some socialists and many others who could be won to the socialist cause, and so, as he believed the ILP needed likeminded allies, he was anxious to establish good relations between the ILP and Common Wealth.[6] Some ILP branches evidently agreed with him, and in November 1942 a joint meeting was held in Essex between the Barking branch of the ILP and the neighbouring Ilford branch of CW which resulted in an accord to help each other at by-elections.[7] A similar meeting took place in Manchester two months later when it was agreed by the local ILP and CW branches to take joint action 'for socialism'.[8]

However, just at that moment the ILP and CW clashed in a by-election contest in Bristol Central. Members of the NAC were becoming convinced that the ILP needed to contest by-elections, even if that meant occasionally competing with the Labour Party, as a way of energising the Party,[9] and this vacant seat was a tempting target. The constituency covered the docks as well as the business quarter, and the Labour Party candidate in 1935 had polled 47 per cent of the votes. The ILP also had a large and active branch in the city and an ILPer on the local council. Therefore on 22 December Head Office asked the Bristol ILP to submit names of prospective candidates to the NAC's by-election committee. The Bristol branch was apparently taken by surprise and replied that it had no candidate to offer, but it soon relented and announced that it was indeed submitting a shortlist for consideration.[10] In the meantime the local press noted that Jennie Lee had been asked to stand as an Independent Labour candidate by members of the local Labour Party who disagreed with the electoral truce, and that she had agreed. She was also going to receive some financial and organisational assistance from CW.[11] Brockway and Padley realised that Lee would be a powerful opponent and far more electorally attractive than John McNair whom the by-election committee had nominated as the Party's candidate. They both tried to persuade Maxton to withdraw the ILP's candidature but he refused.[12]

McNair stood with the ILP's social policy as the main plank of his campaign, but he also reintroduced a measure of anti-war fervour into his speeches that had been conspicuously absent from the Party's election contests of the previous 18 months.[13] However, he was not able to make his anti-war stand an important issue in this by-election. In December 1942 Sir William Beveridge[14] published a report containing his proposed plan for a reconstruction of the social services for the post-war period which was intended to guarantee every citizen, through a system of state-sponsored national insurance, social security 'from the cradle to the grave'. The recommendations appeared to many people to be a revolutionary step forward, and, it has been claimed, the public quickly accepted them as the cause for which the war was being fought.[15] The government, on the other hand, which had originally commissioned the report, seemed less than enthusiastic, and it appeared to be attempting to shelve the proposals. This quickly turned the Beveridge Report into a highly contentious political issue.[16]

Jennie Lee grasped the significance of the report as an election issue and declared that she stood 'for every word, letter and comma' in it.[17] The coalition government's candidate, Lady Apsley of the Conservative Party, also bowed to public opinion and gave the report her support. An observer noted that the election seemed to centre mainly on the question of which candidate was likely to be the most effective champion of Beveridge.[18] McNair and F. Dunn, another independent candidate standing in this election, failed to raise much public interest. While Lee's public meetings were packed,[19] McNair was unable to attract even a small audience,[20] possibly partly because, as an independent observer noted, the ILP's advertising for its meetings during this by-election was 'so insignificant that it could only be found through a determined effort'.[21] McNair and McGovern tried to stir up some publicity by claiming that Jennie Lee had moved to the right since leaving the ILP,[22] and she replied by accusing the ILP of being a pacifist party masquerading as a socialist one. But the ILP was apparently not getting its message across to the voters and it could not for some unknown reason, despite its strong local presence, compete with the efficient and enthusiastic CW's newly-formed organisation.[23] The turnout on polling day was low and Lee received fewer votes than had seemed likely from the response she was getting during the campaign.[24] But she was still second in the poll with 38.2 per cent of the votes cast, forcing McNair into a poor third place with only 7.4 per cent (830 votes). The *New Leader* insisted that support had been switched from McNair to Lee at the last minute because the public had decided that she stood more chance of defeating the government candidate, which would demonstrate their disgust with the government's attitude to the Beveridge Report. The ILP also claimed that its campaign had stimulated the Party in the South West,[25] but there was no disguising the fact that it had suffered a terrible defeat, and perhaps not surprisingly this was the last time the ILP clashed with CW in a by-election contest.

This by-election also seemed to the ILP to show that the Beveridge Report was a key issue. The ILP, like some of the other revolutionary socialist parties,[26] had given the report a rather lukewarm reception initially. The Party's Executive Committee welcomed the report because 'it draws attention to the social insecurity of the workers within the structure of capitalism',[27] but the *New Leader* pointed out that Beveridge's 'Plan' would not destroy poverty and want because it left capitalism, the cause of both these evils, intact. It was, in fact, the paper argued, a palliative designed to maintain the present system in the face of growing social pressure.[28] The Plan was also damned because it had a social insurance basis, and the Party always opposed the idea of the workers paying for the amelioration of the hardship caused by the capitalist system. Moreover, Beveridge assumed that unemployment would be low in the post-war world, which the ILP considered extremely unlikely if the capitalist system was still in use; and he suggested that old-age pensions should be raised to £1 per week after a delay of 20 years while the ILP was calling for pensions of 30 shillings (£1.50p) a week at once. However, certain features of the Plan appeared to the ILP to mark a step forward in social administration, especially the proposed abolition of the Means Test and the introduction of family allowances. And so the 1943 party annual conference decided that it should accept the Beveridge Plan as a 'rallying call'.[29] The ILP Parliamentary Group had already joined with Labour Party backbenchers in February and voted for an amendment proposed by James Griffiths of the Labour Party's NEC proclaiming dissatisfaction with the government's declared policy on the report, and demanding its immediate implementation.[30] Brockway saw this revolt by Labour Party MPs as a portent for the future and immediately began a propaganda campaign aimed at separating the Labour Party, or at least that party's rank and file, from the Conservatives and Liberals in the coalition government.[31] The 1943 ILP 'Jubilee' annual conference called on the Labour Party to break the truce with the capitalist parties and offered ILP support on all issues, except the waging of the war, if it did so.[32]

The next Labour Party conference firmly rejected a call to break the truce[33] and so the ILP's dream of forming a united left front against the Conservatives on the issue of post-war reconstruction was shattered. But the Party had now virtually committed itself to working with left-wing parties against the Conservatives no matter what view the other parties took on the war. This led to a strange opportunistic ILP by-election campaign in Peterborough. The Party had intended to contest this seat with Will Ballantine as its candidate even though the ILP was 'all but unknown in the division'.[34] But Sam Bennett, who was already the prospective constituency Labour Party candidate, decided to resign from his party and fight the by-election. The ILP agreed, despite some dissension in the NAC,[35] to withdraw its candidate and support Bennett, despite the fact he was pro-war. CW also agreed to assist him, and so October 1943 saw the birth of what the CPGB called 'a new two-faced political monster'.[36] It was indeed an odd marriage. CW provided Bennett with £100 towards his expenses and three members of his election team. The ILP gave him £50 and furnished this pro-war candidate with Fred Barton, a Quaker-pacifist ILPer, as his agent. The Party also circulated a programme purporting to be Bennett's which made no mention of the war, while his election address, which was written by the ILP, contained only a passing reference to the need to defeat Hitler. Barton also proved a difficult man for CW to work with even though he had been instrumental in arranging the ILP–CW meetings in Manchester earlier that year. He refused, for example, to allow non-socialists to speak on Bennett's platform, which angered CW leaders, who were anxious to work with all anti-Conservatives and did not themselves accept the title of socialist.[37] Yet despite these difficulties Bennett did quite well. He failed by only just over 1,000 votes to capture the seat and his proportion of the votes cast was four per cent higher than the previous Labour candidate had received in 1935.

In the middle of the Peterborough campaign the London Division of the ILP decided to contest the vacant Woolwich West Conservative-held seat and it asked for, and received, NAC endorsement for Tom Colyer as the candidate.[38] Colyer made Labour unity against the Conservatives the first point of his programme, but he received only limited support from the local branch of CW.[39] It also soon became obvious that Colyer was not intending to fight a conventional campaign. It was already difficult to hold evening meetings because of the blackout, but then Colyer asked his supporters to refrain from using loudspeaker vans so as not to disturb the night-workers in the constituency, and he opposed moves to hold an anti-war meeting near the Woolwich Arsenal.[40] Colyer appeared to be attempting to woo the old-age pensioners in the constituency,[41] and the high point of his campaign came when he presented Maxton with a petition with over four million signatures to be placed before the Commons calling for higher pensions for the elderly.[42] He did put forward the rest of the ILP's current programme in his election address, but his insistence that it should be a quiet campaign had resulted in his candidature being largely ignored by the local and national newspapers. He received 3,419 votes (27.2 per cent of the poll), but the ILP was not impressed.[43] Maxton insisted that the London Division should make amends for what he considered had been a waste of time and money in Woolwich by vigorously contesting the Conservative-held Acton seat which had just become vacant.[44]

Walter Padley was chosen as the ILP candidate in this contest.[45] He fought a far livelier campaign than Colyer on the full revolutionary socialist programme of the ILP, which is perhaps why he did not enjoy the support of the local CW branch.[46] He also made a campaign issue out of the highly unpopular decision of the Home Secretary, Herbert Morrison,[47] in November 1943 to release Sir Oswald Mosley from detention on the grounds of ill health.[48] When interest in this issue began to fade Padley switched his main propaganda effort to a series of personal attacks on his Conservative opponent, the golfing correspondent Harry Longhurst, pointing out his political inexperience and accusing him of being pro-fascist.[49] Padley was attacked in turn because he was a conscientious objector.[50] However, despite all this mud-slinging and the presence of four candidates, the people of Acton seem to have shown little interest in the contest. Only 17 per cent of the registered voters turned out to vote, and, although Padley gained 2,336 votes and beat two of his three opponents, his percentage of the votes cast (28.1) was only about the same as that obtained by Colyer in Woolwich.

While this contest was still underway the NAC met and announced that it had decided to nominate 60 candidates for the next general election, who would stand if the Labour Party had not left the coalition before then.[51] This decision received a great deal of publicity but it is difficult to believe that the ILP could ever have hoped to raise the more than £15,000 it would have needed for this number of contests no matter how many times it appealed for aid in the *New Leader*.[52] It is possible that the announcement was partly a response to CW's earlier declaration that it was planning to put up 75 candidates.[53] But the NAC's announcement did state that the ILP would be willing to reach electoral agreements with other left-wing independents and parties, including the Labour Party if it left the coalition, as long as they did not take an aggressively pro-war line.

Then in December 1943 both the ILP and CW parliamentary groups tabled amendments to the Loyal Address calling for common ownership of the nation's resources. The Speaker refused to call both of these and so the two groups combined to present a composite amendment. Acland led off the debate and was seconded by Maxton. The amendment received few votes, and Labour Party MPs insisted on turning the debate into an attack on the ILP's anti-war record, but nevertheless it could be seen as a possible portent of the future of ILP–CW co-operation. Brockway followed this up by writing an article in *Left* calling for unity among the socialists of the ILP, CW, and the Labour Party on broad issues as the first stage of a mass attack on the capitalist system.[54] And in April *Left* changed from a magazine with an open agenda to being one specifically intended as an organ for the promotion of Left Unity on a socialist basis.

Meanwhile R. W. G. Mackay, the Chairman of CW, had sent out invitations to a conference to be held in London on 8 March 1944 to discuss Left Unity. He had invited a number of Liberals but, although the ILP was not willing to consider forming a Popular Front, the NAC decided nevertheless to send representatives. The Labour Party representatives who had been invited did not attend,[55] and there was only one Liberal present, which suggests that the conference failed as a means of forging Left Unity. However, the ILP and CW representatives agreed that any future action would not only be anti-Conservative but also pro-socialist in aim. There was also some agreement reached on avoiding electoral clashes between them and it was decided to set up united Left Groups to co-ordinate action in the localities.[56] However, just at that moment this unity campaign ran into serious difficulties. The ILP divisional conferences in early 1944 had shown that many rank-and-file ILPers were hostile to the idea of co-operating with the middle-class CW.[57] Then at the ILP annual conference in April Ted Fletcher from the Midlands Division moved an amendment to the NAC's resolution on Left Unity in which he attacked CW because it was 'a middle class party without a socialist ideology', and declared that it was the ILP's job to win the middle class to socialism, not to make electoral agreements, collaborate as national organisations or carry out united action with parties which 'expressed the incapacity of the middle class to completely break with the ideology of the ruling class'. This amendment, which amounted to a vote of censure on the NAC for attempting to reach an agreement with CW, was carried by 55 votes to 43.[58] Some branches decided that they would ignore this decision, and the CW executive resolved to continue co-operating with the ILP as far as possible,[59] but the ILP conference had obviously dealt a serious blow to the NAC's attempt to form a United Front with CW.

In the same month ILP–CW co-operation suffered another knock when Acland wrote an article for *Left* stating that, unless the ILP could counteract the impression it had made that it did not believe that this was a just war, there was little possibility that it could play more than a small role in the drive for Left Unity. Bob Edwards, Chairman of the ILP, replied in the same issue of *Left* that, despite the unpopularity that its anti-war stand roused, the ILP could not consider dropping its opposition to this war because any United Front formed in that way would be based on 'political opportunism and dishonesty'.[60] Thus despite Brockway's continued optimism, and his insistence that the conference decision did not prevent ILPers from co-operating with CW as individuals,[61] it was now clear that the ILP and CW would not be able to work closely while the war continued.

Meanwhile the ILP was determined to carry on with its own election plans even if it could not reach electoral agreements with other left-wing parties. The NAC declared in June 1944 that its election candidates would oppose the government's call for unconditional surrender and would demand instead a socialist peace.[62] The ILP also pledged itself to expose the inequities of capitalism from its election platforms,[63] and issued a list of the constituencies it intended to fight in the next general election. Almost immediately one of these seats became vacant because of the death of its MP. The NAC decided to contest this constituency, the Bilston Division of Wolverhampton, in the resulting by-election. The Party appeared to have a good chance of winning this seat. The constituency, though won by the Conservative Party in 1931 and 1935, had been held by the Labour Party from 1924 to 1931 and still appeared to offer a large potential Labour vote, and seven seats had fallen to left-wing candidates during the previous few months. Moreover, Arthur Eaton, the ILP candidate, who was Secretary of the Wolverhampton branch and the manager of a transport firm in the area, had a strong local organisation and two months in which to campaign. He used this time to publicise the ILP's social, industrial and international policies. Not surprisingly, in view of the fact that the successful D-Day landings, the British and American armies' advances in Italy, and the Red Army's victories on the Eastern Front showed that the Allies were winning the war in Europe, his election literature made no mention of the ILP's anti-war stand, and he concentrated on the Party's demand for more houses for the working class and on its call for the speedy demobilisation of the armed forces. It was an unspectacular campaign, even though he had the support of all the leading ILP speakers, but he collected 9,344 votes (49.1 per cent of the poll) and came within 349 votes of winning the seat. He was immediately adopted by the NAC to fight the seat at the next general election.[64]

The Bilston campaign was hardly over when the British Government ordered its troops to intervene in Greece to help the Greek monarch regain power from the country's communist-led elements in the Resistance. The British Government's interference in this affair led to protests from *The Times* and *Manchester Guardian*, and to another rebellion in the Commons by backbench Labour Party MPs.[65] Unity meetings of the ILP, CW, and the CPGB were held in London to protest against the government's action.[66] Moreover the ILP announced that it would not put forward a candidate in the pending Chelmsford by-election as CW had a strong branch in the constituency and it did not want to 'split the united front on Greece'.[67] The ILP believed that the

Greek issue was a vital one because it thought that the fighting there marked the beginning of the European socialist revolution it was expecting, and it did not wish the British Government to nip this revolution in the bud. The Party therefore announced that it would contest the coming by-elections in two Conservative-held seats – Newport and Bradford East – with the Greek question as one of the main planks of its programme.[68] The Bradford contest was to be delayed for some time but the Newport by-election was expected to be fought fairly quickly. Bob Edwards was chosen as the ILP's candidate and put into the field on 4 March 1945. Edward's original programme featured the Greek question but it also stated the ILP's general policy in much the same way as Eaton's had done. But by the time the campaign began in earnest in late April 1945 the Treaty of Varkiza had (temporarily) ended the Greek Civil War, and so Greece was no longer an electoral issue. Edwards concentrated instead on criticising the Conservative Party's pre-war record.[69] The government's Conservative Party candidate replied by attacking the ILP's anti-war stand, which Edwards was soft-pedalling, and the CPGB distributed leaflets savaging both candidates, and calling on the voters to abstain.[70] Edwards failed to capture the seat, losing by 2,702 votes, though he secured a creditable 45.5 per cent of the poll. But the result was of purely academic interest because the war in Europe had ended on 8 May, a week before the votes in Newport were cast. And that meant that, as the Labour Party had decided at its conference in December 1944 that it would withdraw from the coalition and the electoral truce as soon as the war in Europe was over, in a short time the country would be plunged into another general election. The ILP now had to prepare to meet the supreme challenge of a number of simultaneous electoral contests in an uncertain political climate.

14

The 1945 General Election

The Labour Party's decision in December 1944 to break the electoral truce at the end of the European war and challenge the Conservative Party in a general election brought to the fore again the question of the relationship between the ILP and the Labour Party. Between 1939 and August 1943 the ILP's membership had grown by 30 per cent,[1] but by the end of the war it still only had approximately 2,500 members and so was not in a position to mount a serious challenge to the Labour Party in either the electoral or industrial fields.[2] In November 1943, when the ILP had announced the list of constituencies it intended to fight at the next general election, the Party had made it clear that if the Labour Party left the coalition government it would review its electoral policy and would co-operate 'wholeheartedly with that party in attaining a socialist Britain'.[3] However, the ILP did not make clear what wholehearted support would entail. In view of the position that had been reached in 1939 it was likely that reaffiliation would have to be reconsidered.[4] Indeed the question of reaffiliation had never completely disappeared during the war years. At the 1940 ILP annual conference Tom Taylor and Walter Padley had unsuccessfully tried to persuade the Party to continue negotiating with the Labour Party,[5] and in March 1941 Taylor advised his fellow ILPers not to make the mistake of believing that the ILP would benefit if the Labour Party ever collapsed, for in his opinion it would be the forces of reaction, not those of revolution which would benefit.[6] One month later the ILP's annual conference met and Dan Carradice, the Nelson branch delegate, introduced a resolution proposing affiliation on the grounds that the Party's present isolation was hindering its work at local level and generally forcing it to wait upon events rather than participating in them. Taylor and James Carmichael supported him but the majority of the delegates believed it would be impossible to rejoin the Labour Party at this time because that would mean giving tacit support to the war. Even McGovern, who had been a staunch affiliationist in 1939, took the rostrum to speak against this resolution, and it was easily defeated.[7]

At the 1942 annual conference the Party's confidence was so strengthened by the apparent success of its Socialist Britain Now campaign that the pro-affiliationists, backed on this particular issue by Maxton, had a difficult time convincing a majority of the delegates that it would not be in the ILP's interest to contest by-elections against the Labour Party during the electoral truce.[8] Then at the next year's annual conference a heated debate ensued regarding the NAC's resolution calling on the Labour Party to break the truce with the Conservatives and over what that eventuality should mean for the ILP. The issue of the relationship between the ILP and the Labour Party was further complicated by the growing influence within the North East Division and some London branches of Trotskyists. They called on the ILP to adopt the Fourth International's slogan 'Labour to Power', and work to return a Labour government which, they argued, would soon show the workers how ineffectual gradualism was and thus encourage them to turn towards the revolutionary socialist parties. Harry Wicks, on the other hand, from one of the older ILP–Trotskyist factions, attacked this policy and criticised the NAC's appeal to the Labour Party which he claimed was an attempt to lead the ILP by the nose back into that party. Affiliationists like Padley and Carmichael had to make it clear that while they supported closer relations with the Labour Party they did not support the Labour to Power tactic. This resulted in a strange and confusing mixture of cross-voting on a collection of amendments to the NAC's basic resolution, all of which were lost.[9]

The Labour Party conference held in July 1943 agreed to carry on the electoral truce, but Will Cove MP and some other left-wing members of the party were not happy with what they considered to be a drift to the right manifested in some of the party's other decisions.[10] Cove wrote to the ILP asking it to reaffiliate so that a strong left-wing element would be added to the Labour Party and perhaps help to stop this drift. McNair replied that the ILP could not consider reaffiliation while the Labour Party was still in the coalition, but from the tone of his reply and that of the answers given by Maxton to questions put to him by the *New Leader* on this topic it was obvious that the Party's leaders were keeping this option open.[11] The 1944 ILP divisional conferences, however, showed that the Party's rank and file were seriously split on the question of reaffiliation,[12] and that year's annual conference accepted a compromise resolution from Bridgeton branch which merely called for closer co-operation with the Labour Party when the truce was broken.[13] However, the debate between the pro- and anti-affiliationists continued in the *New Leader* and in *Between Ourselves*. The anti-affiliationists accused the Labour Party of being an undemocratic organisation which was 'the main weapon of the ruling class in subduing the British workers to its will'.[14] The pro-affiliationists replied by pointing out that the Labour Party was the political expression of the bulk of the working class and that it would be impossible for the ILP to play a political role in the future if it remained isolated from that mass party.[15]

Then in December 1944 the Labour Party's NEC took a decision regarding the next general election which seriously weakened the pro-affiliationists' case. It recommended to the Labour Party conference that the party should fight the next election without agreements with other parties. Apparently the NEC was determined not to endanger its party's position by tying it to independent groups which might abandon it at a moment's notice as soon as they found a point on which they disagreed.[16] James Walker for the NEC made it clear to the conference that this decision was meant to include the ILP which he described as a 'walking corpse'.[17] The NAC wrote at once to the NEC asking how this decision affected the prospects of any application to the Labour Party for ILP affiliation.[18] The letter was passed by the NEC to its election sub-committee which considered it along with similar requests from the CPGB and CW. This committee decided to instruct the party's National Agent, G. R. Shepherd, to write to the ILP asking if it would now accept PLP standing orders, and McNair replied that if the ILP did seek affiliation it would be on the understanding that its MPs would accept them.[19] Over a month later Shepherd wrote an 'unofficial' letter to the ILP explaining the problems involved in the proposed affiliation of the ILP, using as an example the difficulties which often arose between the Labour and Co-operative parties which had shared an electoral pact since 1927. This appears to have been intended as a delaying tactic because the election sub-committee endorsed this action and recommended that the NEC should not proceed any further in considering the ILP's tentative approaches until after the ILP's annual conference at Easter.[20]

The 1945 ILP divisional conferences showed the Party was still seriously divided on the question of affiliation.[21] Nevertheless at its next meeting the NAC decided, by eight votes to five, to recommend to the annual conference that the ILP should apply for Labour Party affiliation, on the same conditions as were in operation prior to 1932, from the day the Labour Party withdrew from the coalition government and ended the political truce.[22] No mention was made of the war in the Far East, but this point was raised by Harley Millichap, the ILP's Midlands Division Organiser, when he led the opposition to the NAC's proposal during the annual conference. He was supported by speeches from David Gibson, Arthur Eaton and F. A. Ridley. But this time the pro-affiliationists had the best of the argument. On a composite resolution from Bridgeton, Cardiff, Merthyr, Romford and a number of smaller branches, Carmichael, Padley, Stephenson, Brockway, McGovern and a number of rank-and-file members spoke in favour of affiliation and carried the day by 89 votes to 72.[23] The NAC immediately wrote to the NEC requesting affiliation. The NEC again referred the matter to their election sub-committee for consideration, but in the meantime its policy committee, under the chairmanship of Herbert Morrison (who was also a leading member of the election sub-committee), recommended the rejection of this application.[24] The Labour Party conference which met in May 1945 accepted the NEC's recommendation of December 1944 and decided that the Labour Party should not make any electoral agreements with the CPGB, CW or the ILP, although it was made clear to delegates that negotiations were taking place between the ILP and the Labour Party concerning affiliation.[25] No formal meeting had yet taken place between the NEC and the NAC,[26] but on 30 May the NEC decided that it would not agree to the ILP's request for affiliation at present, although it authorised two of the party's officers to meet ILP representatives to discuss that party's proposals regarding constituency electoral arrangements.[27]

Morgan Phillips, the Labour Party's General Secretary, and G. R. Shepherd, its National Agent, met an ILP delegation led by Fenner Brockway the following day. Brockway said that the ILP wanted the Labour Party to make way for its candidates in Bradford East, Bilston, Barking, Norwich, Kilmarnock, Dundee, Coatbridge, Motherwell, Tradeston, Dewsbury, Merthyr, Newport, Kirkdale, Widnes, Newcastle East, Acton and North Lanark. It is difficult to believe that the ILP expected the Labour Party to give it a clear run in all of these constituencies, and indeed it is unlikely that the ILP could have run contests in all but a few of them.[28] Apparently Brockway intended to use them as bargaining counters, for he soon dropped his demands for unopposed access to all of these seats, and said that the Party would like at least two additional constituencies in Scotland to those where it had sitting members, and that in England it placed its keenest expectations on Bradford East, Bilston, Barking and one seat in Norwich.[29] Phillips and Shepherd pointed out that their party was a democratic organisation which could not force any of its affiliated bodies to withdraw their candidates.[30] There the issue was left. However, the major part of the discussion between the two groups at this meeting concerned the proposed contest in the Shettleston constituency. Although a Labour Party candidate had been under consideration for Campbell Stephen's Camlachie seat earlier in the year,[31] the NEC had decided not to endorse candidates against Maxton or Stephen, and Shepherd had conveyed this decision to the Scottish Secretary of the Labour Party.[32] But a candidate had been endorsed on 16 May to stand against John McGovern in Shettleston.[33] The candidate was a young Army officer, J. Stewart Dallas, who had little previous political experience and whose family were said to be 'greatly surprised when they learned of his nomination as Parliamentary candidate'.[34] It is not clear why the local party decided to nominate someone except that 'it was felt there should be an official Labour Party candidate'.[35] But, despite threats from the ILP representatives that this opposition to McGovern might cause the ILPers in many areas to withdraw their support from the Labour Party nominees, the Labour Party representatives were adamant that they would not withdraw this candidate in Shettleston 'owing to the hostile attitude of McGovern to the Labour Party'.[36] The meeting broke up without agreement having been reached on any issue.

On 4 June the Labour Party election sub-committee met and endorsed the recommendation of its negotiators that the Labour Party should restrict its electoral agreement with the ILP to the Bridgeton and Camlachie seats.[37] The next day the ILP received a letter sent on behalf of the NEC stating that the Labour Party could not accept the affiliation of the ILP at this time because the Labour Party conference had decided that the election should be fought independently of all other parties, and in addition the NEC believed that the ILP's opposition to compulsory military service 'would be inconsistent with the successful conduct of the war against Japanese aggression'.[38] This decision and the Labour Party's refusal to make any other electoral arrangements with the ILP placed the Party in a difficult position. Apparently there was some talk of resurrecting the idea of nominating 60 candidates, but the Executive Committee decided that the main struggle at this election would be between the political Left and Right,[39] and it was agreed that the Party would only fight its own Glasgow seats plus Bradford East, Bilston, Kilmarnock, Tradeston and Kelvingrove. But even this list proved to be too ambitious and the last three seats were abandoned leaving the ILP with five contests. The Executive Committee also announced that, despite the obdurate attitude of the Labour Party, the ILP was recommending that the electors in constituencies where it was not standing should vote for a Labour Party or Common Wealth candidate.[40]

The ILP had published two pamphlets, *A Socialist Plan for Britain* and *A Socialist Plan for Peace*, at the beginning of the year, and these two plans were the basis of the Party's election manifesto.[41] This manifesto closely resembled earlier ILP programmes but it was more specific on certain matters (for example stating the number of houses that it believed could be built each year). In general the manifesto presented the case for a socialist Britain, arguing that only through socialism could the nation's domestic and international problems be solved, but in detail it closely resembled the manifestos of CW, the CPGB, and the Labour Party, particularly with regard to proposed improvements to social services, and in the list of industries to be brought under public control.[42] The main difference between the ILP and the other three parties lay in its attitude to the war in the Far East, for the ILP alone rejected a military solution to the conflict with Japan. But, despite an attack on what the Party called the 'Tory dominated foreign policy of the Labour Party', the ILP's manifesto made little mention of the war and claimed that the most important first step in the creation of a socialist Britain was the defeat of the Conservative Party at the election.[43]

The individual ILPers election addresses differed slightly from the Party's manifesto. Will Ballantine's in Bradford East was possibly the closest to the Party's official programme, although he added a section recording that the ILP had held Bradford East until 1931 and that, therefore, he, and not the official Labour Party candidate, was the true representative of the working class in that constituency.[44] Arthur Eaton, standing in Bilston, made much more than the other ILP candidates of his party's opposition to the war in the Far East,[45] whereas McGovern and Stephen issued addresses 'more on the usual Labour Lines',[46] although unlike their Labour Party opposite numbers they advocated a Scottish Parliament. Maxton's address was more individual, making no mention of the war or of Scottish Home Rule, and concentrating mainly on a personal statement of his international socialist faith.[47] The campaigns also differed greatly. Maxton had such a hold on his constituents that he had no need to campaign in the traditional sense. It was claimed that it was sufficient for him just to show himself in the streets.[48] His contest only cost £165. Stephen also had a quiet campaign, although he had to work harder than Maxton to defeat his Conservative Party opponent.[49] However, McGovern in the neighbouring constituency was having a difficult time. He was opposed by a Conservative, an official Labour Party candidate, an independent, and Peter Kerrigan the National Organiser of the CPGB. The *Glasgow Catholic Herald* also saw fit to remind its readers that, although McGovern was a Catholic, he had violently criticised the Catholic Church during the Spanish Civil War ten years before.[50] But McGovern fought back, holding large meetings and laying about his opponents 'with his customary vigour'.[51]

In the English constituencies the ILP had an uphill struggle. In Bradford East the ILP no longer had the strong organisation that Fred Jowett had been able to call on during the 1930s. The ILP candidate Will

Ballantine had to rely instead on support from Don Bateman and Percy Williams of the ILP Leeds (Armley) branch, and on speakers including Brockway, Edwards and McNair whom he shared with Arthur Eaton, the ILP candidate in Bilston. He received a fillip early in his campaign when James Harrison, an ex-Lord Mayor and a Labour Party member, declared on 14 June that he was supporting Ballantine because Bradford East had always been an ILP seat, and the intervention of a Labour Party candidate was 'a disgraceful waste of time, energy, and money, and endangers the seat being won by a Tory'.[52] Ballantine also attracted some attention when he drove down the route that Churchill was going to take on a visit to Bradford with a placard on his car which read that '2 Churchill cigars = 1 old-age pension'.[53] But Ballantine was attacked by his Labour Party opponent because of the ILP's anti-war stand, and the Labour Party ridiculed the ILP's claim to be a serious opposition party.[54] Eaton in Bilston found himself involved in what he later described as a very dirty campaign.[55] Moreover, Will Nally, his Labour Party opponent, was confident enough of his local support to suggest that a joint meeting of all the representatives of the Bilston Labour Movement should choose between him and Eaton for the nomination as the Labour candidate, the loser having to stand down from the contest. Eaton refused, claiming that the NEC would never agree to it, but he was unable to grasp the initiative in this contest and press coverage of his campaign was small.[56]

The polls in this election closed in most constituencies on 5 July, but counting the ballots was delayed to allow time to receive the armed services' votes. The results, when they were finally announced on 26 July, showed that the ILP had done well in Glasgow. Despite some anxious moments in Shettleston,[57] all three ILP MPs were re-elected with good majorities. In England, however, the results were far from encouraging for the ILP. Ballantine had only polled 5,105 votes (14.6 per cent of the poll) in what had once been an ILP electoral stronghold and the seat had gone to the Labour Party. Eaton had fared even worse, collecting only 849 votes (1.8 per cent of the poll) in a seat he had almost won only ten months before,[58] and it was clear that in England at least the ILP had lost its credibility as an electoral alternative to the Labour Party. Overall the ILP had been more successful than CW or the CPGB,[59] but it was only the Labour Party that had emerged from this election covered in glory.

That party had polled nearly 12 million votes and had won 393 seats, giving it an overall parliamentary majority of 146 seats. The Labour Party had convincingly established its right to be considered as *the* working-class party. It was also the party in power, and a new era was opening.

15

The Way Back

The Labour Party's tremendous victory at the polls in July 1945 was the first of a series of shattering blows that the ILP was to suffer between 1945 and 1948. As soon as the election result was announced rank-and-file ILPers began to leave and join the Labour Party. Some, including Trevor Williams, who had been the ILP's prospective candidate in Barking but had withdrawn when faced with the opposition of a Labour Party candidate, had long favoured a return to the Labour Party and now saw no reason to hold back.[1] Others, like Eddie Milne, who had been an avid opponent of reaffiliation and often spoken from the floor of the ILP annual conference against any moves in that direction, believed now that the Labour Party was the only weapon which the working class had at hand that could be effective against the Conservatives.[2] And many, including Jack Ashley, who had joined the ILP during the war when it had appeared to be the most radical of the left-wing parties, saw that the ILP was now quite powerless.[3] John McNair later wrote that 'it was difficult for some of us to repress a certain amount of regret and even bitterness at these defections', particularly as he noted, quite rightly, that many of these defectors had been 'the most sweeping in their condemnation of the reformist Labour Party'.[4]

The election result also left the NAC confused and divided. At its meeting in Bangor in August 1945 it described the Labour Party's victory as a 'grave moment in the history of the working class' and recorded its general satisfaction at the return of a Labour government,[5] but the Labour Party's rejection of ILP reaffiliation and its decision to oppose McGovern in Shettleston had angered some leading council members. Edwards, who had been a vocal pro-affiliationist for many years, now became a leading member of the anti-Labour-Party group,[6] and Maxton, who had often been ambiguous on this issue, announced to the next ILP summer school that, even if the whole of the Party went over to the Labour Party, he would go on as an independent.[7] But Brockway declared that the election result strengthened the case for affiliation and he proposed that the ILP should reapply at the end of the war in the Far East.[8] The NAC meeting eventually agreed on a compromise resolution which attacked the Labour Party for failing to reach agreement with the ILP and for opposing McGovern and concluded by stating that the ILP would wait for some evidence of a desire for unity from the Labour Party before making any further steps in the direction of affiliation.[9] Thus the council recorded its anger while still leaving the door slightly ajar.

This same council meeting refused to accept a suggestion from Maxton that the Parliamentary Group should table an amendment to the Loyal Address, and it decided instead that a six months' truce should be declared 'on the question of the Labour Government'.[10] This left the Parliamentary Group in a difficult position. It still considered itself to be an opposition party, and it took up the place on the opposition front bench that it had held during the war, much to the chagrin of Churchill who was now the Leader of His Majesty's Opposition.[11] But the council had declared a six months' truce. Therefore the Group's opposition to the government during debates was very mild and this allowed its opponents to charge it with political opportunism.[12]

The NAC had agreed that the ILP still had a role to play as an independent party, yet the general tenor of the discussions at the NAC Bangor meeting was that the Party's immediate role should be that of the propagandist and educational section of the wider Labour Movement without retaining pretensions to mass membership. Then, following six months of confusion and indecision over the ILP's future purpose, darkened still further by the ILP's failure to make any headway against Labour Party opponents in the November 1945 municipal elections,[13] the Labour Party suddenly appeared to be offering the Party a way out of its difficulties. The NEC was under some pressure from its own backbenchers to relax the party's discipline in the Commons now that it had a good majority. On 23 January 1946, therefore, the NEC decided to introduce milder standing orders for the PLP, and then to suspend their operation for a trial period lasting until the end of the 1946–47 parliamentary session.[14]

The *New Leader* was quick to point out that the PLP SOs had been the main issue over which the ILP had disaffiliated in 1932, and that this decision to suspend them would put a different complexion on the question of the relationship between the two parties.[15] Although the standing orders had not apparently featured as an important issue in the affiliation talks of 1945, the NAC meeting on 10 February 1946 announced that, in the light of the 'changed circumstances', John McNair had been instructed to communicate with the NEC again and renew the ILP's application for affiliation.[16] This letter was sent a week later, even though in the meantime the ILP divisional conferences had met and both the London Division, which had previously been evenly divided on the question of reaffiliation, and the Scottish Division, which had recently been a stronghold of pro-affiliationists, had voted against affiliation.[17] This application from the ILP, however, received the support of 100 backbench Labour Party MPs who wrote to the NEC calling on it to accept the ILP back into the fold so that there would be an organisation which could carry out the propaganda and educational work that the bulk of the Labour Party was too busy with administrative duties to undertake.   The NEC rejected this argument saying that the Labour Party 'had now come to maturity as a closely-knit political party with a single organisation, policy and membership ... fully equipped ... for electoral and propaganda purposes'.[18]

Therefore, on 27 March the Labour Party's General Secretary, Morgan Phillips, wrote to the ILP on behalf of the NEC rejecting its application for affiliation on the grounds that the Labour Party was now a unified party which no longer had room within it for a separate party with its own organisation and policies.[19] This decision was endorsed by the Labour Party conference in June.[20] However, it seems likely that the NEC had a more pressing reason for rejecting the ILP's application than its belief that it now administered a self-sufficient party. For a number of years the NEC had been troubled by applications for affiliation from the CPGB. The NEC had consistently rejected these applications because it claimed that the Communists did not accept constitutional action as the way to achieve socialism. It is probable that the Labour Party's leaders were also afraid that once they allowed the CPGB into the party the Communists would attempt to take it over and subordinate it to their aims.[21] The NEC had had little difficulty in rejecting the CPGB's applications in the past because the Labour Party's trade union leaders were often hostile to the Communists and its rank and file generally indifferent on this question. However, during the last four years of the war the CPGB's stock had risen. This was partly because it was able to bathe in the reflected glory of the Red Army, but it was also due to the goodwill that the CPGB had earned through the hard work of its members in the trade union movement, particularly on the production committees.[22] It is likely that the NEC realised that in future it would have a more difficult job convincing party members that the CPGB posed a potential threat to the Labour Party. Therefore it may have decided that the only answer to this problem was to clamp down on all future attempts by parties to affiliate to the Labour Party and thereby catch the CPGB in this blanket decision.

There is some evidence for this assertion. In December 1944 the NEC rejected an application for affiliation from CW. Leading members of the NEC informed acquaintances in CW that this had been done because 'any such affiliation would form a precedent for the communist party's admission'.[23] Moreover, it is perhaps significant that on the two occasions in 1946 when the NEC discussed the ILP's application for affiliation it did so as the next item on the agenda after it had considered a similar request from the CPGB. And its decision on 27 March 1946 to forbid the affiliation of any more parties to the Labour Party was taken after it had been discussing the question of CPGB affiliation but before it had reached the item on the agenda concerning the ILP.[24] The debate at the 1946 Labour Party conference on this decision to prevent any more affiliations also concentrated on the CPGB and ignored the ILP and CW.[25]

Whatever the real reasons for the rejection of the ILP's application for affiliation by the NEC, this decision had a profound effect on the Party's future. Three weeks after the ILP received notification of the NEC's decision it met in annual conference. The New Leader pleaded with the Party to avoid taking any final decisions on the question of the ILP's relationship with the Labour Party until the NEC's proposals regarding affiliation had been published and it was possible to review the situation calmly. However, many in the ILP were apparently not in the mood to wait. There were two rival resolutions for debate. The first, a composite resolution from the Woolwich, Perth, Mosspark, and Kirkdale branches called on the ILP to offer itself as a revolutionary alternative to the Labour Party by all political means, including the fighting of elections. It concluded by demanding that the NAC 'neither ... initiate nor ... entertain any approach or negotiation for affiliation to the Labour Party'. The opposing resolution, also a composite in the names of Bradford, Bridgeton, Hornsey, and Whitehaven branches (which had the backing of the majority of the NAC), called on the NAC to arrange a special conference to consider the ILP's relationship to the Labour Party in view of that party's latest decision, and in the meantime it asked the conference to review the ILP's constitution with the idea of allowing ILPers to become members of the Labour Party as well if they so desired.[26] The second resolution was ably supported by Brockway, Carmichael, McGovern, Stephen, Padley and others, but Colyer, Barton, Gibson and their supporters speaking for the Woolwich resolution carried the day by 74 votes to 60.[27]

Some ILPers now argued that the NEC's decision of 27 March, which stated that no party would be allowed to affiliate which had not already done so by 1 January 1946, finally ruled out the possibility of the ILP reaching a working arrangement with the Labour Party.[28] Brockway, on the other hand, felt that the Party could still try to make some kind of accommodation with the Labour Party, even if it meant turning the ILP into a purely educational body and allowing its members to join the Labour Party for electoral purposes.[29] But having failed to convince the ILP conference with his arguments, he now decided to resign as Political Secretary and Editor of the *New Leader*.[30] He did not leave the ILP straight away, partly out of his regard for Maxton, who lay seriously ill at home in Largs, and partly because he felt he needed time to come to grips with the mental adjustments that would be necessary if he was to abandon a party he had served for 34 years.[31]

Some younger members of the Party did not need time to make these adjustments. Walter Padley, who had been Brockway's closest political associate for six years, and a staunch pro-affiliationist all that time, resigned from the NAC and the *New Leader* board shortly after Brockway and immediately joined the Labour Party. Tom Taylor, who had moved the pro-affiliationist resolution with Padley in 1940 and had been a leading affiliationist ever since, returned to Britain in January 1946 after spending two years in Washington on attachment to the United Nations Rehabilitation and Relief Agency (UNRRA). He had clashed with his ILP colleagues over UNRRA, which they denounced as a tool of the reactionary capitalist governments,[32] and for him the 1946 conference decision to offer the ILP as an alternative to the Labour Party was the last straw. By May 1946 he was a member of the Labour Party.[33] The loss of these leading pro-affiliationists could only strengthen the position of the anti-affiliationists. As early as May 1946 McNair, Edwards, Ridley and the ILP National Organiser, John Hatch, were claiming that the question of affiliation was now dead, and that the future lay with the ILP which would soon become the revolutionary socialist alternative to the Labour Party.[34] Harley Millichap suggested in *Between Ourselves* in June 1946 that the time had come for the ILP to challenge the Labour Party directly in elections. He said that the ILP should avoid the charge of vote-splitting by choosing to stand against Labour Party candidates in contests where the ILP's intervention could not possibly lose the seat for the Labour Movement but where nevertheless the Party could secure 'a reasonable vote on a propaganda fight'.

Almost immediately such an opportunity arose when a vacancy occurred in Battersea North because of the resignation of its Labour Party MP. Hugo Dewar, an ILP–Trotskyist and staunch anti-affiliationist, decided to fight this seat against what the *Socialist Leader* called the reactionary policies of the Conservatives and the reformist domestic and foreign policies of the Labour government.[35] Dewar believed that the only choice before the ILP was 'either to become the nucleus of a new revolutionary party or become a mere, and increasingly impotent, "ginger group" inside the Labour Party'.[36] He saw this by-election as another step in the anti-affiliationists' campaign to wean the ILP away from the Labour Party. Not surprisingly this caused a split in the Party's ranks. Dewar was supported on his platform by the Party Chairman Bob Edwards, and by Ballantine and Colyer, but neither McGovern nor Stephen would speak for him, and Brockway sent his personal good wishes but refused him any political assistance. This lack of support was noted and commented on by the local press who wanted to know where the ILP's MPs were.[37]

Dewar fought the election on the full domestic and international socialist policies of the ILP. He criticised the Labour Party for not introducing socialism and bitterly attacked peacetime conscription, which he said was a tool that the Labour government was using to carry out the Conservatives' foreign policy. He demanded nationalisation without compensation of all the key industries, which he said must then be run under workers' control, and he attacked the Labour government's nationalisation schemes as inadequate and undemocratic.[38] However, his serious and weighty arguments made little impression on this by-election contest. The national newspapers limited their coverage of Dewar's campaign to a short biography of him and a few unimportant details,[39] and the local press almost totally ignored him.[40] Most independent observers appeared to agree that the main issue in this election was the recently introduced bread rationing[41] and it was certainly not international socialism which stirred the electors. Dewar received only 240 votes (1.5 per cent of the poll), the worst result the ILP had had since 1918. George Stone,[42] who acted as Dewar's election agent, admitted that the result was 'a shock and a disappointment' but he argued that the Bexley by-election result, which had been announced during this campaign, had had a profound effect on Dewar's support. At Bexley the Labour Party majority, in what was considered a safe seat, had dropped by ten thousand votes, and Stone claimed that this had induced the electors of Battersea to turn away from Dewar and to support the official Labour Party candidate in case any division in the Labour ranks allowed the Conservative to win the seat.[43] The fear of a Conservative victory, which Stone used to explain his candidate's low poll, was not, however, reflected in any noticeable commitment on the part of the electorate to vote for their Labour Party candidate. He won the election, but the turnout was only 57 per cent. Privately Stone reported to the NAC that in his opinion an error of judgement had been made in contesting this seat. Conscription was not, he said, an important issue with the voters, nor were foreign affairs, and the mass of the people could not differentiate between socialisation and nationalisation.[44]

This result may have been a bitter blow for the anti-affiliationists in the Party, but during the last week of this campaign the whole Party had to endure a terrible shock when it was announced that James Maxton had died on 23 July after a two year fight against stomach cancer. Tributes flowed in from political leaders of all parties[45] and the Commons paid him the rare honour of standing in silent prayer for two minutes after the announcement of his death.[46] Maxton was a committed socialist, a renowned orator and a charismatic figure, but his 'impatience with detail', his reported dislike 'of responsibility and committee work' and his easy-going personality meant he had never been the ideal party leader for the disaffiliated ILP and indeed he never seemed to have seen himself in that light.[47] Moreover, since 1932, the ILP Parliamentary Group, of which he was the undisputed leader, had often acted like an autonomous entity (though it was supposed to abide by ILP conference decisions unless to do so would run contrary to the individual ILP MP's convictions), and had occasionally clashed with the Party as a result.[48] And from having been amongst the most radical sections of the ILP before 1932, Maxton and the Party's other MPs appeared to have gradually drifted away from revolutionary politics towards a more moderate approach. Indeed, R. A. Butler noted in 1944, while nursing his Education Bill through the Commons, that Maxton had gradually become assimilated 'to the wisdom, dignity and atmosphere of this Assembly'.[49] Maxton denied that his spirit had been broken by the House, but it does appear that by 1939 he and his colleagues had become rather tame members of 'the greatest club in the world'.[50] Guy Aldred, a former anarchist and the editor of the socialist publication *The Word*, who had been closely associated with Maxton during the First World War, commented that in his later years Maxton had become too mild and genial, and that his death registered the 'end of an epoch of bogus "red" parliamentarianism'.[51] Nevertheless, Maxton's death meant that the ILP had suffered the devastating loss of its much-loved and irreplaceable figurehead.

But the Party's immediate concern was to find a successor for him as its MP in Bridgeton. This had always been considered the safest ILP seat while Maxton was alive and so it was both an important seat for the Party to retain and a valuable one for the candidate chosen to contest it. However, the choice of candidate was not an easy one. James Carmichael had the best claim. He was a councillor for the Dalmarnock ward of the Bridgeton constituency and he had assisted Maxton with routine constituency work.[52] He was also a lifelong friend of Maxton, who had apparently designated him his heir to the parliamentary seat.[53] Nevertheless, despite all these apparent advantages, Carmichael was not the automatic choice of most of the NAC. He had been for many years one of the leading affiliationists, and, following the recent spate of resignations, the majority of the NAC was now opposed to closer links with the Labour Party. But even among those who supported affiliation there was a fear that, if elected, Carmichael might soon join the Labour Party taking the Bridgeton seat with him.[54] Because of these doubts the NAC members, and other leading ILPers including Brockway,[55] who had come to Glasgow to attend Maxton's funeral, interviewed Carmichael at the Bridgeton ILP rooms. The NAC representatives attempted to secure a pledge from Carmichael that he would not enter the Labour Party while he sat as MP for Bridgeton. It seems he would not give such an assurance and the meeting became heated. Brockway apparently suggested that the Party Chairman, Bob Edwards, might be an alternative choice of candidate,[56] and David Gibson, who was the NAC's Scottish representative, a councillor in the Shettleston Division, and a fervent anti-affiliationist, appears to have pressed his own claim to the seat.[57] However, despite Carmichael's continued refusal to make any pledge, the NAC representatives were eventually forced to give him their unanimous approval after Harry Sergeant and other members of the Bridgeton ILP assured them that the electors of that constituency would not support any ILP candidate who was chosen in preference to Carmichael, and that neither would they![58]

Yet, even if Carmichael was the best ILP candidate for this seat, *The Times* noted that it was by no means certain that he would win, as it was possible that the ILP had retained the seat for so long purely on the personality of James Maxton.[59] Moreover the Labour Party had a strong candidate in John Wheatley. He was the nephew of the John Wheatley who had been the intellectual leader of the Clydeside ILP MPs and the first Labour Minister of Health; and Wheatley was a Roman Catholic in a seat where the Catholic vote had always played an important part.[60] The Scottish Labour Party, however, was divided over the decision to fight this by-election and some of the Scottish Labour Party MPs delayed the writ in the hope that an agreement would be reached between the two parties to avoid a split in the Labour vote.[61] Wheatley had the support of David Kirkwood and George Buchanan, both of whom had previously been disaffiliated-ILP MPs[62] but Emanuel Shinwell, who was a well-known Labour Party figure throughout Glasgow, took no part in the contest even though he was staying in the city at the time. However, the Conservative candidate and the local conservative press insisted on treating the contest as a fight between the Conservative Party and the Labour government and practically ignored the ILP,[63] which tended to push Carmichael from centre stage.

Carmichael was also hindered by his own pro-Labour-Party views. Wheatley quoted from Carmichael's statements calling on the ILP to reaffiliate to show that he was not really serious in his claim to be an alternative candidate to the official Labour Party nominee. Carmichael's own election literature and public utterances added some weight to this argument because, although he was mildly critical of some aspects of the Labour government's foreign and domestic programme, he commended much that it had done and offered himself as a goad to ensure that it continued along the road to socialism. [64] But the ILP fought an energetic campaign. Carmichael was assisted on his platform by McGovern, Stephen, Edwards, McNair and by both Maxton's sister Annie and son James. The Party also brought in members from all over the country to help with the canvassing and propaganda work. Yet the ILP had to admit that the Labour Party was making some progress in this contest,[65] and it was severely shaken by the decision of two of its Glasgow councillors, in the middle of the campaign, to resign from the ILP and join the Labour Party.[66] Nevertheless the Labour Party could not make up enough ground to overtake Carmichael, and the Conservative candidate apparently lost votes to an independent who was a campaigner for Scottish independence. Carmichael won the seat with a slender majority over Wheatley of 1,171 votes and with only 34.3 per cent of the poll. It was obvious that the seat was no longer a safe one for the ILP and many observers believed that Carmichael's victory was simply the result of a number of the electors in the division paying their respects to Maxton by voting for his appointed heir.[67]

As if to underline the unrepresentative nature of this victory, the municipal elections that November resulted in the ILP losing the council seat that Carmichael had held in the Dalmarnock ward for 14 years as an ILPer. The ILP retained only three seats on the Glasgow Council after this contest whereas in 1938 it had held 12 seats. But a greater blow to the Party's strength in that city was delivered by McGovern directly the municipal elections were over. He announced that, as he was at variance with the ILP's policy on various issues, particularly on its attitude towards the Labour Party, he felt that it was his duty to resign from the Party.[68] He later wrote that he had only remained in the ILP until the end of 1946 because he was a close friend of James Maxton and he did not want to leave the Party while Maxton was so ill.[69] After McGovern's resignation was announced both the other ILP MPs confirmed that they were staying in the Party,[70] but there was no disguising the fact that the ILP had been weakened both in Parliament and in the country.

16

Unite or Perish

The death of Maxton and the resignations of Brockway, McGovern and Padley had been serious blows for the ILP to bear. The Party was also beginning to see a marked decline in membership and activity at local level, and McNair noted that the secession of ILPers to the Labour Party had not been matched by any influx of younger members.[1] Brockway, as early as January 1946, had reported to a divisional conference that the Party was beginning to lose members and that the sales of the *New Leader* were dropping.[2] Barking branch, for example, which had been one of the most active ILP centres in the Southern Counties Division, outside of London, during the war years, recorded a dramatic drop in membership for the period from July 1945 to February 1947, and the branch secretary reported that 'the past year had been one of indifference for both the branch and the ILP in general'.[3] Independent observers noted the Party's decline with varying degrees of undisguised glee.[4]

However, just at this moment the ILP enjoyed another of its periodic bursts of energy and launched a new national and international campaign designed to promote the concept of a United Socialist States of Europe (USSE). The idea of a USSE had previously featured in the ILP's international policy as a first step towards the creation of a United Socialist States of the World,[5] and, indeed, the International Bureau of Revolutionary Socialist Parties, to which the ILP had belonged before the outbreak of the war, had had it as one of its ultimate aims. However, as the war was ending and the post-war world was being increasingly discussed, the ILP began a small campaign in favour of a USSE. Edwards and Ridley published a pamphlet on this subject in 1944 and Padley followed with a book a few months later.[6] This literature and the ILP's election propaganda argued that only a socialist united Europe would be able to avoid a return of the old economic rivalries which had led to two world wars in the century.[7]

Then the dropping of two atomic bombs on Japan in August 1945 and the growing friction between the USA and the USSR in the immediate post-war period caused the ILP to adopt a more urgent tone in its propaganda for a USSE. It now claimed that only a united and socialist Europe could prevent the outbreak of a third world war, a war more terrible than the other two because it would be fought with atomic weapons. The ILP argued that a USSE, acting in alliance with India and Africa, could provide a neutral buffer between the two great superpowers and thus prevent clashes which might lead to war.[8] This concept, of a socialist Europe acting as a 'Third Force' working for peace, was to gain some currency amongst the Left in Britain during 1946 and 1947[9] but by then the ILP had been preaching this message for some time. Yet the ILP had been slow to follow up its words with deeds. The Labour Party began holding conferences of European socialists in May 1946,[10] but it was not until December of that year that the ILP declared that the work it had begun in September 1943 was now bearing fruit. The *Socialist Leader* announced that the ILP was preparing a large national campaign of propaganda and meetings to press for the creation of a USSE, and in February 1947 it was calling an international conference to meet in London composed of delegates from working-class 'forces' in Britain, Europe and the colonies.[11]

The ILP's campaign began on a modest scale in the new year under the chilling slogan 'Unite or Perish'. The first international conference met as planned in February. Socialists attended from France, Germany, Holland, Spain and Greece, though not from the colonies. The ILP dominated this conference. Edwards was the chairman and Ballantine, McNair, and Ridley sat with him on the platform. A series of resolutions were passed calling for greater unity and peace, but most of the time seems to have been taken up by delegates making speeches explaining the difficulties faced by socialists in their country. Little would appear to have been achieved, but the leader of the French delegation, Marceau Pivert, said that 'the initiative taken by the ILP in calling the conference had been a splendid act of working class solidarity'.[12] A second conference took place the following June and attracted delegates to Paris from 14 countries including representatives from the colonies. Pivert was elected President and the ILP lost its dominating position, although ILPers retained a number of posts and the Party seems to have been responsible for producing much of the propaganda.[13] Once again little was achieved by this conference, but at least the ILP was reviving its international associations.

Some in the ILP were also anxious to renew its connections with other British left-wing parties. The ILP's contacts with Common Wealth had virtually ceased after the failure of the two parties to form a United Front in 1944. But shortly after the 1945 general election Sir Richard Acland had severed his ties with CW and, along with two thirds of the CW membership, joined the Labour Party. Dr Charles Smith, who had been ILP Chairman from 1939 to 1941, was now Chairman of CW and was anxious to forge closer links with the ILP as he believed both parties could benefit from co-operation. From the autumn of 1945 the two parties did indeed begin to work more closely together, and CW branches assisted ILPers with their municipal election contests.[14] In April 1946 the CW annual conference passed a resolution calling for closer ties with the ILP which led to a joint meeting in London in June between representatives of the two parties 'to discuss methods of co-operation in the interests of socialist action', though the representatives did not have a mandate to plan a merger.[15] The ILP representatives reported to the NAC that they had had a cordial discussion with the CW representatives during which they had agreed on holding joint weekend schools; on exchanging summer school speakers, and on encouraging local branches of the two parties to work together arranging social and electoral activities.[16] Then in August 1946 Dr Smith was invited to address the ILP's summer school and he delivered a lecture in which he made a thinly veiled plea for a fusion between the two parties, because he argued that a combination of the ILP's working-class contacts and CW's ethical appeal for the lower middle class would enable the formation of a far larger socialist party than either the ILP or CW could achieve on its own. His reception from his erstwhile colleagues was mixed, but rumours of a possible fusion between the ILP and CW were in the air.[17]

The two parties held their annual conferences during the same week in April 1947. CW considered a resolution calling on its National

Committee to meet with representatives of the NAC to discuss 'a wide measure of agreement and possible fusion between the two parties to form a single democratic socialist party'. But it was decided to withdraw this resolution and to refer the matter to the National Committee.[18] At the same time the NAC placed before the ILP conference three alternative courses of action for its future relations with CW and asked the Party to choose between them. The first alternative, which had the support of the NAC, was that the two parties should fuse to form a new party called the 'ILP incorporating CW' or else the 'ILP and CW'. The second alternative proposed the establishment of a socialist federation involving the setting up of a permanent joint committee of representatives of the two parties to initiate and organise joint activity on matters of common agreement. The third alternative was that the whole question of fusion or joint activity should be dropped.[19] The debate showed that many branches, even some of those who were co-operating most closely with CW at local level,[20] had retained their distrust of what they saw as a middle-class party.[21] The NAC's recommendation was rejected and the second alternative adopted by a small majority.[22] However, CW was upset by the fact that the ILP seemed insistent that even if fusion should ever be considered it would be under the ILP's name, and so, as local joint activity was already beginning to stagnate, the CW's National Committee decided to take no further action to bring the two parties together.[23] By April 1948 CW's membership had fallen badly and the NAC advised the ILP that in the future effective joint action with CW was highly unlikely.[24]

The 1947 ILP annual conference had destroyed the Party's chance of uniting with CW but it also reopened the old argument regarding the Labour Party. A resolution was passed confirming the ILP's socialist independence and rejecting any further moves towards reaffiliation. James Carmichael promptly handed McNair a letter of resignation and Campbell Stephen threatened to follow suit. Edwards, the Party Chairman, declared that the ILP was facing a crisis and that the only way of avoiding an immediate split was to call a special conference to meet later in the year and discuss yet again the question of the ILP's relationship with the Labour Party.[25] This conference, which met in Manchester in June 1947, had three resolutions to discuss. Ridley moved the first of these which repeated one of the 1946 annual conference resolutions and called on the NAC to present the ILP as an alternative to the Labour Party by all means at its disposal including the fighting of elections. The pro-affiliationist forces now supported a resolution moved by Percy Williams, the Party Treasurer, which, while declaring that the ILP should remain an independent party, called on the conference to vote for the abandonment of electoral contests against the Labour Party and to allow ILPers to have dual membership with the Labour Party. The majority of the NAC supported a compromise resolution which called for the abandonment of electoral activity, except to retain the seats the ILP already held in local government and in the Commons, and to concentrate instead on 'the propagation of the USSE, the need for workers' control of industry, and on the day-to-day struggle of the workers'. The conference voted in favour of the first resolution and thus declared war on the Labour Party.[26] Three weeks later Campbell Stephen resigned from the ILP and applied for admission to the Labour Party.[27]

Clearly the Party and the NAC were still split between pro- and anti-affiliationists. In June 1947 Douglas Rogers, who had replaced Brockway as Editor of the Party's newspaper, resigned. The two factions in the NAC could not agree on a successor and so Bob Edwards suggested that F. A. Ridley and George Stone become joint editors of the *Socialist Leader* as a way of representing both sides.[28] Ridley became responsible for content, while Stone took care of production. The paper, although claiming to give a balanced analysis of the current political scene, began to show a strong anti-Labour-government bias.[29] Then in August the NAC decided to nominate a candidate to contest the Liverpool Edge Hill seat in the coming by-election caused by the death of the sitting Labour Party MP.[30] It had been many years since the ILP had had any support in this Liverpool Division, and its candidate, David Gibson, was the NAC's Scottish Divisional representative whose only connection with the constituency was that he was a railway clerk and Edge Hill contained a large number of railwaymen. The Party announced that it was fighting this election because the Labour Party was 'misusing the honourable name of socialism to describe a policy which is only a modified form of capitalism'.[31] Gibson dismissed the charge that he was splitting the working-class vote, in a seat where the Labour Party only had a small majority, by claiming that the Labour government was abusing its trust by carrying out policies it had inherited from the Liberal and Conservative parties.[32]

Gibson focused his propaganda on the question of peacetime conscription; on a demand for more workers' control of industry, and for increased old-age pensions.[33] He was supported on his platform by Edwards, Annie Maxton, and Mark Foster of the Skipton CW branch. McNair told a local reporter that he believed Gibson was getting solid support from the Old Age Pensioners Association and the local spinsters.[34] Unfortunately for Gibson this support did not manifest itself in the polling booths. He received a mere 154 votes which was less than 1 per cent of the poll and this time there was no disguising the fact that the ILP had done very badly (and wasted the £800 election costs). Gibson was apparently undaunted. He declared that many people in the constituency had agreed with him but their loyalty to the Labour government had made them vote for the Labour Party.[35] The Party put this defeat to one side and prepared to challenge the Labour Party in the forthcoming municipal elections. This was apparently the last straw for James Carmichael who now finally resigned from the ILP declaring that he had never regarded it as a prime duty of the ILP to aid in the defeat of the Labour Party.[36]

The ILP was thus left without a representative in the Commons. But on the day before Carmichael announced his resignation Campbell Stephen died, causing a vacancy in a constituency that the ILP had held, with only one short break, from 1922 until Stephen had left the Party four months before. Bob Edwards had begun to try to wean the ILP away from expensive and ultimately damaging electoral contests, which he believed had created a barrier between the ILP and the wider Labour Movement, and the NAC had declared just before Stephen died that the ILP's primary task should be socialist propaganda.[37] But this seat was too good an opportunity to miss. The NAC promptly chose Annie Maxton as its candidate for the Camlachie contest, and, although she was not everyone's idea of a good choice,[38] she did have the electorally attractive name of Maxton to fall back on if all else failed.[39] She was also the first one in the field. The Labour Party could not agree on a candidate. Its

Scottish Secretary had raised objections to four of the names put forward for selection by the local party. The NEC then chose Tom Taylor, who had only left the ILP less than two years before, as its candidate. However, a number of Labour Party supporters in the constituency declared that they would vote for Maxton if Taylor was the official candidate. He withdrew his name a few days later because of ill health, and it was finally agreed that J. M. Inglis, a local councillor, should stand.[40] In the meantime Maxton had had a month in which to campaign without opposition, and the contest had been thrown open by the intervention of a Liberal and two independents in addition to the Conservative Party candidate.

Annie Maxton campaigned for workers' control of industry and for the creation of the USSE, as well as for the ILP's social programme. But, as in her contest in East Renfrewshire in May 1940, she emphasised her opposition to war and maintained that another war could only be prevented by the introduction of international socialism. She also directed a great deal of criticism at the Labour government 'on the assumption that the working class would never again vote for Unionism'.[41] This had become an article of faith in the ILP since just after the 1945 general election. James Maxton, Edwards, Ridley and others were convinced that the working class would never again elect a Conservative government, and that therefore the future of British politics lay between the Labour Party and those who stood to the left of it.[42] This view was apparently also held by Emanuel Shinwell[43] and possibly some other members of the Labour Party, but even the idealistic SPGB saw that this thesis was not supported by reliable evidence.[44] However, it may explain why some ILPers were willing to see their party split the Labour Movement vote, because they believed that even if the Conservatives won a few seats in this way they were bound to lose the next general election.

In this contest Annie Maxton claimed that it was the Labour Party that was splitting the Labour vote as Camlachie had been an ILP seat.[45] She was supported in her campaign by Edwards, McNair, Dan Carradice of the Nelson ILP branch, Gibson, and her nephew Dr James Maxton. Inglis had the support of James Carmichael, who came from the neighbouring constituency to speak for him on several occasions. The *Daily Telegraph* believed that this was a tactical error because its reporters noted resentment among some of the constituents caused by the fact that Carmichael was now energetically opposing a party he had supported only two months before.[46] Moreover, the ILP was insisting that an MP elected for one party should resign his or her seat on changing party and stand for re-election.[47] It had a field day heckling Carmichael and calling on him to put himself up for election in his new colours. But these attacks on Carmichael may have been a dangerous waste of time from the ILP's point of view because they clouded the issues of the election. The Party had to admit during the campaign that one of the main difficulties it faced was that the electors seemed unable to detect the differences between the ILP's policies and those of the Labour Party.[48]

In the end, despite the ILP's long tradition in the constituency and the large amount of press publicity that the Party had received, Annie Maxton only gained 1,622 votes (6.4 per cent of the poll) which meant that she lost her deposit. She was also blamed for the fact that Inglis lost the seat to the Conservative by 395 votes.[49] But the Scottish Division of the ILP, meeting only a few days after this defeat, was apparently not in the least downcast, and was indeed looking forward to its next battle.[50] Other elements in the ILP, however, were beginning to see the writing on the wall. The leading article in the next Socialist Leader claimed that this defeat in a constituency where the ILP had a strong tradition and a good candidate was further proof, coming as it did after the Party's terrible defeats in Battersea and Edge Hill, that the two-party system had returned to Britain. Its anonymous writer concluded that in the face of the two giant party machines 'the right to fight elections resolves itself into a (constitutional) right to lose deposits!' and finished with a plea that the Party should review its tactics in the light of the political conditions existing in 1948 not in 1893 or 1931.[51]

A majority of the NAC agreed with the anonymous author, and it put a resolution before the 1948 Easter conference, meeting at Southport, calling on the ILP to give up electoral activity in favour of propaganda work. It accompanied this resolution with a report which was both more detailed and more pessimistic than any it had issued since disaffiliation. This report was a sad admission of failure. It noted that since July 1945 the ILP had lost 40 per cent of its branches and members, and now had no presence in the Yorkshire industrial heartlands. The Party's 1945 staff of five full-time Divisional Organisers and one full-time Industrial Organiser had now been reduced to two full-time Organisers. There were no Organisers of any kind in two divisions, and, although the ILP still had members active in their unions, the loss of the full-time Industrial Organiser was making it impossible to co-ordinate industrial affairs. Sales of the Party's literature, including its newspaper, were down, and, although the price of the *Socialist Leader* had been increased by 1d and the Blackfriars Press was making a profit as usual, the Party had an overdraft at the bank for the first time in nine years.[52]

This NAC report indicated that the ILP was suffering from a malaise that was affecting many British left-wing parties at this time. CW had boasted 10,000 members in 1944, but by 1948 it had only a few hundred.[53] The RCP was torn by internal strife and was disintegrating rapidly, and it was finally forced to dissolve and send its remaining members into the Labour Party in August 1949.[54] Even the CPGB had lost some 7,000 members since the end of the war.[55] The NAC blamed this fall in the strength of left-wing parties on 'apathy ... caused by war-weariness and a feeling of self-satisfaction after the election of a Labour Government'.[56] But, whatever the reasons, it was obvious to the NAC that the ILP was losing support at local and national level and could no longer bear the cost of fighting a number of election campaigns from the money the branches raised.[57]

These hard facts had altered the opinions of some of the NAC's key members. Norman Winter, the Midlands NAC member, and F.A. Ridley had both been staunch advocates of the ILP's right, and indeed duty, to continue as an independent party fighting elections in order to provide the workers with a socialist alternative to the Labour Party. They now changed their minds, thus altering the balance within the NAC on this issue, and it was Ridley who moved the NAC's resolution at the ILP annual conference in Southport on 29 March 1948 calling for the termination of electoral activity. He reiterated Edwards' earlier claim that the Party's recent electoral activity had created a barrier between the ILP and the working class which had prevented it from being a successful propaganda body.[58] The NAC resolution also argued that the ILP had enough to do carrying out its propaganda work for the USSE and for workers' control without becoming involved in election campaigns as well.[59] The Scottish divisional conference, however, had already reaffirmed 'the Party's intention to offer themselves everywhere as an alternative to the Labour Party' and it had decided by a large majority to ask the NAC to contest the by-election which was pending in Paisley.[60] Other branches outside Scotland were also loath to give up electoral activity, and so the debate on the NAC's resolution was a long and presumably heated one.[61] The final vote was very close, but the NAC had won. Annie Maxton announced afterwards that the resolution had been carried by only one vote and that she intended to fight this decision as she did not believe that the ILP could 'desert the workers of this country on the strength of one vote'.[62] Many other delegates claimed that if a referendum was taken, a majority of ILPers would indicate that they opposed the ending of electoral activity. Maxton, therefore, tried to get the NAC to change its mind on this issue in view of the closeness of the vote. But the NAC, after a brief meeting, declared that there were no grounds to alter a decision which had been democratically reached by a properly constituted party conference. All that the NAC offered to do was to call a special conference to reconsider this question if it received a request to do so from one third of the Party's branches, and this it was obliged to do anyway under the ILP's constitution.[63]

Most of the newspapers greeted this conference decision as an admission of defeat. Some talked of the ILP having committed suicide and the *Daily Worker* gleefully reported that 'the ILP died today as an electoral force ... secretly ... it was declared a corpse'.[64] Only the *Manchester Guardian* thought that the ILP could survive this change of tactic and emerge with a new role as the conscience of the Labour Movement.[65] McNair tried to disabuse those members of the press who insisted on seeing this decision as marking the end of the ILP's story, but he was unable to get them to publish his reply. He had to be content with a statement in the *Socialist Leader* in which he denied that the ILP was dead or dying, and claimed that it was merely reserving it resources by refraining from pointless electoral activity, while its main purpose for the future would be to work for a United Socialist States of Europe so that a third world war could be prevented.[66] It is impossible to say if anyone outside the ranks of the ILP believed him.

17

Into the Wilderness

The ILP was now committed to directing a large part of its energies towards the creation of a United Socialist States of Europe. However, by mid–1948 the campaign for the USSE it had started in December 1946 was not progressing well. The international conferences only met fitfully and it was apparently impossible for the ILP to sustain a long national campaign on this issue. This was partly due to the cost of such an effort,[1] but there was also insufficient public response to justify the maintenance of the campaign. The ILP had based much of its propaganda for the USSE on the need to create such a union as a neutral bloc that would prevent a third world war which could herald the end of civilisation because of the terrible effects of the atomic bomb. However, the general public in Britain had failed to grasp the full significance of this new weapon, and did not realise that its invention would alter the way in which international affairs would have to be carried on.[2] The Campaign for Nuclear Disarmament (CND) was still ten years away.[3]

The concept of a United States of Europe was not new, nor was it limited to the socialists. There were at least four separate pressure groups operating in the immediate post-war years which were committed to the idea of creating an economically and politically united Europe. These groups – The European Federal Union, United Europe, The Inter Parliamentary Union, and the European Economic Committee – planned to hold a joint conference or 'congress' at the Hague on 7 to 10 May 1948 under the honorary chairmanship of Winston Churchill, who was now an arch-European. The Labour Party's NEC had already advised its party members to avoid the United Europe committee gatherings, which met under Churchill's leadership, and it repeated this advice in connection with the Hague Congress.[4] It was probably for this reason that the ILP's International Committee was asked to act as one of the sponsors for this conference, because the Congress's organisers could then claim that British socialism was being represented. The ILP refused to act in that role but it agreed to send a delegation.[5]

This was a rather strange decision in view of the strong reservations that the ILP had about this gathering. It described it as a 'mixed grill' dominated by bourgeois conservatives from many countries; and at least some members of the ILP believed that Churchill was hoping that a united Europe would be created which could act as a strong ally for the USA against any possible attack by the USSR.[6] This was almost diametrically opposed to the aim of the USSE campaign which had set out to create a neutral bloc between the two powers, and not an ally for one side or the other. Yet the ILP, which had always in the past refused to join with non-socialist groups to form Popular Fronts even for aims in which the Party passionately believed, now participated in a conference with its arch-enemies even though they were possibly pursuing an objective with which it violently disagreed.[7] The NAC claimed that it had agreed to send representatives to this congress so that a socialist voice would be heard,[8] but McNair admitted after the congress that the ILP believed that Europe had to unite or perish, and that if this unity could not be achieved on a socialist basis the Party 'was prepared to accept a federal unity knowing full well that the irresistible development of European and world economy, assisted and spurred on by the workers of Europe, will call for a planned socialist economy'.[9] There seems more than just a hint of wishful thinking in this statement.

Both the dropping of the atomic bomb and the defection of many of the ILP's members after the 1945 general election appear to have strengthened the pacifist elements within the Party (which may partly help to explain the ILP's participation in the Hague Congress). Ethel Mannin, prolific author, anarchist and former member of the ILP, was, for example, writing articles for the *Socialist Leader* at this time in which she put forward an undiluted pacifist case, arguing that it would be better to allow the whole of Europe to fall under the sway of Russian totalitarianism than to fight another war.[10] And between June 1948 and May 1949, when the USA and the USSR were confronting each other over the Berlin blockade, the ILP issued a series of pamphlets with a decidedly pacifist tone. Moreover, David Gibson, a leading ILP pacifist, was elected Party Chairman in 1948 and wrote that he was willing to countenance the whole of Europe overrun by either the forces of capitalism or communism rather than see the world plunged into another war.[11] The NAC now advocated the disbandment of Britain's armed forces and also declared that it was willing to co-operate with any peace movement because the threat of a third world war 'overshadows every other issue and reduces to trivial proportions the differences on long-term policy and tactics which divide the forces of socialism and the peace movements of the world'.[12]

Meanwhile the USSE conferences had become feeble affairs. One conference was held in Paris in June 1948 to which various African nationalist groups sent delegates, and the meeting paid more attention to colonial questions than it did to the creation of a socialist Europe. By the time the next two conferences were held in October and November 1949, in London and Paris respectively, most of the revolutionary socialist groups with which the ILP had been working since the late 1920s had either disintegrated or joined the larger social democratic parties in their countries.[13] The number of delegates attending these meetings had fallen dramatically and many ILPers accepted that the campaign had failed. The conferences were now held under the title 'the Socialist Movement for the United States of Europe' which Ridley claimed was an admission that the movement for the United States of Europe, which had Churchill's backing, had now become firmly established in peoples' minds as *the* movement for European unity, and that the old USSE campaign had just degenerated into a socialist wing of this endeavour.[14]

However, the USSE campaign and the subsequent European unity conferences had never greatly interested the majority of ILPers. Complaints were aired in *Between Ourselves* by members of the rank and file that this campaign was too expensive and was putting the ILP in danger of becoming 'a left screen for British and French imperialism'.[15] Ridley, who had been one of those most closely involved in the early days of the campaign, was complaining by April 1949 that, in view of the fact that the moment had passed when a revolutionary situation might have developed in Europe in the aftermath of the war, 'the United Socialist States of Europe was, for the time being, reduced merely to the status of a propaganda slogan'.[16] For its part, the NAC began to look instead at trying to affiliate to the World Movement for World Federal Government, because that body did not 'specify the economic system' it wished to set up.[17] The ILP had signally failed to turn United Europe into a movement for the USSE, and members of the Party had become concerned about the reactionary tendencies which had infiltrated the United Europe movement, and so in 1950 it was decided to cease any further association with it.[18]

While Edwards, Gibson and McNair were concerned with European unity, the Party's rank and file were showing much more interest in the question of electoral activity at home. Far from settling the question of the ILP's future tactics, the Southport conference decision to cease electoral activity had merely served to strengthen the battle lines. In August 1948 the North East Divisional Council circulated the English branches disassociating itself from this conference decision.[19] Then in November and December of that year a number of articles appeared in *Between Ourselves* attacking the Southport decision and blaming it on the machinations of the pro-affiliationists who, it was claimed, supported this change so that it would be easier for them to steer the ILP back into the Labour Party.[20] At the same time, the NAC was being pressed to call a special conference on this question. It was not, however, until just before the next annual conference was due to meet that the NAC finally received requests for a special conference from the requisite one third of the Party's branches as required by the constitution, by which time there seemed little point in calling an additional conference. The council did issue an appeal for unity in August 1948,[21] and attempted to start an 'anti-war preparations campaign' around which the ILP could unite.[22] However, this patently failed in its objective because some ILPers saw it as an attempt to sidetrack the Party away from the important issues of the day,[23] while those who did discuss this new campaign quickly split into two factions: one which blamed the Russians for the present world tension, the other which blamed the USA. This attempt to unite the ILP proved, therefore, to be almost as divisive as the election debate.[24]

But by far the most serious threat to the unity of the Party came from the Scottish Division. Annie Maxton had been a very vocal opponent of the Southport decision; and David Gibson, even though he was now

Party Chairman, announced at a meeting in Bridgeton just after the Southport conference that he believed that despite the decision to discontinue electoral activity the ILP would be putting up more candidates than ever in the next municipal elections.[25] In September the Scottish Divisional Council asked the NAC to fight the by-election which was pending in the Gorbals division of Glasgow but had this request denied.[26] A month later the Scottish Division called a special conference of its branches to discuss the question of electoral activity, and a resolution calling on the NAC to recommence electoral activity 'because of the sense of frustration which the 1948 decision was creating amongst the Scottish branches resulting in a falling off of activity' was passed and sent to Head Office.[27] A circular stating the Scottish case was also sent to the English branches.[28]

Electoral activity was debated at the divisional conferences which met in January and February 1949. It was an extremely divisive issue in all Divisions, but in Scotland, the North East, and Lancashire the conferences decided in favour of a return to fighting elections.[29] The Scottish Division went further and announced that it was going to contest a number of seats in the next Glasgow municipal elections.[30] A clash between the Scottish Division and the NAC might, in fact, have taken place over this issue during the previous year had not the government suspended the November 1948 municipal elections and altered the polling date to May. Some Scottish ILPers actually stood in municipal by-elections during 1948, but they had done so as members of the Homeless League which was a non-party organisation operating in Glasgow.[31] But now the gauntlet was thrown down, and the Scottish Division made it clear that it intended to direct its main attack against the Labour Party.[32] This move was not strictly unconstitutional, because the majority in favour of ending electoral activity obtained at the Southport conference was nowhere near the two thirds needed to alter the ILP's constitution (which currently listed electoral work as one of the Party's activities). However, it was a potentially divisive move as the Scottish Division was flouting a conference decision.

The 1949 ILP annual conference, which met at Blackpool, received a report from the NAC which again spoke of falling membership, falling revenue, falling literature sales and weakening influence. The council blamed some of the previous year's decline on a lack of enthusiasm within the ILP caused by the continuing sterile debate over the question of electoral activity and it appealed to the delegates to settle this issue so that the work of the Party could continue.[33] The council itself was now in favour of fighting elections and it was the NAC's resolution to this effect which was considered by the conference. Francis Johnson,[34] the ILP's former Financial Secretary, and Don Bateman,[35] the Yorkshire representative on the NAC, attempted to convince the other delegates that fighting elections would merely waste resources which could be used instead for more effective forms of attack on the Labour government, but they were unsuccessful. A majority of the delegates agreed with the representatives of the Scottish Division who claimed that if electoral activity was stopped the ILP would lose its most enthusiastic members.[36] The NAC's resolution was carried by 54 votes to 51.[37]

Tom Colyer remarked in the *Socialist Leader* that this reversal of the Party's earlier decision had come too late for most ILP Divisions to arrange candidates for the May municipal elections; but as the Scottish ILP had already drawn up its electoral plans before the decision was reversed it was able to announce that the Glasgow ILP would be fielding 18 candidates against Labour Party opponents.[38] David Gibson, the one remaining ILP councillor in the city, was faced by Labour opponents, two of whom – Myer Galpern and Robert McAllister – had been his ILP colleagues in the ward only three years before. Gibson, despite being well known and respected locally, lost his seat and the ILP failed to win any of the other contests.[39] That meant that now the ILP did not have a single elected representative in its Glasgow East End stronghold where in 1938 it had had four MPs and 12 councillors.

The terrible results in Glasgow were ammunition for those ILPers who opposed electoral activity. Ridley wrote an article in the *Socialist Leader* ridiculing those who believed that the ILP could defeat the Labour Party in electoral contests. He concluded that the ILP's electoral activity was merely an expensive way of giving election victories to its class enemy, the Conservatives, by splitting the working-class vote.[40] George Stone, the editor of the *Socialist Leader*,[41] agreed with him, and even John Darragh, the Secretary of the Bridgeton branch who six months earlier had vigorously opposed the decision to cease electoral activity, now publicly claimed that the ILP was 'finished as an electoral force'.[42] But there were still a large number of ILPers ready to defend the Party's decision to resume electoral activity and David Gibson issued another appeal for party unity and called on all ILP members to abide by the Party's annual conference decision.[43]

A short time later in October 1949 the *Socialist Leader* declared that the ILP was going to launch an autumn campaign to proclaim its message 'to the very large number of workers in this country' who were becoming 'increasingly interested' in the ILP's fight for international peace and socialism.[44] However, this campaign against a third world war and in favour of the USSE had hardly had a chance to begin when it was announced that there would be a general election in the new year. This meant that the ILP had to abandon most of its other activities in order to prepare for this election in which McNair had already announced the ILP would be contesting seats 'so that the voice of international socialism could be heard'. He had dismissed the claim that the ILP would be letting the Tories in by splitting the Labour vote and had argued instead that the only way to keep the Conservatives out of office for good was by compelling the Labour government to march with the workers on the road to socialism. To this end, he wrote, the ILP had decided to put forward five candidates in Labour Party held seats who would fight on the Party's full socialist programme.[45] Yet in the event, as an independent observer noted,[46] the ILP's pacifist element and its particular agenda 'was well to the fore in this election'. Of the ILP's five original candidates four – David Gibson in Shettleston, Robert Duncan in Bridgeton, Fred Barton in Newcastle Central, and Dan Carradice in Burnley – were pacifists, and the fifth, Tom Colyer in Woolwich East, appealed to the Peace Pledge Union for help with his campaign.[47] All five candidates supported a six point programme drawn up by the PPU which included a call for British neutrality in all future conflicts and a demand that Britain should disarm unilaterally if universal disarmament could not be agreed on. Only two other candidates standing in this general election – Frank Hancock, Independent Socialist in Woolwich East, and Rhys Davis, Labour Party candidate in Westhoughton – were willing to endorse this programme.[48] The two remaining ILP candidates in English constituencies (Colyer withdrew only a short time after announcing his candidature), Barton and Carradice, placed great emphasis on the pacifist side of their programme. Barton, in his election address, stated that the prevention of a third world war was the most important issue in this election, and he was reported in *Peace News* as claiming that the pacifists, socialists, and peace forces in Newcastle, of which he was a part, had embarked upon this general election contest as a 'Peace Adventure'.[49] And Carradice argued that the government's decision to manufacture the hydrogen bomb overshadowed all other issues. His main propaganda effort during his campaign was the organisation of a parade calling on the government to abandon the bomb.[50]

In the English constituencies the ILP was engaged in contests in which it could have little hope of affecting the result as both the sitting Labour Party members had safe majorities. But in Scotland the situation was different. Gibson, who had been chosen to stand against McGovern in Shettleston, had a large local following. Although he had been defeated in the municipal elections the previous May after 15 years as a councillor in one of the Shettleston constituency wards, he had still polled over 3,500 votes. The CPGB had also decided to put up a candidate against McGovern as part of a campaign against the Labour Party which it had started in December 1947.[51] McGovern was thus faced with a strong threat from the Left. But Gibson had to retire early from the contest due to ill health and his place was taken by James Graham from Perth who had little connection with Glasgow. The *Glasgow Herald* noted that McGovern's chances of retaining the seat had been strengthened by this change.[52] Graham presented the ILP's socialist programme well, and tried to make much of the fact that McGovern had won the seat as an ILPer, arguing that the MP should have resigned when he changed parties and fought a by-election. But apparently few constituents showed much interest in that particular question.

The ILP also tried to make this a major issue in the Bridgeton contest in view of Carmichael's defection to the Labour Party only two years before. Robert Duncan, the ILP's candidate, was the Scottish Division representative on the NAC but he was not a well-known figure in Glasgow. He had unsuccessfully tried to hold Carmichael's council seat in 1946 when Carmichael became an MP, and he had been equally unsuccessful in an attempt to win a seat in the 1949 municipal elections.[53] He was not a strong candidate, but he was assisted in his campaign by Annie Maxton who attracted the interest of the local newspapers because of the bitterness of her attacks on Carmichael.[54] The ILP also played heavily on the memory of James Maxton. The ILP rooms in Bridgeton carried large pictures of Maxton in its windows and the constituency was covered with posters which appealed to the electors to 'Be Faithful to Old Faithful'.[55] Duncan did not even bother to have normal poll cards printed but instead had his supporters give the voters a card bearing a picture of James Maxton.[56] The ILP Scottish Divisional Secretary, Betty McCrimmon, later denied that the Party was attempting to use Maxton's name to win votes. She claimed that it was used merely 'to emphasise the philosophy of fundamental socialistic ideas which the ILP has always put before the electorate, and for which James Maxton had fought consistently all of his life'.[57] It was a distinction that was far from obvious.

This appeal to sentiment did the Party little good. Duncan polled 1,974 votes (5.8 per cent of the poll), losing his deposit and leaving Carmichael with a safe seat. McGovern also easily warded off the challenge from the ILP, with Graham finishing bottom of the poll with only 1,031 votes (2.5 per cent of the poll). It was obvious to even the most sympathetic observer that the ILP's electoral strength in Glasgow had been broken.[58] But the Glasgow results were still far better than those recorded by the ILP in the English contests. Neither ILP candidate put a dent in the Labour Party MP's majority. Barton collected 812 votes (2.1 per cent of the poll) in Newcastle and Carradice a mere 295 (0.5 per cent of the poll) in Burnley. It was true that all the left-wing parties had done badly. The CPGB had lost its two MPs, and the Labour Party's majority had fallen from 147 to 5 seats (even though its number of votes had increased). But the ILP had argued for the last five years that when the people became disillusioned with the Labour Party they would turn to a party further to the left, at which time the ILP would have its chance. Instead it had been the Conservative Party that had gained, not the Left.[59]

Yet the Party refused to alter its tactics to meet this changed circumstance. The NAC report to the 1950 annual conference was even gloomier than it had been the year before. The ILP had lost more branches and more members,[60] and only the Scottish Division could still afford to employ a full-time Divisional Organiser. The Party's literature sales were also falling. The NAC had only been able to maintain the sales of the *Socialist Leader* at their 1949 level by reducing the price of the paper which meant that it was now unprofitable.[61] The Party's magazine *Left* was running into difficulties and only one more edition was ever printed, and *Between Ourselves* had only been published once since the beginning of the year because few ILPers now bothered to send in material. Only the Blackfriars Press was in a healthy position.[62] But the conference still passed, by a majority said to be the largest recorded for such a decision for several years, a resolution moved by the North East Division, which opposed forming any links with the Labour Party and committed the ILP to presenting itself on all possible occasions, including in elections, as a socialist alternative to the Labour Party.[63]

These brave words doomed the ILP to continued isolation from the mass of the working class. Moreover, the ILP was now very weak. It had no MPs and only half a dozen municipal representatives in the whole of Britain, and the defections of Bob Edwards and Will Ballantine to the Labour Party after the general election[64] reduced still further the ILP's negligible industrial strength. With less than 1,500 members the ILP was no longer a threat to the Labour Party or to the CPGB but it continued to talk and act as though it was a major political force,[65] while most other parties and political commentators treated it with the same mixture of mild contempt and hilarity normally reserved for small fringe political groups.[66] When the Korean War broke out in the autumn of 1950 the ILP could do little more than give lip-service to its revolutionary socialist ideals while pleading wholeheartedly for Britain to stay neutral.[67] The political landscape had changed but the ILP was apparently unable or unwilling to follow suit.

18

Epilogue

———————

The general election of 1950 had shown that the ILP was no longer an electoral force. But although the election was a bitter experience for the Party it was a happy one for four ex-ILPers. Both James Carmichael and John McGovern were returned in their constituencies with safe majorities and they were joined in the House of Commons by Fenner Brockway, who was now Labour Party MP for Eaton and Slough, and by Walter Padley who held the Ogmore seat for the Labour Party. However, in the short time since these men had left the ILP they had begun to diverge politically and could not now form a left-wing phalanx within the Labour Party as they might have done had the ILP affiliated in 1945.[1]

John McGovern had probably undergone the greatest change in political outlook. For the first few months after he left the ILP McGovern still voted with Carmichael and Stephen against the Labour government's proposals to introduce peacetime conscription.[2] But McGovern had long been suspicious of the Soviet Union, and even claimed during the Second World War that Russia was a greater threat to Europe than Hitler's Germany.[3] Then the tension between the Soviet Union and the Western Allies leading up to the Berlin blockade in June 1948 caused him to reconsider his attitude towards national defence,[4] and he announced to the Commons that, although he had opposed the war against Germany, he would be forced to support a war against the Soviet Union because he did not believe that life would be worth living under communist totalitarianism.[5] He now began to support conscription,[6] and in 1950 announced that he was 100 per cent behind the British and American governments in their struggle against communism in Korea; and he called on the British Government to suppress the CPGB, which he claimed was a branch of the Russian government used to organise sabotage in Britain.[7] In 1954 he joined the

Moral Rearmament Movement and began touring the world preaching that only revitalised Christianity could defeat communism.[8] By 1958 his local Labour Party was receiving complaints from the PLP and his constituents about his poor Commons attendance,[9] and in September 1959 he gave up his seat. He had resigned from the PLP in February 1959, and announced that, to his knowledge, of the 186 Labour Party MPs in the Commons, 26 were communists or fellow travellers and another 75 would 'throw off their democratic masks and join the communist world' if the democratic powers began to lose the struggle against the Soviet Union.[10] He began praising the Conservative prime ministers Harold Macmillan and Sir Alec Douglas-Home, and in 1964 he announced that in future he would vote Conservative and advised all workers to do the same.[11] He died in 1968 largely un-mourned by his former socialist colleagues.[12]

James Carmichael remained closer to his socialist faith and he continued to oppose conscription,[13] though his position on the Korean War cannot be discerned from the ambiguous speeches he made on this topic in the Commons.[14] He was now a backbench Labour Party MP concerned primarily with the problems of Scotland in general and of his constituency in particular.[15] He was not considered an outstanding orator and made little impression in the Commons during the next ten years, partly because ill health kept him from being a very active member.[16] He retired for health reasons in 1961 and died five years later.

Fenner Brockway continued to work with the ILP in the USSE campaign after leaving the Party and retained many of his international socialist ideals.[17] He spoke in the Commons against conscription,[18] and was a leading member of CND and the movement for world peace.[19] However, he specialised in colonial affairs.[20] He frequently attempted to introduce Bills in Parliament against racial discrimination, and his support for increased 'coloured immigration' is said to have cost him his seat at the 1964 general election.[21] He then accepted elevation to the House of Lords though he had scornfully rejected a similar offer a few years before.[22] He continued to use the Lords and the printed page as his main platforms in his continuing fight against capitalism and imperialism until his death in 1988 aged 99.[23]

Brockway's friend and political comrade in arms, Walter Padley, also remained active for some time in the USSE movement. But from 1948 until 1964 he was President of USDAW, and much of his time was taken up with union affairs.[24] His maiden speech in the Commons was an assertion of his continued faith in left-wing socialism and particularly in the socialisation of industry.[25] But ill health and his union work seem to have often kept him away from the Commons during his first years as an MP. In 1956, however, he was elected on to the NEC, of which he remained a member for 22 years, and he was Chairman of the Labour Party from 1965 to 1966 and of the Labour Party Overseas Committee from 1963 to 1971. He was Minister of State for Foreign Affairs from 1964 until 1967 but did not hold office again. Padley gradually moved away from his revolutionary socialist past and in 1961 he tried to form a 'centre party' within the Labour Party with the object of reconciling the Left and Right which had been divided over the question of unilateral disarmament.[26] He continued to move to the right so that by 1966 an observer remarked that it was difficult to believe he had ever belonged to the ILP, and he became known as a doctrinaire anti-communist and expert on the activities of left-wing splinter groups.[27] He retired from Parliament in 1979 and died in 1984.

Other ex-ILPers entered Parliament during subsequent years. Bob Edwards was the Labour Party MP for Bilston and later Wolverhampton South East from 1955 to 1987, but, although he was a supporter of CND in the late 1950s[28] and retained his interest both in Spanish affairs and in the idea of a united Europe,[29] he tended to concentrate on his union duties, first as the General Secretary of the Chemical Workers' Union from 1947 to 1971, and then as a National Officer of the Transport and General Workers Union.[30] He is, however, credited with playing a leading role in the introduction of the Clean Air Act, the Trades Description Act and the Matrimonial Property Act.[31] He died in 1990 aged 85.

Myer Galpern was an ILP councillor in Glasgow until he resigned from the Party in 1947, though he quickly regained his seat for the Labour Party. He was subsequently both Lord Provost of the City of Glasgow from 1958 to 1960 and Deputy Lord Lieutenant of the County of the City of Glasgow from 1962. He replaced John McGovern as Labour Party MP for Shettleston in 1959 and sat for that constituency until he was created a Life Peer as Lord Galpern of Shettleston in 1979.[32]

He died in 1993 aged 90. At the same election in 1959 Charles Loughlin, an ILPer until 1946 and an USDAW colleague of Padley, was returned as the Labour Party MP for West Gloucestershire, a seat he held until he retired in 1974. He was Parliamentary Secretary for the Ministry of Health from 1965 to 1967, Joint Parliamentary Secretary for the Ministry of Social Security from 1967 to 1968 and Parliamentary Secretary for the Ministry of Public Buildings and Works from 1968 to 1970.[33] He died in 1993. A year after Loughlin was elected, another USDAW member and ex-ILPer, Eddie Milne, became Labour Party MP for Blyth. He was to gain nationwide fame during the 1970s because of the allegations of corruption he made against both the Blyth Labour Party and an ex-ILP colleague T. Dan Smith. Smith, having been expelled from both the ILP and the RCP, joined the Labour Party and worked his way up through the local council in Newcastle to become the Chairman of the Northern Economic Planning Council, and he was also a very successful businessman. He was eventually tried and convicted on corruption charges in connection with building contracts. After a spell in prison he became a researcher, lecturer and broadcaster on a number of topics and died in 1993.[34]

Eddie Milne, meanwhile, was not adopted as the official Labour Party candidate for Blyth in 1974 but he fought two elections in that year as an Independent Labour candidate, amidst great media interest, winning in February but narrowly losing to the official Labour Party candidate in October. The media referred to his local organisation as the Independent Labour Party but he had no connections with the ILP. [35] He died in 1983. Neil Carmichael, the son of the ILP's last MP and himself an ex-member of the Party, entered Parliament in 1962 for the Glasgow Woodside constituency as one of the first MPs elected as a 'whole-hogging' CND supporter.[36] He was the Labour Party MP for Glasgow Kelvingrove from 1974 until 1983 and a junior minister from 1974 to 1976 as Parliamentary Secretary for Transport, then Parliamentary Secretary for Technology, and later Under Secretary for the Environment. In 1983 his constituency was abolished and he was created a Life Peer as Lord Carmichael of Kelvingrove. He died in 2001. His brother-in-law, and an ex-member of the Tollcross ILP, Hugh Brown, was a left-wing Labour Party MP for Glasgow Provan from 1964 until 1987, and was also

Parliamentary Under Secretary of State for Scotland from 1974 until 1979. He retired in 1987 and died in 2008.

Jack Ashley, who made a great reputation for himself as a champion of the disabled, was elected as Labour Party MP for Stoke-on-Trent South in 1966 having served his original political apprenticeship as Secretary of the Widnes ILP from 1944 to 1945.[37] He was Secretary of State at the Department of Health and Social Security from 1974 to 1976 and a member of the NEC for the next two years. He retired from the Commons in 1992 and was created Baron Ashley of Stoke. He died in 2012. Tom Taylor also had a highly successful career after leaving the ILP. He became President of the Scottish Co-operative Wholesale Society in 1965, and later a member of the Glasgow Railways Board, a director of a bank, a member of the Scottish Television Board and of the Scottish Economic Council amongst other posts. He served as Chairman of the Forestry Commission from 1970 until 1976 and was a Life Peer as Lord Taylor of Gryfe from 1968 until his death in 2001. As he once remarked, it was a long way from the ILP Guild of Youth, where he wore a red shirt and carried the red flag, to the red benches of the House of Lords.[38] Many of these ILP alumni in Parliament retained personal friendships from their days in the ILP, but they were never able to form a politically coherent group within the Labour Party and give any kind of leadership to the Labour left-wing.[39]

In the 1950 general election four Communists and one Liberal standing as candidates claimed to be recent converts from the ILP, but most of those who left the Party during the post-war years and remained politically active seem to have joined the Labour Party.[40] It is one of the paradoxes of ILP history that Fred Barton and David Gibson, who had both fought the hardest during the period from 1938 to 1950 to keep the ILP independent from the Labour Party, became prospective Labour Party candidates just before their deaths in the mid–1950s, while Don Bateman and Emrys Thomas,[41] who were staunch affiliationists in the same period, remained members of the ILP to the bitter end.[42]

The ILP went through a difficult period after 1950. The Scottish ILP was in particularly straitened financial circumstances at the end of 1950 having fought and lost two expensive contests in the general election and a by-election in Glasgow Scotstoun in September.[43] But it insisted on

continuing to fight municipal and parliamentary contests against
Labour Party candidates, which resulted in lost deposits for the ILP and
increasingly bitter relations with the Labour Party and Labour press.[44] In
the 1951 general election Duncan and Graham again contested the
Bridgeton and Shettleston seats respectively, but came a poor third in
both cases, and in England Barton again stood in Newcastle but fared no
better than his Scottish colleagues. Indeed each ILP candidate received
virtually the same number of votes as in 1950.[45] Meanwhile the internal
debate about the ILP's relationship with the Labour Party continued to
rumble on. In 1952 Don Bateman tried unsuccessfully to persuade the
ILP to co-operate with the Bevanite wing of the Labour Party,[46] and in
1954 the NAC again decided to recommend that the Party eschew
electoral activity and allow ILPers to have dual membership with the
Labour Party, only to have its advice rejected by the next ILP annual
conference.[47]

The ILP contested two seats in the 1955 general election. This time
George Stone stood in Bridgeton and H S Birkett represented the ILP in
Bermondsey. Both men lost their deposits.[48] These ILP candidates still
called for workers' control of industry and for other socialist measures,
but the main burden of their message was pacifist. The Party had passed
a resolution at the 1951 annual conference, despite a great deal of
opposition from non-pacifist delegates, declaring that the ILP was
opposed to all wars.[49] ILP election addresses subsequently contained a
call for British neutrality in the event of another war, and for the ending
of the manufacture of nuclear arms.[50] Yet by now few newspapers
bothered to mention ILP candidates which meant that the propaganda
value of these electoral contests was greatly reduced. Even inside the
constituency where the contest was being fought, it was unlikely that
many people heard the ILP's message because the Party was no longer
strong enough to mount large campaigns, and sales of the *Socialist
Leader* had fallen to a few thousand copies a week.

In the late 1950s the Party became involved with CND, although it was
too small to have any influence on the direction that movement took, and in
1962 it issued a pamphlet in collaboration with the libertarian left-wing
group Solidarity[51] supporting the civil disobedience tactics of the anti-
nuclear weapons group the Committee of 100.[52] The pamphlet spoke of

using the strike weapon in the fight against the manufacture of the hydrogen bomb and of utilising this agitation as a stepping stone towards social revolution. But the ILP seemed to be suggesting that this revolution could take place using the pacifist civil disobedience techniques of Gandhi without the need for any violence.[53] In 1965 a survey of the British political left claimed that the ILP was in a poor way politically, with its policies confused and antiquated and its membership standing at a mere 250.[54] But the Blackfriars Press was thriving[55] and rising land prices had made the Party's property holdings very valuable. The ILP was now said to be the richest party per capita in Britain, [56] and the tales of its wealth became truly fabulous.[57] The media, however, showed little interest in the Party and gave scant coverage to its demonstrations in the 1960s against apartheid in South Africa and the Vietnam War.[58]

In 1970 the ILP finally gave up electoral activity[59] and issued a pamphlet called *Towards Socialism* in which it reiterated its social, industrial and international policies, which had changed little since 1938, and scorned parliamentary action in favour of 'organised subversion' designed to encourage 'contempt for the social and economic system and actions designed to undermine the political credibility of those in power'. The pamphlet did not clarify what was meant by 'organised subversion', but it did state that after a period in the 1950s and 1960s when the ILP had not been making new recruits it was now attracting young people into its ranks. By February 1974 the Party was claiming that it had 600 members and that the circulation of the *Socialist Leader* was running at 3,500 copies a fortnight.[60] But despite this growth and its more aggressive sounding revolutionary stance,[61] the ILP was apparently losing confidence in the appropriateness of independent action. At its 1974 annual conference the Party finally agreed to allow ILPers to have dual membership with the Labour Party, and in May 1975 it made the fateful decision to cease independent political activity entirely. It changed its name to Independent Labour Publications and became an educational trust, publishing house and pressure group within the Labour Party.[62] Thus ended over 80 years as an identifiable political party and over 40 years of attempting to offer itself as an alternative to the Labour Party. The long wait for the workers to turn to the ILP was finally over.

19

Conclusion

With hindsight it is clear that when the Independent Labour Party hesitated on the brink and then took a step back from reaffiliation to the Labour Party in 1939 it unwittingly doomed itself to virtual extinction. Inside the Labour Party the ILP might have once again become a vocal part of the Labour Left and exerted some kind of influence, no matter how small, on the direction the Labour Party took, while at the same time acting as a propaganda and educational arm of the Labour Movement. But instead outside the Labour Party the ILP proved to have no function and no future. Of course, if it had reaffiliated in 1939 there could have been a heavy price to pay. The endless arguments over any possible rapprochement between the two parties that dominated this period show that there were many in the ILP who regarded the Labour Party as irredeemably reformist and were unlikely to have worked happily within it. Moreover, possibly even more ILPers might have found it impossible to function in a party that was supporting what those ILPers believed was an imperialist war. Some might have found a way to work with the Labour Party's pacifists, but it is difficult to know what they could have actively campaigned about during those war years without falling foul of both the Labour Party's leadership and the bulk of that party's rank and file. It seems likely, therefore, that reaffiliation in 1939 would have led to another wave of branch and membership losses.

What is certain, however, is that by remaining outside the Labour Party in 1939 and again (if reluctantly) in 1945 and 1946, the ILP could only hope to be able to establish itself as a revolutionary socialist alternative to that party to which the workers would flock in time of need. But at no time between 1932 and 1950 did the mass of the British working class turn towards revolutionary socialism as a way of solving its social, economic or political problems. Moreover, even those workers who did believe in revolutionary change were unlikely to join the ILP. The CPGB was well established before the ILP disaffiliated in 1932 and was able to offer the Bolshevik Revolution as proof of its revolutionary bona fides and the Soviet Union as a working model of the kind of society that it proposed should replace capitalism. That party was also active in the factories, and its propaganda through the *Daily Worker* and its numerous pamphlets reached far more people than the ILP's material ever did. During the Second World War the CPGB became an enthusiastic supporter of the war effort and seemed temporarily to be accepting the political status quo, but workers who found that party too conservative could always look to the Trotskyist factions who could lay claim to the same Bolshevik tradition but offered a different analysis of the world scene and arguably a more radical programme than either the CPGB or ILP. The ILP on the other hand did not have a revolutionary tradition to call on, and it was not always clear what the Party meant by revolutionary socialism. When it finally began to formulate its radical position towards the end of the 1930s, while many of its social policies would have been familiar to British workers, and, indeed, during elections voters often found it difficult to differentiate between the ILP's and the Labour Party's domestic programmes, the picture which emerged of the kind of revolution it envisaged and the type of society it wanted to build was an unfamiliar one. It did not draw on the apparently tangible Soviet model but instead seemed to be advocating a mixture of state socialism together with a form of libertarian socialist cum neo-syndicalist society which it hoped could be brought about by the same kind of popular uprising in Britain that had occurred in Catalonia. It was a model unfamiliar to most British workers and just as importantly it seemed to leave the ILP with little to do but mount propaganda campaigns and wait for the workers of Britain and Europe to rise up spontaneously and bring this new society into existence.

Moreover the ILP did little to establish its revolutionary credentials. Partly as a result of its passionate belief in local autonomy, it never adopted the kind of close-knit centrally led organisation often favoured by revolutionary groups. Moreover, despite stigmatising the Second World War as an imperialist conflict that should be opposed by the working class, it failed to formulate a revolutionary policy to offer to the workers of Britain, seemingly content instead, because of its libertarian socialist leanings and faith in the people's innate political sense, to follow the workers' lead. The Party's leaders, particularly Maxton and the other ILP MPs, refused to countenance any illegal action or to encourage revolutionary defeatism and the majority of the rank and file of the Party showed no inclination to take a truly radical stand on the war or on any other issue. The Party's wartime propaganda often sounded pacifist rather than revolutionary, and its anti-war message became confused and diluted as it apparently came to accept that socialist uprisings against the fascist and capitalist governments would not take place in Europe, and that an Axis victory could have an unacceptably adverse effect on the international working class movement.

The ILP's anti-war stance during the Second World War was, of course, both the signature difference between it and the Labour Party and a major stumbling block in its attempt to present itself as the party of the working class. Its position on the war was not unique, could be justified by reference to socialist theory, and proved attractive to a number of left-wing pacifists. Yet while such a stand might have had some appeal to the man and woman in the street during a war that, like the First World War, could be convincingly represented as a struggle between rival 'Great Powers' competing for global markets and dominance on the world stage, it was a much harder argument to make when Britain and its allies were faced by three militaristic foreign powers who seemed bent on over-running, dominating, and in many cases exterminating, other peoples. And while today, as the passage of time has meant more is known about the darker aspects of the history of the British Empire, particularly with regard to India and the African colonies, the idea that this same imperialism was an evil comparable in some ways to fascism might just possibly receive a moderately sympathetic hearing (though a 2014 YouGov poll suggested a majority of Britons still felt the empire was something to be proud of), it would have been more difficult for most British people in the 1930s and early 1940s to accept this comparison between the two, particularly as it appeared that Britain was in the process of loosening its grip on India, and, it was often claimed, bringing the benefits of good government and modern infrastructure to other parts of the empire. Moreover, even now, it seems highly unlikely that the majority of British people would accept the notion that fighting the Nazis and their allies was wrong or unnecessary!

Clearly, after the Second World War, Maxton's death proved to be an important factor in the rapid decline of the ILP, not only because some people had remained in the Party purely because of their personal attachment to him, but also because it presaged the loss of both the ILP Parliamentary Group and the loyalty to the ILP of voters in Glasgow's East End. Although by 1946 the ILP MPs appear to have drifted away from their radical political stance of 1932, and occasionally clashed with their party members as a result, a group in the Commons, even if it represented the more moderate wing of the Party, was obviously of great propaganda value to the ILP, particularly when one of its members was as charismatic and newsworthy as Maxton. While the ILP had its MPs its voice was heard, even though the message was occasionally muffled or distorted. When the Parliamentary Group finally dissolved in 1947 the mass media lost interest in the ILP and in future its message could only be heard faintly, if at all, outside the ranks of the faithful.

But arguably after 1947 the Party was left with deeper underlying problems than just the loss of its parliamentary representation. As the war had not provoked a socialist uprising in Britain, or indeed revealed any substantial working-class interest in revolutionary socialism, the ILP faced the post-war world with little to do but chase shadows. The USSE campaign proved to be insubstantial and the ILP's attempt to present itself as a viable alternative to the Labour Party was fanciful. It was, moreover, somehow indicative of its predicament that the ILP should expend so much time and energy arguing about fighting elections against the Labour Party when it apparently had long believed that representation in the Commons could do little to forward the cause of socialism, and, furthermore, it was becoming increasingly clear that it gained little propaganda value from these contests. Yet this internal dispute was in reality an embodiment of the key question of whether or not the ILP still had a role to play as an independent party attempting to challenge the Labour Party by conventional means.

Indeed, the Party had been divided since 1938 between those who wanted the ILP to rejoin the Labour Party and act as a left-wing ginger group, and those who believed it should offer itself as a revolutionary, or at least radical, socialist alternative to that party. This conflict came to a head after the 1945 general election had shown that the Labour Party had established itself in a seemingly impregnable position as *the party* of the working class. Those who saw the ILP's rightful place as a Labour Party ginger group believed they had been vindicated by the election results, while even many of those who had previously favoured remaining independent now had to admit that their position was untenable and joined the exodus from the ILP. Yet there remained an element which refused to accept this analysis, or to compromise with the reformist Labour Party, and so fought to maintain the ILP's independence.

As the individual pro-affiliationists and those who had lost their faith in independent action left to join the Labour Party after 1945, it allowed those in the ILP who were hostile to that party to strengthen their hold and drive the ILP down what proved to be the road to the political fringes. This trend may have been reinforced by the increase in the influence of the pacifists and unilateral disarmers within the ILP in the 1950s whose platform seemed to swamp the Party's more general socialist message. Yet by the late 1950s and early 1960s, when CND began to gain support, particularly within the political left, the Party was no longer strong enough to play a leading role in that movement. Indeed by the 1960s only the ILP's wealth differentiated it from the other left-wing fringe groups, and, despite a small revival in the early 1970s, it still could not effectively compete with the Trotskyist parties in attracting young revolutionary socialists. Perhaps, therefore, its decision to rejoin the Labour Party as an educational body and pressure group in 1975 was a logical one, if sadly belated. At least its supporters were no longer transfixed waiting for the workers to sweep them to power as ILPers had been for much of the time since 1932.

SECTION 3

Appendix,
Chapter Notes
and Bibliography

Appendix:
The ILP and Local Government

Throughout this period the ILP never lost sight of the importance of local government where many of the day-to-day political problems had to be tackled. The ILP had contested municipal elections from its earliest days, and fighting local elections was often seen by its branches as at least as important an activity as contesting parliamentary elections.[1] By 1932 the Party had several hundred members serving on local councils with their main concentration in Scotland and the North of England.[2] After disaffiliation the vast majority of these local councillors decided to remain with the Labour Party and give up their ILP nomenclature. The ILP chose, however, to continue to be involved in local government partly because of the opportunity it gave for propaganda work, and partly to achieve some practical gains for the workers, or at least expose the evils of the capitalist system in the attempt. There was also a feeling in the ILP that it would be important for the working class to seize control of the organs of local government to ensure the success of the socialist revolution. It was at local level, after all, that many of the laws passed at Westminster were put into effect and so, if this level of government was not under workers' control, the ILP argued, the forces of reaction would be able to block many of the measures passed by a socialist government.[3]

It is perhaps surprising, in view of both the ILP's strong advocacy of local autonomy, and its neo-syndicalism, that only a few members of the Party ever hinted that local government might replace Parliament as the main vehicle for the capture and control of political power by the workers.[4] But official ILP policy in this period stated that workers' councils, set up independently of any established form of government, should be the main political weapon of the working class[5] and the Party had no blueprint for the kind of governmental structure that should be set up in the aftermath of the socialist revolution. There was not even an articulated ILP view on the correct relationship between local and central government under the existing capitalist system. On the one hand the ILP abhorred the national government's tendency to override local government decisions and impose its own policies, and yet on the other the Party continually pressed central government to accept responsibility for the financing and administration of those social services which had traditionally been one of the main justifications for local government.[6]

It was therefore not a revolutionary socialist but a radical reformist programme that the ILP espoused in the 1932 municipal elections.[7] At this election ILPers stood against Labour Party candidates as well as against Conservatives and Liberals. The ILP's programme was similar in many ways to that of the Labour Party, but the Party maintained that all the social improvements it advocated could be achieved at once and did not have to form part of a long-term programme of gradual progress as the Labour Party claimed. This was mainly because the ILP believed that the rating system should be scrapped in favour of a local income tax, which would enable local councils to raise large additional sums of money immediately, without penalising the working class, to pay for all the extra services the ILP advocated. It is noticeable that the ILP was always less concerned with the level of rates being charged than it was with the level of services being provided. Its councillors usually called for bigger budgets than the other parties and unlike the Labour Party it did not offer to cut the rates of non-working-class residents.[8] The ILP was concerned, though, to ensure that the money raised from the rates was used to provide social services and not wasted on entertainment, luxuries and other non-essentials.[9]

The ILP's programme was not attractive enough, however, to save it from a massive defeat in the 1932 municipal elections; and defections to the Labour Party followed by those electoral losses reduced the ILP's tally of local councillors to less than 30 in the whole of Britain. Amongst the groups and individuals who survived this purge two ILPers were saved in Bradford and the Party's representation on the council increased to four from 1938 to 1939.[10] Tom Markland kept the ILP's flag flying on the Derby Council until 1950, and May Edwards sat on the Chorley Council as an ILPer until she resigned from the Party in that same year. Other small groups remained on district councils and on one or two small town councils. There were usually, for example, three or four ILP councillors on the Bedwas and Machen Urban District Council throughout the 1930s; and until 1950 in Barrhead near Glasgow four ILPers, led by Annie Maxton, constituted the official opposition on the town council to the Conservatives. Moreover from 1945 to 1947 a temporary electoral agreement between the Labour Party and the ILP allowed Will Ballantine and two ILP colleagues to hold seats on the Perth Council.[11] And in Northern Ireland during the mid–1940s four ILPers held seats on district councils; one on a county council, and the ILP was briefly the official opposition on the Armagh town council.[12]

But there were four areas, Glasgow, Merthyr, Norwich and Great Yarmouth, where the ILP managed to maintain or build a relatively strong council presence after 1932. Glasgow seemed the most promising of these centres. In 1931 the ILP held 44 seats on the council. After disaffiliation only seven of these councillors remained with the ILP and one of those returned to the Labour Party within three months. The ILP had, though, a strong organisation in Glasgow and it was able at the 1932 municipal elections to win two additional seats. These were held in subsequent elections and other gains were made until by 1936 the Party had 14 seats, though they were concentrated within the parliamentary constituencies of the ILP's MPs. From 1933, when the Labour Party became the largest group on the council, until 1942, when the defection of two ILPers to the Labour Party finally gave that party an overall majority, the balance of power on the council was held by the ILP group. The ILPers tried to use this position to force the Labour Party group to adopt more radical social policies. The ILP councillors attacked, for example, the Labour Party's council budgets because they claimed that those budgets allocated too much money to entertainment facilities and not enough to unemployment relief and housing. Yet although the ILPers could combine with the Conservative Party group to defeat the budgets they could not follow this up by getting their own proposals accepted. The Conservatives would not support measures which were more radical than those they had just helped to vote down and the Labour Party group refused to accept them either. The ILP group was eventually forced, therefore, to give its support to the Labour Party's original proposals.[13] The ILP councillors used their clashes with the Labour Party in the council as propaganda material against gradualism and claimed that they caused the Labour Party group to be bolder in some of its reforming measures.[14] But the ILPers were not able to get their own measures adopted and a growing feeling of frustration seems to have gripped the group. Three members returned to the Labour Party during the Second World War and three more within one year of the war's end. Electoral defeats accounted for the rest of the ILP's seats, and, as the local branches were no longer strong enough to mount effective electoral contests,[15] by May 1949 the Party's council group in Glasgow had disappeared never to return.

In Merthyr, Labour was in control of the council before 1932. This town had been an ILP centre since 1900 when Keir Hardie had been asked by local working men to represent it in Parliament. In 1932 its MP, Richard Wallhead, disaffiliated from the Labour Party with the ILP, though he returned to that party in 1933.[16] Only two of Merthyr's 25 Labour councillors, however, disaffiliated with Wallhead and one of those began standing as an Independent Socialist in 1935. But in the 1932 municipal elections the ILP captured a second seat in the Plymouth ward, and, after the two ILP councillors, James Davies and Claude Stanfield, had nursed the ward for two years, B. M. Davies won a third seat for the ILP at a by-election. The ILP was to retain these three seats until 1950 though it was never able to capture seats in any other wards. The ILP's position on the Merthyr Council should have been weaker than in Glasgow, for in Merthyr the Labour Party always had a majority. Indeed the Labour Party did prevent any ILPer from becoming an alderman or chairman of a council committee. Yet the ILP was not without influence. The Merthyr Labour Party group was left-wing and so fairly sympathetic to the ILP's policies. Stanfield and a new ILP colleague, D. J. Protheroe, were able, therefore, to convince the council to abolish 'test work' for relief applicants and to complain to the central government about the 1934 rating scheme because it did not give enough relief to the poor. The Labour Party group was also willing to be persuaded by the ILP councillors to issue free milk to the children of the poor and unemployed.[17] There were many defeats for the ILP group but the few victories enhanced the stature of these ILPers.[18] The Party seemed invincible in its Plymouth ward stronghold until 1950 when both the local ILP branch and the ILP councillors decided to enter the Labour Party.[19]

Over the other side of Britain in Norfolk the ILP had strongholds in Norwich and Great Yarmouth. The Norwich branch was formed in 1894 and by 1910 there was an ILP MP representing the city and ILPers sat on both the town council and on the Board of Guardians.[20] After disaffiliation Norwich became the largest of the ILP's local branches with a reputed 500 members, and that figure rose to 930 by February 1946.[21] The Party was never, however, as strong in Norwich as those numbers suggest. It did have an active branch,[22] but from its earliest days the Norwich ILP operated the Keir Hardie Hall social club, and to join this popular club one had to become a member of the ILP by paying the Party's affiliation fee in with the club's subscription. Many non-socialists, therefore, became nominal members of the ILP so that they could sit and have a drink in this pleasant venue.[23]

Three Norwich ILP councillors disaffiliated from the Labour Party in 1932, though two of them were defeated by Labour Party opponents at the next municipal elections. In 1933, however, G. F. Johnson, the NAC representative for East Anglia, was elected to serve in the Catton ward. The ILP took advantage of Johnson's local popularity to nurse this ward and in 1934 A. E. Nicholls captured a second seat, while Arthur South gained another in that ward in 1935.[24] During the first two years after disaffiliation relations between the ILP and the Labour Party in Norwich, both inside and outside the council chamber, were very bad with both sides accusing the other of betraying the working class movement.[25] But the balance of political forces within the council was so close that the ILP decided that only the Conservatives were gaining by this conflict and offered the Labour Party an electoral truce.[26] The Labour Party rejected this offer and so in the 1935 general election Fenner Brockway stood in Norwich for the ILP against both Labour Party and Conservative candidates. He lost his deposit and the Conservative held the seat. When the ILP approached the Labour Party again, however, the offer of an electoral truce was warmly accepted[27] and in future the ILP was given a free run in the Catton ward while in return it ceased opposing Labour Party candidates in other wards. In 1937 the sole surviving ILP councillor from those who had disaffiliated in 1932, Dorothy Jewson, resigned but, despite being given a clear run by the Labour Party, the ILP was unable to retain her Westwick ward seat. Yet in February 1939, with Labour Party support, Johnson was elected an alderman, and another ILPer, W. Channell, was returned unopposed in Johnson's old seat to bring the ILP group's strength back to four.

This electoral truce seems to have helped the ILP and the Labour Party in Norwich to draw closer together. They held joint meetings and the ILP council group rarely attacked the Labour Party in the council chamber. Even when the Labour Party gained control of the council and the ILP criticised the rate of progress achieved in the field of social services, there was little real enmity, and in general the two groups worked closely together.[28] In 1941 South resigned his seat to join the RAF. His ILP replacement, W. T. Hardment, lost the seat to a Liberal in 1947. In the same year A. Barley, who now held Johnson's old seat for the ILP, joined the Labour Party, and two years later Johnson decided to retire from public office. This left A. E. Nicholls as the sole remaining ILPer on the council. He was unhappy with the ILP's decision to recommence electoral activity against the Labour Party and at a meeting of the local branch in November 1949 he announced his resignation from the ILP. At the same time the branch decided that in future the social club would become an independent organisation open to anyone who subscribed to the principles of socialist democracy.[29] This decision, and the defection of Nicholls and many of his colleagues to the Labour Party, reduced the branch membership from 700 to just 9.[30] The ILP limped on in Norwich for a few more years but it made no attempt to recapture any of the council seats it had lost.

During the 1930s the Norwich ILP had helped revive the ILP in nearby Great Yarmouth. The ILP had an active branch in Yarmouth during the first two decades of the century and had had some electoral success. But by 1932 there was not a single representative of the Labour Movement on the council and a Conservative–Liberal electoral truce operated to ensure the status quo. A few independents had been successful in winning seats but the small local Labour Party contested few council elections. After disaffiliation the local ILP branch with 50 members on its books[31] and with a great deal of encouragement from the Norwich ILP branch, decided to contest municipal elections for their propaganda value.[32] L. A. Everett, a Yarmouth ILPer, stood unsuccessfully for election to the council in 1932 and 1933. In 1934 he was joined by L. F. Bunnewell who stood against a Labour Party candidate. The two parties were clashing locally at this time because the ILP claimed that the Labour Party had abandoned socialism in order to win votes while the Labour Party accused the ILP of capturing the local Labour Club which had originally been established as a non-party organisation.[33] As a result the two parties continued to challenge each other in some wards though neither was strong enough to field more than a handful of candidates. But in 1936 with the international situation worsening the two parties came together to hold a series of anti-war meetings. This spirit of co-operation was extended to the electoral field.[34] They collaborated without success at the 1936 municipal elections, but in 1937 both parties managed to get one candidate elected and within a few weeks, with ILP help, the Labour Party won two council by-elections.[35] This small left-wing group, led by Councillor Bunnewell, began to challenge the Conservative majority on every major issue and public interest in council business greatly increased.[36] In 1938 F. H. Stone won another seat for the ILP and the Labour Party gained three more. Then just before the wartime electoral truce came into effect[37] the ILP secured yet another seat through a by-election, and Bunnewell and Stone were leading figures in the opposition to the Conservative majority on the council between 1939 and 1945.[38]

Then in the 1945 municipal election the ILP gained five seats and Bunnewell and Stone were elevated to the Aldermanic Bench.[39] The Labour Party also increased its representation and the Labour-ILP alliance just failed to win a majority on the council. The ILP group worked closely with the Labour Party councillors for the next five years, but it gradually dwindled in size. One member defected to the Labour Party in 1947 and another seat was lost to the Conservatives. Then in 1950 the ILP's decision to field candidates in the general election against two of its former MPs caused three other members of the ILP group to join the Labour Party.[40] The two remaining ILP councillors, Bunnewell and E. Burgess, continued to co-operate with the Labour Party group, but believed that the ILP still had its own contribution to make to the working-class movement. However, the defections had left the ILP branch in Yarmouth very weak.[41] In 1964, when Bunnewell was again made an alderman, the ILP was unable to find anyone to contest his seat at the resulting by-election. Then Burgess lost his seat to a Conservative in 1968 and made no attempt to regain it. Bunnewell was re-elected in 1970 when his term as an alderman expired and he held his seat on the new Yarmouth Borough Council which was formed in 1973. But it had been many years since the ILP had had a branch in the town[42] and Bunnewell's electoral support was clearly based on his personal popularity and not on his membership of the ILP.[43]

Unfortunately, it is not possible now to gauge how effective the various ILP councillors were as advocates on a day-to-day basis for the individual local residents and community groups they represented, but in general the ILP does not appear to have been able to achieve much politically through its municipal activities, notwithstanding the occasional practical and propaganda successes of some individual members. In Chorley, for example, May Edwards fought a long and bitter campaign as a lone ILP councillor to try to persuade the council to raise its expenditure on the provision of free milk to nursing and expectant mothers and to infants amongst the town's poor and unemployed. She failed, though the expenditure on this item did gradually rise. But she had roused public opinion and when she mounted a similar campaign in 1937 to try to force the council to provide school meals for the children of the poor and needy, she enjoyed the wholehearted support of the local press and of a substantial number of local people. When in December 1940 the council finally agreed to set up school feeding centres in the town the local press declared that this was solely as a result of her campaign.[44] But May Edwards achievements, and the few successes of Stanfield and Protheroe in Merthyr, were the exceptions that proved the rule.

Some ILPers blamed their lack of local government success in part on the Party's municipal programme.[45] It was a programme based firmly on the Party's social policies decided at its annual conference, and it was one which was to be used by the ILP, with just minor changes introduced in

1938 and 1945, from 1932 until 1950.[46] But local conditions varied so much that it was difficult to produce a programme nationally that was more than just an outline of desired improvements. A pressing problem in Glasgow, for example, would not necessarily be so important in Yarmouth, and a programme which was applicable to Merthyr might be inappropriate in Norwich.[47] Moreover, most of the problems considered by local councils involved routine matters like road maintenance, street lighting and refuse collections, and did not lend themselves to the propagation of revolutionary socialist principles. Even on issues like housing or unemployment, which had a higher propaganda potential, ILP councillors quickly found themselves ruled out of order and effectively gagged if they attempted to turn debates on these questions into a general attack on the capitalist system.[48] There were some issues, of course, which did allow room for propaganda. The ILP councillors in Glasgow and Merthyr, for example, opposed the provision of school facilities for Officer Training Units or Cadet Corps because they claimed that schools should not encourage militarism amongst schoolchildren. Before the war ILP councillors in East Anglia also challenged every item of expenditure on the Air Raid Precaution scheme because the ILP claimed that the only way to protect people from air raids was to end capitalism, the real cause of all wars.[49] In this way ILP councillors made their anti-war views heard, though it was only in Merthyr that the ILP council group actually voted on a resolution to end the war,[50] while in other towns the ILP councillors just announced their opposition to this latest capitalist war.

Local ILP groups also reacted in different ways to the political problems they faced. The ILP officially opposed the municipal electoral truce set up at the beginning of the war,[51] for example, and in some areas the more active branches or Federations tried to put forward candidates whenever a vacancy arose on their local council.[52] In Yarmouth both the ILP and the local Labour Party put up candidates every time a Conservative seat fell vacant as they felt that the truce was artificially protecting the Conservative majority on the council.[53] In Glasgow, on the other hand, the ILP group accepted the co-option of members on to the council without comment, while in Merthyr the ILP appealed to Herbert Morrison to support their claim to a seat which had fallen vacant following the death of an ex-ILPer who had defected to the Labour Party after the municipal electoral truce had begun.[54] Moreover in Norwich the ILP group agreed an electoral truce with all the other parties on the council even before the official municipal electoral truce came into effect.[55]

There were also local differences concerning the Party's attitude to office holding. The Glasgow ILP group accepted a decision made at the 1932 Scottish divisional conference that no party member should accept any kind of municipal office until the ILP had a majority on the particular council.[56] This decision stood until 1940[57] and in the meantime the Glasgow ILP group was subjected to frequent attacks from their political opponents who claimed that the refusal to take office was proof that the ILP was not willing to accept any form of responsibility.[58] The English and Welsh ILPers did not have the same restriction, and indeed the ILP in Merthyr complained bitterly because the dominant Labour Party group would not allow Stanfield to become an alderman or the chairman of any council committee.[59] In Yarmouth Stone and Bunnewell were chairmen of council committees and both accepted places on the Aldermanic Bench, despite Bunnewell's assertion that it was an antiquated and undemocratic office,[60] while in Norwich Johnson served two consecutive terms as an alderman apparently without suffering any pangs of conscience.

Yet in some ways the experience of the English and Welsh ILP office holders exonerated the 1932 Scottish Division's decision. Despite being Chairman of the Health Committee Bunnewell could not persuade the Yarmouth Council to give serious consideration to his proposals for the expansion of the local health services and, in retrospect, he did not believe that he had ever achieved much in his council work.[61] But perhaps the difficulties of holding office without having real power or influence were most clearly demonstrated by the dilemma of those ILPers who were elected to mayoral office. In Merthyr, for example, the office of mayor was filled on the basis of seniority and ILPers held that position from 1937 to 1938, from 1947 to 1949 and from 1949 to 1950. And in 1947 Stone was Mayor of Yarmouth because that office circulated between the various parties on the council and the ILP's turn had come.

But the mayor of any town is traditionally non-party-political for his or her term of office which meant that the ILPers could not use their time in the limelight to propagate ILP policies, nor could they avoid fulfilling duties which would normally have been anathema to an ILPer. Thus J. Davies, during his term as Mayor of Merthyr was forced, despite the ILP's anti-militarism, to plead with the government to build a munitions factory in the town because his local council coveted the job opportunities that such a factory could bring. And after the war the ILP Mayors in both Merthyr and Yarmouth had to make speeches at Remembrance Day Services talking about 'the war for democracy' even though as ILPers they believed that the Second World War had been fought to protect profits not freedom.[62] Only Stanfield while Mayor of Merthyr from November 1947 to May 1949 refused to abide by the rule of strict political neutrality. He could not avoid receiving Field Marshal Montgomery when he came to Merthyr on a visit, but Stanfield made his own opposition to war plain in his speech of welcome.[63] He also intentionally missed meetings with local industrialists at which he would have been expected to praise the success of their capitalist ventures.[64] Yet when he did not attend these functions the duty merely devolved to his deputy who was also an ILPer![65] Stanfield was bitterly attacked by the local press for bringing politics into what was supposed to be a non-political job and told he should not have accepted the office.[66] It is questionable, therefore, how valuable his stand was as a propaganda weapon for the ILP.

Yet this was in many ways typical of the dilemma that faced all ILPers engaged in local government. If they stood aloof and stuck to their revolutionary socialist principles they could be accused of being irresponsible or attacked for taking on roles which they had no intention of fulfilling. But if they made the compromises necessary to play an active part in council work they ran the risk of having to abandon most of the propaganda opportunities provided by being in the public eye, which had been one of the main incentives for standing for office in the first place. Yet, at the same time, these compromises did not necessarily ensure that the ILP would be able to achieve its social programme through this local government work because during this period the Party never obtained a strong enough position on any council to push through its own measures. It is small wonder that ILP councillors began drifting back to the Labour Party within a short time of disaffiliation or that barely a handful remained in the whole country by 1950.

Notes

Chapter 1

1. B. Winter, *The ILP: A Brief History* (1982), p.2.
2. R. E. Dowse, *Left in the Centre* (1966), pp.20–34, and H. Pelling, *A Short History of the Labour Party* (1961), pp.43–44.
3. Dowse op. cit., p.37.
4. James Ramsay MacDonald (1866–1937), joined the ILP in 1894, became an MP in 1906 and prime minister 1924, 1929–1931 and 1931–1935.
5. Dowse op. cit., p.48. For a fuller discussion of the ILP—Labour Party relationship, see Dowse, op.cit. pp.35–48, and I. Bullock, *Under Siege* (2017), pp.27–66, and passim.
6. John Wheatley (1869–1930), ex-miner, publican, publisher, and intellectual leader of the Clydeside MPs from 1922 to 1930.
7. James Maxton (1885–1946) joined the ILP in 1904, and was its 'leader' from 1932 until his death in 1946.
8. David Kirkwood (1872–1955), engineer, MP and staunch trade unionist.
9. Campbell Stephen (1884–1947), clergyman, teacher and a barrister before becoming an MP.
10. Bullock op. cit., p.29; Dowse op. cit., p.47.
11. For the ILP radicals' beliefs see Chapter 3.
12. Dowse op. cit., p.93.
13. Ibid., p.106. Dowse, p.14, calls those opposed to subordinating the ILP to the Labour Party 'dissidents'; I prefer the term 'radicals'. Bullock op. cit., p.159, says many ILPers were impatient with the Labour Party and disliked its desire to impose its tepid approach on ILP MPs.
14. G. Brown, *Maxton* (1985), p.19; W. Knox, *James Maxton* (1986), p.58.
15. Clifford Allen (1889–1939) pacifist, wartime conscientious objector, and later Treasurer and Chairman of the ILP.
16. H. N. Brailsford (1873–1958) journalist, writer, and editor of the *New Leader* 1922–26. He left the ILP in 1932.
17. J. A. Hobson (1858–1940), Liberal intellectual who joined the ILP in 1919 because of its anti-war stand.

18. Dowse op. cit., p.130, p.132, pp.212–215.
19. Ibid., pp.141–146, pp.216–7; G. Brown op. cit., pp.208–9; Knox op. cit., p.72.
20. Emanuel (Manny) Shinwell (1884–1986), leading Scottish ILPer and later minister in the first three Labour governments. See Dowse op. cit., pp.156–7 for Shinwell's part as organiser of the pro-Labour-government ILP MPs.
21. Dowse op. cit., pp.156–157, and *New Leader*, 22 November 1929.
22. J. Jupp, *The Radical Left in Britain 1931–1941* (1982), p.22; Dowse op. cit., p.161; and NAC Minutes 23 April 1930 and 12 July 1930. The NAC also demanded that in future ILP MPs should seek its permission to take office and then relinquish office if instructed by it.
23. Dowse op. cit., p.159 (though they could abstain).
24. Jupp op. cit., p.23 and NAC Minutes 12 June 1931.
25. Jupp op. cit., p.23; Dowse op. cit., p.162. In 1931 19 ILP candidates stood without Labour Party endorsement.
26. Jupp op. cit., p.23. Maxton in Bridgeton, John McGovern in Shettleston, R. C. Wallhead in Merthyr Tydfil, George Buchanan in Gorbals and David Kirkwood in Dunbarton Burghs. The last two were officially trade union candidates but were still refused Labour Party endorsement.
27. Dowse op. cit., p.184. The ILP annual conference had voted against both disaffiliation and unconditional affiliation! The special conference may have been swayed by the Labour Party's hard line on the PLP SOs.
28. Winter op. cit., p.10.
29. Dowse op. cit., p.185; B. Pimlott, *Labour and the Left in the 1930s* (1986), p.43, and G. Brown op. cit., p.310.
30. See N. A. Holdaway, *The Adelphi*, May 1934, p.138, and G. Cohen, *The Failure of a Dream* (2007), p.54.
31. Dowse op. cit., p.185; Jupp op. cit., p.35. Kirkwood joined the PLP in August 1933, see D. Kirkwood, *My Life of Revolt* (1935).
32. Cohen op. cit., p.5 and passim.
33. (Archibald) Fenner Brockway (1888–1988), Indian-born journalist and writer. He joined the ILP in 1907, was active in his opposition to the First World War, and later was an MP and member of the House of Lords.
34. Fred Jowett (1864–1944), founder of the Bradford ILP, former MP and member of the first Labour government.
35. John Middleton Murry (1889–1957), writer, essayist and critic, member of the ILP from 1931 to 1934, an 'ethical Marxist' and pacifist.

36. Cohen op. cit., pp.95–102. Some members of the ISP rejoined the ILP during the Second World War.

37. Ibid., pp.102–8 and pp.204–5. The RPC was riven by internal disputes and left behind a rump called the Communist Unity Group (Bullock op. cit., p.203).

38. See Chapter 9, note 15. The NAC organised a plebiscite of the membership. Only 38 per cent took part, and of those only 56 per cent supported Maxton and the Parliamentary Group's position.

39. Cohen op. cit., pp.106–7. N.B.: some Trotskyists, including Hugo Dewar and Harry Wicks, had been members of the ILP since the late 1920s or early 1930s, though they also seem to have been involved with the Trotskyist elements of the CPGB during part of that time; see R. Groves, *The Balham Group* (1974).

40. Dr Charles Smith (1895–1984), a teacher; awarded the Military Medal in the First World War for carrying wounded through a blanket barrage.

41. See also Brockway's comments on the impact of factionalism during that period in Cohen op. cit., p.81.

42. R. Barltrop, *The Monument: The Story of the Socialist Party of Great Britain* (1975), p.7, pp.9–10 and p.12.

43. Dowse op. cit., pp.51–54 and p.191.

44. Jupp op. cit., p.41.

45. Dowse op. cit., p.189; *New Leader,* 19 May 1933 and 17 August 1934; and F, Beckett, *Enemy Within: the Rise and Fall of the British Communist Party* (1995), p.44. The CPGB had 'undercover' members in the ILP during 1933–34 (Cohen op. cit., p.87). The CPGB downplayed the ILP's part in the Cable Street 'battle'.

46. See P. J. Thwaites, 'The ILP Contingent in the Spanish Civil War', *Review* (1987).

47. B. Crick, *George Orwell: A Life* (1982), pp.329–330.

48. P. Broue and E. Temime, *The Revolution and the Civil War in Spain* (1972), p.286 and p.289, and *Daily Worker* 9 September 1937.

49. Pimlott op. cit., p.98; Cohen op. cit., pp.133–8.

50. Jupp op. cit., pp.107–108.

51. Jupp op. cit., p.80; Dowse op. cit., p.198 and H. Pelling, *The British Communist Party* (1975), pp.98–99. The ILP favoured the setting up of a 'Workers' Front' instead (Cohen op. cit., p.137.)

52. For the ILP's growing disillusionment with the Soviet Union, see Bullock op. cit., pp.265–295.

53. R. P. Arnot, *Labour Monthly* October 1936, quoted in Dowse op. cit., p.197.

54. Bullock op. cit., p.313.

Chapter 2

1. J. Clayton, *The Rise and Decline of Socialism in Great Britain 1884–1924* (1926), p.82.

2. A. J. B. Marwick, 'The Independent Labour Party 1918–32', B.Litt. thesis (1960), p.24.

3. The wards were Shettleston and Tollcross, and Parkhead; the branches Parkhead, Shettleston, Springfield, and Tollcross.

4. See note 16. In 1942 Melksham branch had two members (Bristol and Gloucestershire Federation Minutes 25 April 1942); in 1944 Sparkbrook branch had 11 members, Perry Common 26, Selly Oaks 3 (Birmingham and District Federation Minutes 11 May 1944).

5. Interview D. Bateman. But the Bristol and Gloucestershire Federation had its very first meeting on 25 April 1942 and boasted five active branches. Federation meetings consisted of the Chairman and Secretary of each branch plus one branch delegate for each 25 branch members or part thereof, and the Federation's annually elected officials, but only the delegates could vote (Birmingham Federation Constitution).

6. For the geographical boundaries see P. J. Thwaites, 'The Independent Labour Party 1938–1950', PhD thesis (1976), footnote 8, pp.11–12. In the late 1940s the ILP had branches in Northern Ireland, but there were too few members to constitute a Division.

7. The ILP lost 128 branches in Scotland and 14 in Lancashire in 1932. After the split, which came over the question of co-operation with the CPGB, the Lancashire ILP was further reduced from 72 branches in 1932 to approximately 20 by 1935 (R. E. Dowse, *Left in the Centre* [1966], p.185).

8. This Division contained the Norwich branch which insisted that people wanting to use its Keir Hardie Hall Social Club signed up as ILP members.

9. By 1939 ILP HO was unclear whether some Welsh branches still existed as nothing had been heard from them (Francis Johnson, letter to A. Berry, 15 March 1939), and during the war H. Davies complained to Brockway, 25 September 1940, about how difficult it was to get reports from the Welsh branches (FJC ILP/4/1939/31 and ILP/4/1940/28). By 1941 there were only seven active branches, contributing less than £30 in fees (NAC Minutes 30 July 1940 and 11 April 1941).

10. Treasurer, Industrial Organiser etc. (see East Anglia Division Minute Book 1932 to 1960). The Federations had a similar group of officers, and Executive Committees, e.g., Birmingham and District Federation Constitution.

11. At this time they were invariably male. This section is based on an interview with D. Bateman, voluntary part-time Organiser, Yorkshire Division 1942–1943.

12. Until a new branch could be formed the recruit was accepted as a 'National Member' and paid their fees direct to ILP H.O. (e.g. see FJC ILP/4/1938/3).

13. Walter Padley complained that a single Organiser in a large Division could not be expected to do everything (NAC Minutes 11 April 1941).

14. Barking Branch Minutes 25 March 1942, letter to the London Division complaining that Padley, the London Organiser, was costing the branches a great deal of money but was very rarely in the Division!

15. NAC Minutes 21 May 1938 and Organisation Committee Minutes 14 June 1941.

16. In 1933 they could send one delegate for every 50 members; this had reduced to one for 35 by 1938 and one for 25 members in 1942.

17. E.g., over the question of electoral activity in 1949; see Chapter 17.

18. When a plebiscite was called re the Parliamentary Group's actions over Abyssinia in 1936 (see Chapter 1) only 38 per cent of the ILP membership sent in their ballots.

19. The General Secretary was responsible for organisation, propaganda, arranging the NAC and other committee meetings and taking minutes, arranging annual conferences and summer schools, writing official ILP letters and running the Head Office.

20. This paid post appears to have been created for Brockway so he could provide political input for the NAC. Both Secretary posts were combined when Brockway resigned in 1946. The 1945 ILP constitution removed the Political Secretary's right to an NAC vote.

21. H. Pelling, 'The story of the ILP', *Popular Politics and Society in Late Victorian Britain* (1968), p.123. Before 1906 the whole NAC was elected by the annual conference.

22. Much of this paragraph is based on G. Cohen, *The Failure of a Dream* (2007) pp.45–46, and Dowse op. cit., pp.80–1.

23. An Executive Committee was established in 1920 but abolished in 1924 (I. Bullock, *Under Siege* [2017], p.246).

24. Bullock op. cit., p.260.

25. Cohen op. cit., p.205, talks of the Inner Executive being abolished after the Abyssinian dispute, but the term was still in use in 1938 and it may have remained theoretically the body charged with leading the ILP *in extremis*.

26. The NAC met just before and just after annual conference and during the first fortnight in June, August, November and February.

27. For some idea of the number and scope of these sub-committees and boards see NAC Minutes 11 April 1939.
28. Bullock op. cit., p.246. I have not found an example of its use.
29. *ILP Constitution and Rules 1936*, pp.4–5.
30. E.g. Barking Branch Minutes 3 April 1943 for the reaction to a suggestion from the Divisional Council on how its members should vote in a London Co-operative Society election.
31. E.g. on electoral activity and reaffiliation to the Labour Party (see Chapter 1).
32. *ILP Constitution and Rules 1936*, p.2.
33. This had been introduced in 1923 by Clifford Allen (see Marwick op. cit., p.147).
    In 1934 the rates were set at:
    25 members or under £1
    26–50 £2
    51–75 £3
    76–100 £4
    Over 100 members pro rata
    See letter from Francis Johnson to Mark Simpson, 2 Division stating the Division's 1937–1938 share of the affiliation fees and Quota Fund, FJC ILP/4/1938/4. The calculation of equivalence between £1 in say 1940 and today is tricky, but some sources suggest that a 1940 £1 was the equivalent of £40 in 2020, and so 1 shilling = £2 and 1d = 17p (roughly).
34. *New Leader* 5 May 1933; the suggested rates were:
    Income below 30 shillings per week contribution Nil
    Income 30s to 50s ½d per day
    Income 50s to 90s 1d per day
    Income over 90s 2d per day
    Gladys Martin, London Division, complained (letter to Francis Johnson 21 June 1940) that most members should pay 2/6d per week, but were in fact contributing one shilling [1/-] (FJC ILP/4/1940/14).
35. The extra going to the branch to help it meet its obligations (interview D. Jobson).
36. E.g. letter from Francis Johnson to Dr Charles Smith 15 March 1940 FJC ILP/4/1940/8 and NAC Minutes 30 July 1939, 15 June 1946 and 7 August 1948. To meet their financial obligations, branches and Federations often resorted to Bazaars and 'Bring and Buy Sales', e.g. see ILP Glasgow Federation Bridgeton Branch Social Committee Cash Book April 1935 – October 1953 and Birmingham and District Federation Minutes 11 January 1945.

37. The *Labour Leader* was established by Keir Hardie in 1889. In 1893 it became the official paper of the ILP. Its name was changed to the *New Leader* on 14 September 1922 and to the *Socialist Leader* on 22 June 1946.
38. File No. 106263, Companies House, London.
39. File No. 5774R, Register of Friendly Societies.
40. Interviews Dr C. Smith and N. Carmichael and Companies House File No. 287026.
41. *NAC Report to Annual Conference 1915*, p.19.
42. In 1938 the value of these investments was £6,550 (letter from A. Sudbery to Francis Johnson 31 March 1938, FJC ILP/4/1938/15).
43. File No. 141267 Articles of Association, Companies House.
44. *New Leader* 9 November 1934 and *The Times* 27 June 1936.
45. E.g. see correspondence re Tottenham branch's property, 12–14 March 1939, FJC ILP/4/1939/27A–30 and re West Ham and Leyton branch 19 January – 4 March 1950 FJC ILP/4/1950/6, /9–10,/16–25.
46. E.g. donation of £1,450 (letter from W. Stafford to F. Johnson 7 March 1950, FJC ILP/4/1950/27).
47. Interviews Bateman, Carmichael, Smith. For an example of their 'donations' see Francis Johnson Correspondence, letters from W. Stafford 27 June and 17 August 1950, ILP/4/1950/32, /43, when it amounted to £1,844.
48. The Financial Report 28 February 1942 shows affiliation fees £155.18.1 and donations £1,790.18.3.
49. Norwich for example never received money from the NAC for its election expenses, and paid out £700 on alterations to its premises (*New Leader* 1 March 1939). And South West Ham branch in 1938 loaned £100 to the London Division (letter from D. Springer to John Aplin 21 January 1938, FJC ILP/4/1938/2).
50. See East Anglia Division Minute Book 12 April 1931 passim.
51. Letter to author from B. Lea 22 June 1975, and Bullock op. cit., p.85. From 1926 until his death in 1946, James Maxton was the public face of the ILP, but not its formal leader, though he was always very influential in the party.
52. Bullock op. cit., p.80 suggests there may also have been a 'provincial' versus 'metropolitan' element at play.
53. The London and South East Division contained both working-class and predominantly middle-class branches (e.g. Hampstead) and the balance between them is unclear.
54. The ILP Parliamentary Group was also predominantly drawn from

those in middle-class occupations: Maxton had been a schoolteacher, Stephen a barrister and priest, and, later, Carmichael had been an insurance agent and secretary. McGovern had been a plumber, though he too became an insurance agent.

55. *Forward* 14 April 1934, and interview Carmichael. Women were also underrepresented in the NAC for most of this period (Cohen op. cit., p.49).
56. Interviews Carmichael and E. Sword. ILP summer schools provided some political education, but were also social events. Few members of the working class, however, could afford the cost of the schools (£2.15/- a week or 8/6d a day), or obtain a paid holiday from their jobs.
57. See McGovern's attack on Brockway at the 1939 conference, in *New Leader* 19 April 1939, and Dowse op. cit., p.82.
58. Brockway also may not have been universally trusted. He was considered too intellectual by some working-class ILPers and too 'Bohemian' for some middle-class ones (interviews A. Hambly, D. and R. Jobson, and H. Sergeant).
59. Dr Charles Smith, while Party Chairman, claimed that 'the lack of central control ... is one of the ILP's chief weaknesses' (*Between Ourselves*, July 1939). In 1948 Percy Williams blamed many of the party's problems on the continuing electoral contests with the Labour Party, and ended his Treasurer's report with an appeal to the NAC: 'we have been elected leaders of the Party, for the sake of Socialism let us on this occasion LEAD!' (NAC Minutes 7/8 August 1948).

Chapter 3

1. John Paton, *Left Turn* (1936), p.389.
2. *New Leader* 21 April 1933 and 18 May 1933. For the intended purpose of workers' councils see R. E. Dowse, *Left in the Centre* (1966), p.190. For the debate surrounding them within the ILP see G. Cohen, *The Failure of a Dream* (2007), pp.100–101, pp.111–118, and I. Bullock, *Under Siege* (2017) pp.213–216 and passim.
3. See G. Brown, *Maxton* (1986), p.261 and G. Cohen, *The Failure of a Dream* (2007), p.64, pp.111–115. In 1933 the NAC declared Parliament was 'an instrument of government of the Capitalist state' and could not be the main instrument of its destruction (Bullock op. cit., p.218). Some ILPers, however, including Fred Jowett, Elijah Sandham and the Unity Group, believed in parliamentary work and opposed the ILP's focus on revolutionary action (Cohen op. cit., pp.99–100 and p.118).

4. *New Leader* 17 February 1933. This may partly explain the disaffiliated ILP's lack of interest in parliamentary and electoral reform as espoused by Jowett (Bullock op. cit., pp.13–17, p.335).

5. E.g. during the war McGovern used his parliamentary privilege to enter Army camps and other restricted areas to obtain information about the way conscientious objectors and others were being treated, which he could then use for propaganda purposes; see for example in HC 371 col. 677–6, 6 May 1941 and HC 379 col. 1231, 5 May 1942.

6. *New Leader* 21 April 1933.

7. Ibid., 1 November 1935, 22 April 1938 and 23 June 1945. Douglas Moyle (*Between Ourselves* July 1939) argued, however, the Party should withdraw from parliamentary activity because 'it is the "mistakes" which get the publicity' (e.g. Maxton congratulating Chamberlain over the Munich Agreement). Jowett also did not accept the 'propaganda argument', saying that 'if democracy has any use for Parliament it is to make it work and not talk' (Bullock op. cit., p.89).

8. See Chapter 5.

9. John Paton in *New Leader* 15 July 1932 and Editorial *New Leader* 22 July 1932.

10. N. Wood, *Communism and British Intellectuals* (1959), pp.37–74.

11. G. Cohen op. cit., pp.127–127 and Bullock op. cit., p.184.

12. Interview H. Sergeant.

13. Interviews D. Bateman and Dr C. Smith, who devised this course to help ILPers understand the theoretical aspects of socialism.

14. Interview T. Taylor.

15. Maxton in *New Leader* 9 February 1934; G. Brown, *Maxton* (1988), p.312 and W. Knox, *James Maxton* (1987), pp.147–148. F. Brockway, *Outside the Right* (1963), p.182 (my emphasis).

16. *New Leader* 1 May 1943.

17. Brockway in *New Leader* 26 March 1937 and Editorial *New Leader* 5 December 1942 said: 'The ILP is not doctrinaire in acceptance of Marxism ... but it DOES base its policy on the class struggle, which is Marxism in action'.

18. *New Leader* 19 March 1933. John Aplin claimed there were at least half a dozen definitions within the ILP of 'revolutionary socialism', Bullock op. cit., p.229 and p.334, p. 339 doubts if the ILP could ever have reached a clear position on this question.

19. *New Leader* 19 March 1933.

20. Speech reported in *Glasgow Eastern Standard* 23 February 1935, and for Smith's position see Bullock op. cit p.227.

21. *Yarmouth Mercury* 2 September 1939.
22. Maxton called on the people to end the war the same way that hooligans stop a football match: 'by breaking on to the pitch' (see *New Leader* 26 August 1944, and interview Sergeant). But Maxton always argued that socialism could be achieved in Britain without violence (Brown op. cit., p.174, p.263.)
23. Compare with the pluralist thinkers; see D. Nicholls, *The Pluralist State* (1975), p.6, p.11.
24. *New Leader* 19 August 1933, quoted in Brown op. cit., p.263.
25. J. Jupp, 'The Left in Britain 1931–41' M.Sc. thesis (1956), p.299 and interview W. Padley.
26. Peter Kropotkin (1842–1921), Russian anarcho-communist and writer.
27. John McNair in *ILP 1893–1943: Jubilee Souvenir* (1943), p.1. McGovern was an anarchist in his youth.
28. See J. White, 'The meaning of anarchism', in *Controversy* July 1937 and McNair on workers' control in Spain in *Controversy*, October 1936, pp.10–12. Syndicalism was intended to replace capitalism by organising workers and their industries into syndicates, so that the workers thereby owned and controlled their industries. Anarcho-syndicalism added a political element to this idea to rob the state of economic and social power.
29. See I. Deutscher, *Stalin* (1970 edition), pp.138–82, and P. J. Thwaites, 'The Independent Labour Party Contingent in the Spanish Civil War', *Review* (1987).
30. *New Leader* 22 April 1938.
31. Syndicalism enjoyed some popularity before the First World War but was later modified by G. D. H. Cole and others into 'Guild Socialism', which advocated workers' control of industry through trade-related guilds. Support for this idea waned after 1924.
32. Resolutions to this effect were passed at the 1935, 1936 and 1937 conferences.
33. Brockway, *Workers Front* (1938), p.206.
34. Brockway noted this later in *Forward* 3 May 1947.
35. E.g. F. A. Ridley, 'Anarchism and Marxism', *Controversy* August 1938, pp.216–7 and Brockway op. cit., p.206.
36. E.g. see George Orwell's and Dr Smith's views on the Second World War (Chapters 9 and 11 respectively), or Maxton on the need for the ILP to remain independent (Chapters 8 and 14).
37. See G. Cohen, *The Failure of a Dream* (2007), pp.41–44 for the importance of the ILP's social activities during the period 1932–1939;

these were, of course, curtailed somewhat during the war. In the 1970s I met ex-ILPers who were still friends, despite having different political views in the 1930s and 1940s. However, personality clashes and factionalism could also drive ILPers apart; see Cohen op. cit., pp.204–5, and the often turbulent relationship between Maxton and Brockway.

38. *Tribune* 14 February 1947.
39. Interviews N. Carmichael and E. Sword.
40. See attacks by the Socialist Party of Great Britain (SPGB) in *Socialist Standard* April 1938 passim.
41. Both the Socialist Labour Party (SLP) and the SPGB were formed from splits in the Social Democratic Federation in the period 1903–1904, and both refused to co-operate with any other party; see R. Barltrop, *The Monument* (1975).
42. E.g., on the question of the workers' control of industry. For a history of British Trotskyism see J. Callaghan, *The Far Left in British Politics* (1987).
43. *RCP Internal Bulletin*, April 1946.
44. See F. Brockway, *Inside the Left* (1942) p.237 and interviews Taylor and Bateman. For 'machinations of the CPGB', A. J. B. Marwick, 'The ILP in the 1920s'. *Institute of Historical Research Bulletin*, Vol. XXXV (1962), p.72.
45. E.g., A. J. P. Taylor, *English History 1914–45* (1965), p.548, D. Martin, *Pacifism* (1965), p.129, and A. Calder, *The People's War* (1971), p.68.
46. It always opposed capitalist wars, but sent a contingent to fight in the Spanish Civil War; see P. J. Thwaites op. cit.
47. E.g., the CPGB from 1939 to 1941, and see Chapter 9.
48. E.g., *Norwich Mercury* 4 May 1940, also E. Mannin, *Privileged Spectator* (1948), p.232.
49. See for example *New Leader* 8, 15 August 1940, and Maxton HC 367 col. 749 5 December 1940. Maxton always resented being called a pacifist; he was anti-war because he believed wars were fought solely in the interests of the rich and powerful (W. Knox op. cit., p.138).
50. See NAC Minutes 23 April 1943 for setting up of the armed forces branch and NAC Minutes 15 December 1940 which state that the ILP neither urges, nor seeks to dissuade, socialists from joining the armed forces.
51. Smith warned his colleagues about this (NAC minutes 27 July 1940).
52. NAC Minutes 25/26 May 1940 and 27/28 February 1943.
53. The ILP Chairmen during this period were David Gibson 1948–1950, Fred Barton 1951–1953, Annie Maxton 1953–1958 and Fred Morel 1958–1961.
54. J. McNair, *James Maxton: The Beloved Rebel* (1955), p.312.

55. E.g., three ILPers, J. Davies, B. M. Davies and W. W. Herbert, were lay preachers in Merthyr and ILP town councillors. There were 'Quaker' branches of the Party in Birmingham and Norwich (interview A. South). The ILP did not apply any religious test to its members, although F. A. Ridley, in *Socialism and Religion* (1948), hinted that a socialist party might have to do so if it was to purify itself.
56. Interview J. Morel.
57. Fred Barton, for example, was a Quaker pacifist and a revolutionary socialist who advocated using non-violent methods to defeat all opposition.
58. *Merrie England,* published in 1893, comprised a series of articles on a socialism based on the principles of human justice.
59. William Morris (1834–1896) textile designer, poet and revolutionary international socialist. In 1946 the NAC's Scottish representative gave his heroes as Morris, Keir Hardie and James Maxton (letter from J. Taylor to F. Johnson 20 November 1946, FJC ILP/4/1946/27).
60. R. H. Tawney (1880–1962) educator, influential author and an ethical and Christian socialist.
61. Middleton Murry wrote articles for the *New Leader* on the 'Fundamentals of Marxism' but emphasised the ethical aspects of Marx's teachings (Bullock op. cit., p.207).
62. E.g. the ILP attacked a government ban on the *Daily Worker* in 1941 because the ban was unjust although it strongly disagreed with nearly all that that paper printed.
63. Bullock op. cit. p.11.
64. *ILP Constitution and Rules 1933,* p.2, and Fred Jowett *New Leader* 27 November 1936.

Chapter 4

1. *ILP Constitution and Rules 1933*, p.4.
2. J. Jupp, 'The Left in Britain 1931–41' MSc thesis (1956), p.578.
3. Some ex-ILPers still believed 30 years later that the Party could have played a leading role in this work for the Labour Movement after 1932 (interviews B. Edwards, N. Carmichael and W. Ballantine).
4. Mass Observation (MO) reports nos. 111 and 1983, and *New Leader* 10 January 1948.
5. G. F. Johnson, *New Leader* 2 April 1937.
6. Contests in areas where the ILP had little support were considered pointless by local branches (interview J. E. Thomas).

7. See Barking Branch Minutes 14 May 1942. ILPers chosen as union representatives to the Trades Union Congress (TUC) could propound ILP views, e.g., see P. J. Thwaites 'The ILP 1938 to 1950' PhD thesis (1976) p.231 footnote 1 for a record of some of Walter Padley and Bob Edwards speeches expressing their ILP views in TUC Reports from 1938 to 1946. In 1944 the Birmingham Federation managed to persuade local trade union branches to accept ILP speakers at their meetings (Minutes 14 December 1944).

8. See Division 5 (East Anglia) Minutes 29 June 1941. There was also, of course, often a purely altruistic motive behind these actions.

9. E.g. *Merthyr Express* 17 December 1932.

10. *Yarmouth Mercury* 6 July 1946.

11. *Glasgow Eastern Standard* 27 November 1948.

12. CPGB members apparently dominated the NUWM even though the ILP was the larger party at that time.

13. *Glasgow Eastern Standard* 22 February 1947, for example, contains adverts for regular Bridgeton ILP public meetings.

14. See Barking Branch Minutes 28 September 1944.

15. Editorial *Merthyr Express* 9 June 1945.

16. Barking Branch Minutes 18 April 1947.

17. E.g. on USSE, ibid., 13 March 1947 and *NAC Report 1942*, p.7.

18. E.g. Division 5 Minutes 26 June 1938.

19. Ibid., 14 January 1933 notes the Divisional Council had refused to put forward the name of a local ILPer for this panel 'until he had further experience as a Divisional speaker'.

20. Interview Ballantine. Occasionally a speaker was put up in a hotel, e.g. Division 5 Minutes 12 April 1931 re a visit from Dr Campbell (Stephen?). McNair complains, in *Life Abundant*, p.56, that, because ILPers were often poor and could not afford heating, he had to stay in cold bedrooms; and that as many of them were total abstainers he could not get a drink after a meeting!

21. E.g. NAC Minutes 15/16 December 1940; 9/10 August 1941 and 27 April 1943.

22. E.g. they were in places too difficult to reach easily from London or Glasgow.

23. Particularly Wales and the South West Division. McNair, op. cit., p.289, says he travelled on average 20,000 miles a year and always addressed more than 100 meetings.

24. See R. E. Dowse, *Left in the Centre* (1966) pp.130–133, pp.141–146 and Chapter 12.

25. And, it is claimed, frequently gained converts (interviews W. Padley and Ballantine). McNair, op. cit., p.290, says Maxton would insist McNair did the donkeywork of speaking first, usually for an hour. Maxton himself doubted the efficacy of public meetings as a recruiting tool (NAC 8/9 August 1942).

26. Division 5 Minutes 29 June 1941 report from Ipswich Branch: '(We) posted 100 bills to advertise McGovern meeting … A large amount of chalking had been done'. It became too expensive to have any graphic work on the posters (interview D. Bateman). MO Report 111 p.13 noted that some of the slogans were amusing, e.g. 'The Front Trench 14/- a week, The Front Bench £5,000 a year'. The ILP also stuck 'fly posters' over opponents' announcements (Barking Branch Minutes 8 March 1947).

27. Tom Taylor used a parade of children, Annie Maxton of women during their respective election campaigns. McNair bought six loudspeakers. Two were kept in Glasgow, two in the Midlands and one each in Yorkshire and on Tyneside (NAC Minutes 11 December 1944).

28. MO Report 1015 p.7. Mass Observation, a social research organisation set up in the UK in 1937, was active until the mid–1960s and revived in 1981.

29. For ILP branch banners see ETV film of NUWM marches in 1934.

30. Organisation Committee Minutes 12 August 1945.

31. McNair, op. cit., p.289, says that he sometimes travelled over 200 miles to find he was addressing a meeting of only 10 or 12 people. In 1948 Percy Williams, the Party Treasurer, remarked that ILP public meetings probably attracted 5,000 people a year in total out of a population of 44 million (NAC Minutes 7/8 August 1948).

32. Division 5 Minutes 29 June 1941 and 1 February 1942. An anti-war meeting in Conway Hall, London on 7 September 1940 addressed by McGovern was disrupted by an air raid (R. Challinor, *The Struggle for Hearts and Minds* [1995], p.57).

33. *New Leader* 30 May 1940.

34. Ibid. Some pamphlets cost more, e.g., 3d, 6d or 1/-.

35. Division 5 Minutes 3 September 1932.

36. 'New Lamps for Old', *New Leader* 30 May 1940.

37. In 1943 Padley titled a pamphlet on economics 'The Real Battle for Britain' and Edwards called a survey of the Chemical Industry 'War on the People'.

38. Barking Branch Minutes 14 May 1942.

39. *NAC Report 1942* p.14 says 7 issued in the year and *NAC Report 1944*

p.16 says 9 were issued in the year.

40. E.g. J. McNair, *Socialist Britain Now* (1942) and *What the ILP Stands For* (1945).
41. E.g. F. A. Ridley on the history of the Christian church, and Padley on economics.
42. See C. Day Lewis *Buried Day* (1960) p.215 for his view on the CPGB's language.
43. E.g. H. Brannan and T. Stephenson, *The Miner's Case* (1942).
44. Jupp op. cit. p.299.
45. Interview Bateman, who said an edition usually ran to 5,000 copies; though few pamphlets sold more than one edition, some ran to four. But Common Wealth sold as many as 45,000 copies of some of their pamphlets (A. Calder, 'The Common Wealth Party 1942–45' D.Phil thesis [1968] vol. 2, p.113). Until it was destroyed in the Blitz, the ILP had a retail outlet called the Socialist Bookshop within its London Head Office building.
46. Brockway, *Socialism over 60 Years* (1946) quotes extensively from that paper.
47. See *Barrhead News* 10 January 1936 and *New Leader* 4 April 1940. The Bristol and Gloucestershire Federation (Minutes 25 April 1942) briefly published its own industrial newspaper, *Shop Steward*, in 1942.
48. E.g. Division 5 Minutes Norwich 9 February 1941. Birmingham Federation inserted locally printed 'slips' into the *New Leaders* they sold (Minutes 8 June 1944).
49. Jupp op. cit., p.280 and p.555 gives *Tribune* sales as 25,000 per week and *Daily Worker* sales as 80,000 a day.
50. *New Leader* 12 January 1940.
51. See Chapter 11.
52. Barking Branch Minutes 28 August 1947.
53. Pre-war ILP Cycle Clubs were a popular social outlet and outings might be combined with *New Leader* sales campaigns (G. Cohen, *Failure of a Dream* [2007] p.42).
54. But Norwich branch, with 500 members on its books, only sold 600 *New Leaders* a week (Division 5 Minutes 1 February 1935).
55. During the Second World War, according to the Imperial War Museum, there were apparently some 34 million changes of address recorded in Britain!
56. Saltcoats Minute Book letter from ILP Head Office November 1945, and *The Times* 4 February 1974. By 1948 sales were already below 8,000 and dropping (NAC Minutes 7/8 August 1948).

57. Being a weekly paper, it occasionally gave extensive coverage to strikes (e.g. the 1945 dock strike) which were over before it was published! See Barking Branch Minutes 1 March 1945.

58. The *Socialist Leader* 5 October 1946 defended its coverage of foreign news by arguing that the world was shrinking to such an extent that 'nowadays we have just got to take notice of what is happening everywhere in the world'.

59. See G. Thayer, *The British Political Fringe* (1965), p.147.

60. E.g. *New Leader* 30 August 1947 and passim.

61. The *Daily Worker* also relied on subsidies; see Viscount Camrose, *British Newspapers and their Controllers* (1947), pp.76–77. In Division 5 Minutes 6 February 1950 the NAC is reported as saying that the *Socialist Leader* was losing £13 per week.

62. Barking Branch Minutes 2 March 1944, and NAC Minutes 30 July 1938 and 9/10 February 1946. Birmingham Federation attacked the newspaper on several occasions e.g., for its poor content, pro-Labour Party bias, and its anti-Soviet Union bias (Minutes 13 December 1945, 12 February 1948 and 11 November 1948).

63. Interview Carmichael; also H. Dewar, *Between Ourselves* March 1941 and Birmingham (City) Branch Minutes 1 September 1949.

64. *New Leader* 8 July 1938.

65. NAC Minutes 21 May 1938.

66. T. Williams, *Between Ourselves* July 1941.

67. E.g. McGovern HC 388 col. 846 8 April 1943 debate 'Supply Civil Estimates BBC (Propaganda)'. See also *Newcastle Journal* 22 May 1950 and *The Times* 17 April 1956.

68. E.g. *New Leader* 30 May 1940 and *Glasgow Eastern Standard* 27 September 1941. The ILPers were not the only ones to put great faith in the power of radio propaganda to win the war (see D. Stafford, 'The Detonator Concept: British Strategy SOE & European Resistance After the Fall of France' [1975]).

69. *New Leader* 11 August 1945.

70. Interviews Carmichael, Edwards, Ballantine, Mr and Mrs H. Brown, A. Nicholls.

Chapter 5

1. E.g., *Norwich Mercury* 23 December 1933; J. Walker, Chairman's speech, *Labour Party Conference Report 1941*, p.111, and Herbert Morrison, *Labour Party Conference Report 1943*, p.168.

2. G. F. Johnson, *Norwich Mercury* 23 December 1933.
3. *New Leader* 16 October 1936.
4. *ILP Conference Report 1930*, p.106, A. J. B. Marwick, 'The ILP in the 1920s', *Institute of Historical Research Bulletin* Vol. XXXV (1962), p.74.
5. Municipal Programme, *New Leader* 16 October 1936.
6. R. Barker, *Education and Politics* (1972), p.67 for the debate on common schools.
7. M. Galpern, *New Leader* 28 August 1943; and ILPers vote on the Common Wealth amendment to the Education Bill (HC 398 col. 774 21 March 1944) calling for all parents to send their children to a local education authority school.
8. NAC Minutes 12/13 February 1944.
9. Apparently Maxton, McGovern, Stephen and Buchanan pledged during the 1931 general election to support Roman Catholic Schools (I. Bullock, *Under Siege* [2017], p.191).
10. *Yarmouth Mercury* 24 April 1943.
11. HC 279 col.1042 22 June 1933 and HC 308 col. 683 18 February 1936.
12. HC 398 col. 803 21 March 1944 and interview L. F. Bunnewell.
13. E.g. McGovern's election address 1935.
14. The ILP did not believe that full employment was possible under capitalism because investments could not keep up with consumption (LSE file Beveridge/9A/15/7).
15. *Socialism in Our Time* in R. E. Dowse, *Left in the Centre* (1966), p.213. See also I. Bullock, *Under Siege* (2017), pp.99–139 for a discussion on the ILP and the Living Wage. It was to be £5 per week in 1944 (LSE Beveridge/9A/15/7).
16. G. Buchanan HC 279 col. 811 21 June 1933.
17. Maxton HC 398 col. 1625 30 March 1944 and C. Stephen HC 322 col. 469 8 April 1937.
18. *Shop Steward Pamphlet* (1943) No. 2.
19. R. Challinor, *The Struggle for Hearts and Minds* (1995), p.60.
20. Women were underrepresented on the NAC 1938–50, and the ILP's separate women's NAC and other decision-making bodies were disbanded as a result of annual conference decisions in 1933 and 1934 (G. Cohen, *The Failure of a Dream* [2007], pp.49–50).
21. W. Knox, *James Maxton* (1987), p.37 and J. Hannan, 'Women and the ILP 1890–1914', in D. James et al. (eds), *The Centennial History of the Independent Labour Party* (1992) for a view of the ILP's early support for women's rights.
22. E.g. McGovern's election address 1935. Campbell Stephen was

particularly vocal in his calls for increased old-age pensions, e.g. see HC 352 col. 2034–8 1 November 1939. The ILP called him the 'pensioners' MP', *New Leader* 30 June 1945.

23. G. Latham, *Labour Party Conference Report 1937*, p.164.
24. Stephen HC 352 col. 2034–8 1 November 1939.
25. *New Leader* 16 October 1936.
26. Item 1 Municipal Programme, *New Leader* 13 October 1945.
27. See C. Stephen HC 404 col. 1475 8 November 1944.
28. Buchanan HC 281 col. 512 10 November 1933.
29. *New Leader* 16 October 1936.
30. LSE Beveridge/9A/15/7.
31. *New Leader* 22 September 1939 and Maxton HC 346 col. 1391 27 April 1939 on the conscription of wealth. £500 pa equates to approximately £31,000 pa in 2020. The 1939 average annual salary was £180 pa. So the 100 per cent tax rate would have been levied on incomes over 2½ times above the average wage. But this calculation is not straightforward, because £500 was the cost of an average house in 1939!
32. This section is taken from the ILP's *A Socialist Plan for Britain* (1945).
33. LSE Beveridge/9A/15/7.
34. F. Brockway, *The Way Out* (1942), p.2, 'a Socialist Britain would distribute money … according to the number of mouths to be fed and would be based on a national estimate of the wealth – that is on the productive capacity of the workers … and national resources'.
35. See W. Padley, *The Economic Problem of the Peace* (1944), p.159.
36. F. Brockway, *Socialism Over 60 Years* (1946), p.383 for Jowett's economic theories.
37. *New Leader* 27 November 1943 contains an attack on Keynesian economics.
38. R. E. Dowse, 'The ILP and foreign politics 1918–23', *International Review of Social History* vol. VII (1962), p.46 (my emphasis).
39. HC 386 col. 941 3 February 1943.
40. C. Stephen, *Norwich Mercury* 23 January 1932, and *Socialist Britain Now* (1942).
41. LSE Beveridge/9A/15/7.
42. *A Socialist Plan for Britain 1945*, p.10, and J. McNair, *New Leader* 15 October 1949.
43. The SLP organ *Socialist* October 1939 said the ILP appeared to expect 'the capitalist leopard to change its spots'.

Chapter 6

1. *ILP Constitution and Rules 1933*. Moves to insist that ILPers join unions were defeated, e.g., Ipswich resolution to East Anglia divisional conference, East Anglia Division Minutes 1 February 1941.
2. *What the Party Stands For* (1935), p.12. In fact the ILP had never succeeded in winning over the trade unions or in attracting large numbers of trade unionists into its ranks, see G. Brown, *Maxton* (1988), p.311.
3. NAC Minutes 31 October 1942. Federations could also have (unpaid) Industrial Organisers, e.g., Harley Millichap's report, Birmingham Federation Minutes 12 October 1944.
4. NAC Minutes 12/13 August 1944 and 24/25 February 1945.
5. See G. Cohen, *The Failure of a Dream* (2007), pp.56–62. For the loss of Padley, Ballantine and Edwards see Chapters 15 and 17.
6. J. Aplin in *New Leader* 2 July 1937.
7. *What the Party Stands For* (1935), p.13.
8. *New Leader* 23 July 1937 and *Socialist Leader* 16 August 1947.
9. I. Bullock, *Under Siege* (2017) p.338 says that the ILP was conspicuously lacking tact and patience when dealing with the trade unions. Despite trying to form alliances with trade unionists (see M. Brown, *The ILP Centenary: Still Making Socialists* [1996], p.5), the ILP angered many trade union leaders by its attacks on both the Labour Party and on the TUC leadership (Dowse op. cit., pp.86–89).
10. H. Dewar in *Between Ourselves* April 1941. In 1942 the Bristol and Gloucestershire Federation (Minutes, 25 April 1942) briefly published its own newspaper, *Shop Steward*, for sale outside the Bristol Aeroplane Company's factories, which attempted to present the ILP's 'line' to the BAC shop stewards.
11. For the CPGB's influence in industry, see H. Pelling, *A History of British Trade Unionism*, p.215, and Cole, *A History of the Labour Party from 1914*, p.394. The NAC wished to replace the CPGB-dominated National Shop Steward Council with a militant Shop Stewards' Committee, (NAC Minutes 27/28 February 1943).
12. B. Edwards, *Workers! Freedom or Servitude?* (1941), p.22.
13. Pelling op. cit., pp.102–3.
14. J. McNair, *What the Party Stands For* (1944), p.13. Later the NAC said the ILP supported the 'closed shop' when unionism was under threat, but not to obtain a monopoly for the General Workers' Union (NAC Minutes 26/27 October 1946).

15. *Socialist Leader* 5 November 1949.
16. Ibid.
17. *A Socialist Plan for Britain* (1935).
18. J. Aplin, *New Leader* 16 April 1937, said Lenin had drawn a parallel between the UK First World War Shop Stewards' Committees and the Russian Soviets.
19. *New Leader* 1 August 1940.
20. Ibid., 11 October 1941.
21. *ILP Conference Report 1943*, p.21.
22. N.B.: At this time Sir Stafford Cripps, President of the Board of Trade in the Labour government, was saying that the British workers were not ready to run their own industries even if that was desirable, *The Times* 28 October 1946.
23. The one thing ILPers seemed to agree on was that there should be no compensation paid when industries were taken over (Organisation Committee Minutes 12 August 1945).
24. HC 430 col. 309 14 November 1946.
25. *Socialist Leader* 12 April 1947 and W. S. Wigham, *Socialist Leader* 24 July 1948 and *Between Ourselves* October 1946 passim.
26. It was still unclear whether industrial democracy would precede or follow the revolution. In *New Leader* 30 May 1942 an anonymous writer said they would occur simultaneously.
27. N. Winter, *Workers' Control* (1947), *Socialist Leader* 12 April 1947 and ILP Conference Report quoted in *Socialist Leader* 3 April 1948.
28. NAC Minutes Easter 1948.
29. *Socialist Leader* 11 December 1948.
30. Ibid., 12 April 1947. The ILP agitated on day-to-day issues but insisted that workers' control was the only worthwhile reform for industry.

Chapter 7

1. G. D. H. Cole, *A History of the Labour Party From 1914* (1948), pp.6–7.
2. A. J. B. Marwick, 'The Independent Labour Party 1918–32' B.Litt. thesis (1960), p.97, p.105, p.117 and R. E. Dowse, *Left in the Centre* (1966), pp.53–59.
3. NAC Minutes 27 November 1927, quoted in Marwick op. cit., p.279.
4. Ibid., p.280. The parties were the Norwegian Labour Party, the Polish Bund, the Polish ILP, and Left elements of the Dutch Social Democrats.
5. NAC supplement 1934. F. Brockway, *Inside the Left* (1942), p.284 claims the 'London' Bureau was originally intended as a bridge between the

other two Internationals. It was called at different times the Left International Committee, the International Bureau for Revolutionary Socialist Unity and the International Left Bureau (G. Cohen, *The Failure of a Dream* [2007] p.164).

6. R. E. Dowse op. cit., p.191. I have drawn heavily on Dowse and Cohen op. cit., pp.163–166, for this section.

7. B. Edwards, *Controversy* December 1936, p.49. Bureau members also went to meetings of the International Workers' Front Against War in 1939 (Cohen op. cit., p.167).

8. *New Leader* 18 February 1938.

9. Cohen op. cit., p.168 and I. Bullock, *Under Siege* (2017) pp.279–285.

10. For its members see the *ILP Conference Report 1938* and Cohen op. cit., pp.166–170.

11. *Economist* 5 August 1944, p.181. This group, also known as Archeo-Marxists, derived their name from their paper the *Archeion Marxismou*.

12. For the break-up of the ILL see *American Socialist Appeal* 18 January 1941.

13. Brockway, *Inside the Left* (1942), p.284 admits that the Bureau's HQ moved to Paris in January 1939 partly because 'five of the refugee parties' had their headquarters there.

14. The International Workers Front Against War was still claiming to be receiving messages from inside occupied Europe in June 1941 (NAC Minutes 14/15 June 1941).

15. East Anglia Division Minutes 9 February 1941.

16. *New Leader* 29 May 1943.

17. *New Leader* 4 September 1943. By early 1944 foreign socialists were telling the ILP the time was not ripe for a new International (NAC Minutes 12/13 February 1944).

18. The ILP gave platforms to Jomo Kenyatta (1889–1978) and the West Indian socialist George Padmore (1903–1959), who were both anti-colonial activists. In 1946 the ILP campaigned for the release of Spanish Republicans held in UK POW camps (R. Challinor, *The Struggle for Hearts and Minds* [1995], p.97).

19. NAC Minutes 9/10 February 1946 and 19 April 1946.

20. C. Stephen HC 383 col. 1412 11 September 1942.

21. HC 380 col. 2068 24 June 1942.

22. HC 390 col. 873 10 June 1943. Newfoundland had gone bankrupt.

23. As it did for others on the Left, e.g. R. Sorenson, 'The operation of imperialism in India is in essence no different from the operation of fascism in Germany' (*Labour Party Conference Report 1934*, p.227). See

also *Labour Monthly* August 1939 and September 1942.

24. P. S. Gupta, *Imperialism and the British Labour Movement 1914–1964* (1974), p.41.

25. Marwick op. cit., p.205.

26. *ILP Conference Report 1926*, p.53.

27. Gupta op. cit., p.258.

28. E.g., Maxton HC 276 col. 1076 29 March 1933 and HC 383 col. 581 11 September 1942, and Padley in *New Leader* 15 August 1942.

29. Though Maxton always asserted that he wanted to see a socialist government set up in India as a result of self-determination (W. Knox, *James Maxton* [1987], p.89).

30. HC 288 col. 361 11 April 1934. He said he could understand loyalty to causes and principles, but only prejudice in favour of geographical areas.

31. *New Leader* 15 April 1940.

32. NAC Minutes 8/9 August 1942.

33. *Forward* (quoting Maxton) 12 October 1940.

34. I. S. Wood. 'The ILP and the Scottish National Question', in D. James et al. (eds), *The Centennial History of the Independent Labour Party* (1992), pp.65–66. Maxton moved a resolution at the Scottish ILP conference calling for self-government for Scotland (*New Leader* 13 February 1943). After his death Maxton was criticised by R. E. Muirhead (1868–1964), President of the Scottish National Party, for not using his considerable talents to obtain Home Rule for Scotland (letter to F. Johnson, 29 April 1948, FJC ILP/4/1948/8).

35. HC 389 cols. 1810–11 27 May 1943.

36. Wood op. cit., p.71.

37. *New Leader* 16 March 1946.

38. Ramsay MacDonald had favoured devolution for Scotland, Wales and the English regions in 1920 (Bullock op. cit., p.53).

39. NAC statement 14 October 1920 quoted in Marwick op. cit., p.135.

40. *ILP Conference Report 1921*, p.85 and Marwick op. cit., p.135.

41. The party's support for Eire may also have been coloured by its need to retain Roman Catholic votes in Glasgow (W. Knox op. cit., p.123).

42. Anonymous article, *Controversy* October 1936 Vol. 1 No. 1, p.13.

43. Executive Committee Minutes 18 December 1942.

44. Manifesto on Palestine, NAC Minutes 4/5 August 1946.

45. Maxton's speech in Glasgow reported in *Forward* 24 November 1945.

46. C Stephen HC 326 col. 2345 21 July 1937 and *New Leader* 8 January 1944. This Committee included the Scottish Zoologist Sir Peter

Chalmers Mitchell (1864–1945), the journalist H. W. Nevinson (1856–1941), the Labour politician D. N. Pritt MP (1887–1972), and the Labour Party supporter Gavin Henderson, 2nd Baron Faringdon (1902–1977).

47. Brockway op. cit., p.292, admitted that 'you cannot apply general principles to Palestine'.
48. Dowse op. cit., p.99. For Maxton's views on foreign policy, see Knox op. cit., p.46.
49. Conference Report in *Socialist Leader* 22 May 1948.
50. The ILP propaganda often suggested socialism could advance country by country.
51. See Chapter 1.

Chapter 8

1. Financial Statement NAC Minutes 28 February 1938. The deficit would be met by property sales and a grant from the Blackfriars Press.
2. In 1935 the ILP fought 17 seats, won four and lost eight deposits. Only in Merthyr did an ILP candidate (Claude Stanfield) do reasonably well in a Labour-held seat.
3. See Maxton's admission to the NAC in August 1939, in I. Bullock, *Under Siege* (2017), pp.310–13.
4. George Buchanan (1890–1955), patternmaker, trade unionist and ILP MP 1922–1939.
5. *New Leader* 8 January 1937.
6. Divisional Conference Chairman's Report, East Anglia Division Minutes 12 February 1939.
7. F. Brockway, *The Workers' Front* (1938), p.13; G. Brown, *Maxton* (1986), p.310.
8. Or the 'February Uprising', which consisted of armed clashes in Austrian cities 12–16 February 1934 involving conservative forces and the Austrian army against socialists.
9. Letters in J. Middleton's ILP File in the Labour Party Archive from NEC members.
10. *Labour Party Conference Report 1935*, p.29, p.140.
11. *Controversy* November 1936.
12. Brockway op. cit., p.19.
13. James Carmichael (1894–1966) was Maxton's constituency 'minder' in Bridgeton and replaced him as its MP.
14. *Controversy* August 1937.

15. *New Leader* 22 April 1938.
16. F. Brockway, *Inside the Left* (1942), p.274.
17. Brockway favoured a federated system for the Labour Party (*New Leader* 1 April 1938). Bullock (op. cit., p.310) believes there was no new enthusiasm in the ILP for the Labour Party just resigned acceptance that affiliation seemed inevitable.
18. Tom Taylor (1912–2001) was later a member of the House of Lords.
19. The Guild of Youth (1924–1939) catered for those too young to join the main party.
20. Jennie Lee (1904–1988) ILP MP for North Lanark 1929–31, and Labour MP for Cannock 1945–1970; minister from 1964 to 1970 and then member of the House of Lords.
21. NAC Minutes 15 April 1938 and 21 May 1938.
22. NEC Minutes No. 303 25 May 1938.
23. John McGovern MP (1887–1968).
24. Aplin was the London Division NAC representative and an influential ILPer.
25. George Dallas (1868–1961), formerly an MP and in 1937 Chairman of the NEC.
26. Barbara Ayrton Gould (1896–1950), member of the NEC and later an MP.
27. George Latham (1875–1942) MP, member of the NEC and Labour Party Treasurer from 1936 to 1942.
28. Hugh Dalton (1887–1962), Chairman of the Labour Party and minister in the second and third Labour governments.
29. Harold Laski (1893–1950) writer and political theorist, former member of the Socialist League and in the NEC from 1937 to 1949.
30. James Middleton (1878–1962), General Secretary of the Labour Party from 1935 to 1944.
31. James Walker (1883–1945), Trade Unionist and MP.
32. This description of the meeting is based on a report in Middleton's ILP File, JSM/ILP/31.
33. NEC Minutes No. 344 22 June 1938.
34. NAC Minutes 30 July 1938 and *NAC Report 1938–9*, p.9.
35. *NAC Report 1938–9*, p.10.
36. *Daily Herald* 25 July 1938.
37. Ibid., 1 September 1938. McGovern's disagreement with the NAC is not recorded in its minutes, and at that point the NAC was still negotiating with the NEC.
38. A. J. P. Taylor, *English History 1914–45* (1965), pp.426–9; E. Wiskemann,

Europe of the Dictators (1966), pp.142–151.

39. *New Leader* 30 September 1938 and F. Brockway, *Socialism over 60 Years* (1946), p.347.

40. Neville Chamberlain (1869–1940), Conservative Party MP and prime minister 1937–1940.

41. *Daily Herald* 3 October 1938.

42. Maxton spoke without notes and apparently always regretted these words (interview W. Padley). For the text of his speech see HC 339 col. 193–7 4 October 1938, and for more background Brown op. cit., pp.292–296.

43. E.g., *Daily Express* 5 October 1938 and *Sunday Times* 9 October 1938.

44. J. McGovern, *Neither Fear Nor Favour* (1960), pp.127–8, and HC 339 col. 528–533 6 October 1938.

45. *The Times* 7 October 1938 and *Manchester Guardian* 7 October 1938.

46. *Daily Worker* 8 October 1938.

47. *The Times* 8 October 1938.

48. *NAC Report 1938–9*, p.3, and Divisional Conference Reports, *New Leader* 10 February 1939.

49. HC 340 col. 150 1 November 1938.

50. *Glasgow Eastern Standard* 18 December 1938.

51. *New Leader* 4 November 1938.

52. Published by the ILP 1933–1950 but open to any contributor, unlike *Between Ourselves* which was purely an internal bulletin. It was called *Left/Controversy* in April 1939 and *Left* after that.

53. Brockway op. cit., pp.326–8.

54. Hugo Dewar (1908–1981), Trotskyist, writer and educator, joined the ILP in 1928 and co-founded the Marxist (Marxian) League with F. A. Ridley and others in 1930(?).

55. *Glasgow Eastern Standard* 11 February 1939 said he voted against it at the Scottish divisional conference, but his position seems more ambivalent than that; see *Between Ourselves* August 1939.

56. Interview Dr C. Smith.

57. *New Leader* 10 February 1939. Brown op. cit., pp.289–290 indicates the conditions being sought by the ILP.

58. *NAC Report 1938–9*, p.10.

59. *The Times* 11 April 1939.

60. *New Leader* 14 April 1939. The NAC set up another negotiating team of Maxton, Brockway, Smith and McNair, though it did not act because the NEC refused further talks.

61. Letter 24 April 1939 in Middleton's ILP File, JSM/ILP/34.

62. *NAC Report 1939–40*, pp.18–19.
63. *New Leader* 11 August 1939.
64. Cohen (op. cit., p.161) believes conference would have voted for affiliation. The Party voted overwhelmingly against affiliation at the 1940 Conference (see *New Leader* 28 March 1940), but by then the Labour Party was supporting the war.
65. *NAC Report 1939–40*, p.4.

Chapter 9

1. R. E. Dowse, *Left in the Centre* (1966), p.11.
2. Ibid., p.20.
3. E. H. Carr, *The Bolshevik Revolution Vol. 3* (1953), Note E 'The Marxist attitude to war', pp.549–556.
4. See 'Tyranipocrat Discovered' in C. Hill, *Puritanism and Revolution* (1968), p.152.
5. J. A. Hobson, *Imperialism* (1902), quoted in D. Martin, *Pacifism* (1965), p.83.
6. V. I. Lenin, *Imperialism, the Highest Stage of Capitalism* (1916), p.73, pp.85–86, and *Socialism and War* (1915), p.9, p.16, p.24.
7. Organisation of socialist and labour parties formed in 1889.
8. Carr op. cit., p.561 and Chapter 7.
9. Dowse op. cit., pp.21–22, on which the first part of this section is based.
10. George Lansbury (1859–1940), pacifist ILPer, member of the second Labour government and leader of the Labour Party 1932–1935.
11. Dr Alfred Salter (1873–1945), medical practitioner, ILP and Labour Party MP 1922–23 and 1924–1945.
12. Tom Johnston (1881–1965), Scottish socialist, journalist, MP and Under Secretary of State for Scotland 1929–31.
13. See for example T. Jowitt and K. Laybourn, 'War and Socialism: the experience of the Bradford ILP 1914–18', in *The Centennial History of the Independent Labour Party* (1992), pp.166–176.
14. The ILP saw the League of Nations as a fraud intended to preserve imperialism (W. Knox, *James Maxton* [1987], pp.120–121).
15. Dowse op. cit., p.195. Maxton argued that 'workers' sanctions' would be indistinguishable for most people from League of Nations sanctions (G. Brown, *Maxton* [1988] p.278).
16. Karl Liebknecht (1871–1919), German socialist, co-founder with Rosa Luxemburg of the Spartacist League and the German Communist Party.

17. Robert (Bob) Edwards (1905–1990) led the ILP Contingent in Spain, was Party Chairman 1942–48, Trade Unionist and a Labour MP 1955–87.
18. For a discussion of the ILP's role in the Spanish Civil War see P. J. Thwaites, 'The Independent Labour Party Contingent in the Spanish Civil War', *Review* (1987), and C. Hall, *'Not Just Orwell': The Independent Labour Party Volunteers and the Spanish Civil War* (2009). W. Knox (op. cit., p.122 and p.125) argues the ILP was inconsistent when it refused to support Abyssinia because it was not a socialist state, yet supported the non-socialist Spanish Republican government even after the suppression of POUM.
19. Hall op. cit., p.76.
20. HC 316 col. 77 29 October 1936.
21. In 1943, for example, the NAC pointed to the suppression of democratic liberties it claimed was taking place under the Allied Military Government for Occupied Territories, and the Allies' recognition of Prime Minister Pietro Badoglio and King Victor Emmanuel III as leaders of the liberated Italy to show that the Allies were not fighting for democracy (NAC Minutes 6/7 November 1943).
22. *New Leader* 22 April 1938.
23. Knox op. cit., p.132. The Central Board, set up in 1939 under the chairmanship of Fenner Brockway, continued supporting conscientious objectors until 1960.
24. NAC Minutes 23 April 1943 for the first report from the armed forces' Branch. 'The ILP neither encourages socialists to join the armed forces, nor seeks to dissuade them from doing so' (Chairman's statement, NAC Minutes, 14 December 1940). Some ILPers saw the benefit of having ILPers in the armed forces because they could possibly 'educate' their non-socialist comrades in arms (see A. Sudbery, *Between Ourselves*, July 1939).
25. E.g. 'George Orwell', the writer Eric Blair (1903–1950). See 'Autobiographical Note' 17 April 1940 in S. Orwell and I. Angus (eds), *The Collected Essays, Journalism and Letters of George Orwell*, Vol. 2 (1971), pp.38–40, and R. Spraggins interview.
26. *New Leader* 29 April 1938 and 20 June 1940.
27. Ibid., 1 February 1941.
28. Ibid., 19 September 1940 and *Left* February 1941.
29. Letter to Geoffrey Gorer 15 September 1937, in Orwell and Angus (eds) op. cit., Vol. 1 (1970), pp.317–318.
30. *New Leader* 30 September 1938 for the Manifesto's text.

31. Dowse op. cit., p.34.
32. Clement Attlee (1883–1967), Limehouse MP, Leader of the Labour Party 1935–1955, prime minister 1945–1951, and elevated to the peerage in 1955.
33. J. Jupp, *The Radical Left in Britain 1931–1941* (1982), p.164. Despite its hatred of fascism, the ILP MPs continued to vote against rearmament (Dowse op. cit., p.199).
34. Sir Stafford Cripps (1889–1952), Solicitor General in the second Labour government, wartime Ambassador to the Soviet Union, and minster in the third Labour government.
35. *Labour Party Conference Report 1935*, p.156.
36. Aneurin (Nye) Bevan (1897–1960), former coal miner, firebrand speaker and MP, served in the third Labour government. See report of a speech by Bevan in *Norwich Mercury* 21 September 1935.
37. E. Estorick, *Stafford Cripps* (1949), p.132, and Bevan in *Norwich Mercury* 21 September 1935.
38. *Labour Party Conference Report 1937*, p.209.
39. See *Tribune* 1 January 1937, 15 January 1937, 16 February 1938, 10 February 1939, 17 March 1939, 28 April 1939 and 19 May 1939.
40. Ibid., 8 September 1939.
41. See G. Orwell, 'The Lion and the Unicorn' in Orwell and Angus (eds) op. cit., Vol. 2 (1970), p.113; J. B, Priestley, *Postscripts* (1940), 14 July 1940 and 21 July 1940.
42. *Labour Monthly* November 1938.
43. See H. Pollitt, *How to Win the War* (1939) and *The Times* 9 September 1939.
44. *Daily Worker* 5 and 7 October 1939.
45. *Labour Monthly* August 1941. Harry Pollitt, who was the CPGB General Secretary, and J. R. Campbell, the Editor of *The Daily Worker*, both previously demoted because they opposed the Imperialist War line, were now reinstated as party spokesmen, as their views were in agreement with the party again.
46. See for example J. R. Campbell, *Socialism through victory: A reply to the policy of the ILP*, (n.d.) in which he called the ILP's opposition to the war 'a hotchpotch of pernicious nonsense', and 'a pro-Fascist policy thinly camouflaged by a few rotten tatters of socialist phraseology'.
47. Boris Souvarine (1895–1983), French Marxist and journalist.
48. Rosa Luxemburg (1871–1919), Polish Marxist theorist and revolutionary socialist, co-founder with Karl Liebknecht of the Spartacist League and the German Communist Party.

49. *Labour Monthly* January 1942.
50. *Militant* September 1939 and January 1940.
51. *Socialist Appeal* October 1939.
52. Ibid., July 1941.
53. The Social Democratic Federation (1881–1911), Britain's first organised socialist party.
54. R. Barltrop, *The Monument: The Story of the Socialist Party of Great Britain* (1975), pp.52–54.
55. *Socialist Standard* June 1938, July 1938 and October 1939.
56. Ibid., July 1941.
57. Ibid., October 1939.
58. *Socialist* August 1939 and January 1941.
59. Ibid., June 1941.
60. S. Morrison, *I Renounce War* (1962), p.28.
61. *Peace News* 17 November 1939.
62. W. O. Brown, *The Hypocrisy and Folly of this War* (n.d.).

Chapter 10

1. Even so the *New Leader* 5 September 1939 was quoted on the German radio because of its attack on British imperialism and the BBC broadcast the anti-Nazi messages received by the ILP from German socialists printed in the paper (F. Brockway, *Inside the Left* [1942], p.348). J. McNair (*Life Abundant*, p.301) claims the *New Leader* was heavily censored during the first few weeks of the war.
2. *New Leader* 15 September 1939.
3. See H. Pelling, *A History of British Trade Unionism* (1963), p.210, p.213.
4. See HC 351 col. 3 passim 24 August 1939.
5. *ILP Conference Report 1935*, p.17.
6. *ILP Conference Report 1938*, p.27.
7. Interviews W. Ballantine, B. Edwards.
8. *Daily Telegraph* 26 March 1940.
9. McGovern admitted he could not bring one factory in Glasgow out on strike (HC 347 col. 133 8 May 1939).
10. Interview T. Taylor, who had worked in Austria and helped socialists escape the Nazis. McNair and Brockway had also been involved in this work. For the messages see *New Leader* 15 September 1939.
11. Some ILPers wanted to believe it was true to justify their stand (interviews Ballantine, N. Carmichael). For McGovern's denunciation see HC 351 col. 705 13 September 1939.

12. *Final Agenda ILP Conference 1939*, pp.48–9; *New Leader* 12 January 1940; and interview H. Sergeant.
13. J. Jupp, 'The Left in Britain 1931–41', M.Sc. thesis (1956), p.355. Actually the Inner Executive still existed, at least in theory, and should have led the Party under those circumstances. Other groups made plans to go underground – see D. Hyde, *I Believed* (1950), p.91 re CPGB; J. Higgins, 'Ten Years for the Locust: British Trotskyism 1938–1948' (1963) re WIL, and S. Morrison, *I Renounce War* (1962), p.38 re PPU.
14. Interviews Brockway and Edwards. See also F. Brockway, *Outside the Right* (1963), pp.18–19.
15. Interview Brockway.
16. Interview Ballantine.
17. J. McNair, *James Maxton: The Beloved Rebel* (1955), p.287. The NAC (Minutes 1 August 1938) had resolved that 'The ILP should remain throughout a war situation as an open and legal organisation'.
18. Interview Carmichael.
19. The Parliamentary Group had already announced that it would do nothing to baffle those running the war thus apparently ruling out any 'revolutionary activity' (HC 351 col. 43 24 August 1939).
20. Interview Ballantine.
21. McNair (1955) op. cit., p.286, and *Life Abundant*, p.301.
22. Interviews Ballantine and Brockway.
23. CAB WP (44) 202 5 April 1944, 'The Trotskyists in Great Britain'.
24. *New Leader* 6 June 1940. Brockway claimed one of his meetings was broken up because of a piece of staged-managed 'public disturbance'. McNair reports (*Life Abundant*, p.302) that the only time he was stopped from speaking was on Hyde Park Corner by 'Stalinists' just after the German invasion of the USSR.
25. Defence Regulation 39B.
26. HC 352 cols. 1829–1902 31 October 1939 and *Manchester Guardian* 29 November 1939.
27. CAB 66 WM 49 (39) 14 16 October 1939 discussion on anti-war groups.
28. Particularly on the CPGB e.g. CAB WP 169 (41) 18 July 1941; CAB WP (43) 109 13 April 1943.
29. C. Cross, *The Fascists in Britain* (1961), p.145.
30. E.g. the Party was not mentioned in the Home Secretary's memo on anti-war propaganda CAB WPG (39)36 14 October 1939, discussed CAB 66 49 (39) 14 16 October 1939.
31. Jupp op. cit., p.166 and NAC Minutes 17 September 1939.
32. *New Leader* 6 October 1939.

33. David Lloyd George (1863–1945), Welsh Liberal MP, Chancellor of the Exchequer 1908–1915, prime minister 1916–1922.
34. H. W. S. Russell (1888–1953), later 12th Duke of Bedford.
35. A. Calder, *The People's War* (1971), p.66; H. Pelling, *Britain and the Second World War* (1970), p.56.
36. *New Leader* 6 October 1939. For the reaction of British socialists to this war see Chapter 9 and P. J. Thwaites, 'Revolutionary Opposition to the Second World War', *Review* (1986).
37. See *Norwich Mercury* 23 December 1939 and *Peace News* 5 January 1940 and 15 March 1940.
38. McGovern HC 358 col. 1307 13 March 1940; Maxton in *Glasgow Eastern Standard* 28 December 1940, and W. Knox, *James Maxton* (1987), p.140.
39. *Daily Herald* 25 March 1940 and *New Leader* 25 March 1940.
40. *New Leader* 6 October 1939.
41. Interview Brockway.
42. *New Leader* 24 November 1939.
43. See *New Leader* 20 October 1939. He got 6.3 per cent of the poll, but a Gallup poll noted that 17 per cent of the people they questioned would have approved of peace talks with Germany (H. Cantril, *Public Opinion 1935–46* [1951], p.1135).
44. *New Leader* 3 December 1939 and *Stretford Guardian* 1 December 1939.
45. *New Leader* 24 November 1939.
46. Ibid., 1 December 1939.
47. *Stretford Borough News* 24 November 1939 says he left the Labour Party over its attitude to the call for a Popular Front against Fascism.
48. *Stretford and Sale Advertiser* 8 December 1939 and *New Leader* 8 December 1939.
49. Calder op. cit., pp.86–7 says that public opinion was 'strangely unimpressed by anti-Russian propaganda'.
50. *New Leader* 8 December 1939.
51. Letter to *New Statesman and Nation* 16 December 1939.
52. *New Leader* 15 December 1939.
53. *Manchester Guardian* 8 December 1939.
54. The BUF never got more than 3 per cent of the poll (Cross op. cit., p.191).
55. *New Leader* 15 December 1939.
56. Jupp op.cit., p.166.
57. *New Leader* 2 February 1940 said that Southampton was considered too large! *New Leader* 8 March 1940 gave no reason for not fighting Leeds.

58. Ibid., 15 December 1939. Letter from F. Jowett to Dr C. Smith, 15 March 1940 noting the ILP now had many nominal branches and the cost of the postage for circulars sent to them more than absorbed their contribution to ILP Head Office (Francis Johnson Correspondence (FJC) ILP/4/1940/8).
59. *New Leader* 12 January 1940.
60. *Daily Express* 3 February 1940.
61. W. Max Aitken (1879–1964), Canadian-British newspaper publisher and politician.
62. Beaverbrook lectured to the 1930 ILP summer school and see his letter to Maxton November 1931 in A. J. P. Taylor, *Beaverbrook* (1972), p.321.
63. T. Driberg, *Beaverbrook: A Study in Power and Frustration* (1956), p.247.
64. J. McGovern, *Neither Fear Nor Favour* (1960), pp.133–4 and Taylor op. cit., p.403.
65. Cantrill op. cit., p.1135.
66. McGovern op. cit., p.133 claims Beaverbrook promised £500 a seat. Taylor doubts that he would have offered the ILP money; see *Beaverbrook*, p.403.
67. Annie Maxton (1916–1977[?]), sister of James Maxton, teacher and trade unionist.
68. Ratified by Scottish Divisional Council 2 days later (*Barrhead News* 29 March 1940 and *The Renfrew Press* 29 March 1940).
69. *Tribune* 14 May 1940; MO Report No. 111, p.1.
70. *New Leader* 11 April 1940. See J. MacCormick, *Flag in the Wind* (1955), p.96 and p.103 for the Scottish National Party and the war.
71. *New Leader* 4 April 1940.
72. *The Renfrew Press* 29 March 1940.
73. *New Leader* 2 May 1940 (emphasis in original).
74. MO Report No. 111, p.1.d.
75. MO Report No. 111 p.13.
76. See *The Renfrew Press* 19 April 1940.
77. *Manchester Guardian* 20 May 1940.
78. She got 8,206 votes, 19.3 per cent of the poll, which the ILP claimed was the highest anti-war vote ever polled by any political party (NAC Minutes 25/26 May 1940). She did not, however, capture many of the 21,475 Labour Party votes and 6,593 SNP votes from the 1935 election.
79. Taylor op. cit., p.405. Beaverbrook did not reply until 17 May.
80. *The Times* 14 May 1940.
81. Maxton and Edwards favoured contesting seats again by December 1940 (NAC Minutes 14/15 December 1940), and in the Commons the ILP

Group continued to vigorously oppose the government, e.g. HC 360 col. 1507 13 May 1940.

Chapter 11

1. Sir Oswald Mosley (1896–1980), Conservative and then Labour MP, founded the British Union of Fascists in 1932.
2. C. Cross, *The Fascists in Britain* (1961), p.145.
3. CAB 66 memo from Home Secretary 267 (41) 14 November 1941 and Cabinet discussion 17 November 1941 115(41) 5. *The Word* August 1940 said that M. Kavanagh, an anarchist, was arrested under this regulation.
4. CAB 66 WP (40) 482 23 December 1940.
5. E.g., *New Leader* 12 January 1940, 'Government Prepare to make Britain Totalitarian' and *New Leader* 26 January 1940, 'Churchill schemes to spread the war'.
6. *Peace News* 31 May 1940 and S. Morrison, *I Renounce War* (1962), p.53.
7. *New Leader* 13 October 1939 had the word 'British' struck out of an attack on imperialism, probably by the printers as similar attacks later were not censored.
8. The records of the Association have been destroyed (W. H. Smith & Sons *Trade Circular* vol. 34. No. 865 8 June 1940, p.7).
9. *New Leader* 19 September 1940 and interview F. Brockway.
10. To 11,000 copies, *New Leader* 3 October 1940.
11. MEPOL 2/3130 quoting Regulation 39E 28 November 1939.
12. MEPOL 2/6260 14 May 1940 memorandum from Commissioner's Office A signed by Phillip Game, Commissioner.
13. Particularly in London and Glasgow. Many ILPers were killed in Glasgow in the Blitz in March 1940 (letter from W. Stewart to F. Johnson 28 March 1940, ILP/6/4/6).
14. See *New Leader* 5 and 12 September 1940 and East Anglia Division Minutes 9 February 1941, Norwich Branch Report.
15. Interviews W. Padley, A. Hambly, R. Jobson, A. Nicholls, L. F. Bunnewell.
16. *Forward* 14 September 1940.
17. HC 361 col. 20–8 21 May 1940.
18. The ILPers had their own Commons room. The ILP MPs had been recognised as a separate group by the Speaker after disaffiliation and Maxton and McGovern sat on Committees (see e.g. McGovern re civilian injury compensation, NAC Minutes 27/28 February 1943, and Maxton re Electoral Reform, NAC Minutes 12/13 February 1944).

19. See P. J. Thwaites 'The ILP 1938 to 1950' PhD thesis (1976), p.206 footnote 38 for some examples of their interventions.
20. See Chapters 9, 11 and 12.
21. HC 367 col. 695 passim 5 December 1940. See G. Brown, *Maxton* (1986), p.299; W. Knox, *James Maxton* (1987), pp.142–3.
22. *New Leader* 14 December 1940. Only the ILP MPs, W. Gallacher (CPGB) and two pacifists voted for the amendment.
23. *Peace News* 9 May 1941 and 6 June 1941, and Brown op. cit. pp.299–300.
24. *Glasgow Eastern Standard* 8 February 1941; *Forward* 15 February 1941; and see an attack on this speech as a betrayal of socialist principles in *American Militant* 22 March 1941.
25. NAC Minutes 25/26 May 1940.
26. *New Leader* 16 May 1940.
27. HC 373 col. 966 23 July 1941.
28. *New Leader* 15 August 1940 and 24 October 1940.
29. A. Calder, *The People's War* (1971), p.566.
30. In 1941 ILP Bradford City Councillors used scientific experts to expose the poor quality of the shelters built in Bradford (R. Challinor, *The Struggle for Hearts and Minds* [1995], p.63).
31. Many ILPers in safe parts of the country opened their homes to bombed-out ILPers (NAC Minutes 14/15 December 1940).
32. Walter Padley (1916–1984), trade unionist, ILP London Organiser and NAC member; later Labour Party MP and government minister.
33. *New Leader* 10 and 17 October 1940, and 7 November 1940.
34. See *Daily Worker* 8 July 1940, 20 August 1940, 9 September 1940; *Labour Monthly* October 1940, and Calder op. cit., p.283.
35. *New Leader* 28 December 1940.
36. S. Orwell and I. Angus (eds), *The Collected Essays, Journalism and Letters of George Orwell* (1968) Vol. 2, p.23.
37. J. Lee, *This Great Journey* (1963), p.187.
38. *New Leader* 30 May 1940 and *Left* September 1940, p.258.
39. *Tribune* 19 June 1942. She continued to oppose ILP policy after May 1940 and was disowned by the Party in September 1941 (NAC Minutes 6/7 September 1941).
40. J. Jupp, 'The Left in Britain 1931–41', MSc thesis (1956), p.244. Also interview N. Carmichael, and East Anglia Division Minutes 12 January 1940 passim. In the first 6 months of the war the ILP received 1,000 membership applications (Challinor op. cit., p.11) and by 1942–43 membership was at 1936 levels (P J Thwaites, 'The ILP 1938–1950', PhD thesis [1976], Appendix 1, p.25).

41. This paragraph is based on an interview with Dr Charles Smith. He was inspired to join the ILP after hearing Brockway speak.
42. *New Leader* 14 April 1939.
43. Ibid., 6 October 1939 and *Left* November 1939.
44. Interview D. Bateman.
45. Coincidently the June 1940 edition of *Left* contained Dr Smith's last defence of the ILP's anti-war position. Smith later claimed he agreed to support the Party's anti-war line in 1939 on the strict under-standing that its opposition would be purely political and would do nothing to weaken the struggle against Hitler (see letter to Professor Vincent, 11 April 1971, Don Bateman Collection (DBC), DM1532/Q4/8).
46. *New Leader* 27 June 1940.
47. Ibid., 25 July 1940.
48. A copy exists in FJC ILP/4/1940/18 and letter/25 from the Ministry of Information 12 August 1940.
49. *New Leader* 8, August 1940.
50. Ibid., 15 August 1940.
51. See *New Leader* 29 August 1940 and NAC Minutes 14/15 December 1940.
52. *Left* October 1940. Smith replied that perhaps he might have a different view on the issue if he was in Mexico rather than in London.
53. J. McGovern, *Neither Fear Nor Favour* (1960), p.155, p.158, Brown op. cit., pp.299–300, and Knox op. cit., p.143 for a fuller discussion of this incident.
54. *New Leader* 14 April 1941.
55. J. C. Hatch, *New Leader* 10 October 1940.
56. Challinor op. cit., pp.196–198 discusses this dichotomy within the Party.
57. See F. A. Ridley in *Between Ourselves* October 1940.
58. V. I. Lenin, *Collected Works* vol. XVIII (1966), p.194, p.197.
59. Ridley, *Between Ourselves* October 1940. F. A. Ridley (1897–1994), author, public speaker, former Trotskyist, ILPer circa 1938–1950.
60. Smith in *Left* November 1939 said 'the revolutionary socialist sees his chief hope in the difficulties of his capitalist rulers attacked simultaneously by a foreign state, by revolting colonial subjects . . ., and by the British workers determined not to fight any longer'. See also W. Padley in *Left* October 1940.
61. NAC Minutes 14/15 December 1940.
62. Interview Padley, who said he would have opposed invasion with force.
63. Interviews W. Ballantine, N. Carmichael and Padley.

64. McGovern HC 357 col. 1601 22 February 1940 and conference decision quoted in *New Leader* 19 April 1941.
65. *New Leader* 1 and 8 February 1941.
66. *Between Ourselves* January 1941 and *The Times* 12 April 1944.
67. T. Williams, *Between Ourselves* July 1941.
68. NAC Minutes 14/15 June 1941. ILP Head Office in St Brides Street was destroyed by an incendiary bomb, and later reopened in Finchley Central (McNair *Life Abundant*, p.299).

Chapter 12

1. A. J. P. Taylor, *English History 1914–45* (1965), p.529.
2. *Labour Monthly* July 1941.
3. E. Shinwell, *I've Lived Through It All* (1973), p.168.
4. *New Leader* 28 April 1941.
5. F. Brockway, *Outside the Right* (1963), pp.19–20.
6. *New Leader* 19 January 1941. For the ILP's changing attitude to the Soviet Union see I. Bullock, *Under Siege* (2017) pp.279–295.
7. *NAC Report on Russia 1942*, p.13 and *New Leader* 11 April 1942.
8. NAC Minutes 9/10 August 1941, 1/2 November 1941, and *NAC Report on Russia 1942*.
9. *Left* March 1942, and interview J. Aplin.
10. The by-election committee initially comprised Maxton, McGovern, Jowett, Brockway and McNair.
11. NAC Minutes 9/10 August 1941 and *New Leader* 23 August 1941.
12. The Party did register an increase in membership (*New Leader* 3 September 1941).
13. *Lancaster Guardian* 3 October 1941. The NAC originally thought this contest inadvisable, (NAC Minutes 9/10 August 1941), but Brockway had polled 9,043 votes (31.6 per cent) in 1922.
14. *New Leader* 11 October 1941, *Manchester Guardian* 8 October 1941 and *Daily Telegraph* 13 October 1941.
15. Interview F. Brockway.
16. See *Socialist Appeal* November 1941 and *Manchester Guardian* 14 October 1941.
17. *Lancaster Guardian* 10 October 1941.
18. And attacked the ILP – see *New Leader* 4 October 1941 and interviews B. Edwards and W. Padley.
19. *New Leader* 25 October 1941. In 1935 the Labour Party candidate polled 20 per cent, so where was the effect of the absentee vote?

20. Padley claimed he suggested adding the word 'Now' (interview Padley). *Socialist Standard* December 1941 described it as 'just the old reformist trash'.

21. Called his 'Lancaster Charter'; see *New Leader* 11 October 1941.

22. *New Leader* 15 November 1941.

23. *Daily Herald* 28 November 1941 called it the ILP's 'annual trip to the moon'.

24. E.g. HC 376 col. 935 27 November 1941 G. Jones (Aberdeen North Labour MP).

25. HC 376 cols. 912–971 27 November 1941. Sir Richard Acland (1906–1990), consecutively a Liberal, Common Wealth and Labour MP.

26. E.g. debate on Common Ownership HC 395 col. 1039 8 December 1943.

27. See HC 395 col. 1037 8 December 1943 for an attack by Silverman on the ILP.

28. E.g. debate on equal pay for women teachers HC 398 col. 1368 28 March 1944.

29. NAC Report 1942, p.9.

30. MO Report A 1015, p.2.

31. Ibid., p.7.

32. Ibid., p.2.

33. *New Leader* 13 December 1941, MO Report A 1015, p.8 and *Edinburgh Evening Dispatch* 5 December 1941.

34. Taylor op. cit., p.540.

35. R. Challinor, *The Struggle for Hearts and Minds* (1995), p.78; T. Dan Smith, *An Autobiography* (1970), pp.21–22.

36. The ILP was 'well satisfied with the result' (*New Leader* 20 December 1941).

37. *New Leader* 3 January 1942, 21 February 1942, 7 and 14 March 1942, and 11 April 1942.

38. See *Socialist Appeal* March 1942, *WIL Internal Bulletin* 12 March 1942 and *New Leader* 27 December 1941 and 3 January 1942.

39. Interview N. Carmichael. His father, James, resigned as full-time Organiser for Scotland in 1938 because the Division could no longer afford his salary.

40. Financial Reports February 1942 and 1943, NAC Report 1943, p.5.

41. Challinor op. cit., p.85.

42. *New Leader* 11 April 1942, *Cardiff Times* 28 March 1942 and MO Report No. 1227 25 April 1942.

43. *The Times* 10 April 1942. The ILP replied by producing Speakers' Notes

on 'CP Provocation', but Fred Jowett in a letter to J. McNair, 17 May 1942, objected to what he saw as an attack on Stalin and Russia while in a life-and-death struggle with the Nazis (ILP/6/6/11).

44. E.g., *Western Mail* 10 April 1942 described ILP policy as 'a farrago of political trash'; *The Times* 11 April 1942 described the ILP's policy as 'defeatism ... disguised as socialism'.

45. *New Leader* 11, 18 and 25 April 1942, and interview Brockway.

46. *New Leader* 2 May 1942.

47. *Forward* 25 April 1942. Patrick Dollan (1885–1963) was expelled from the ILP in 1932 and joined the Labour Party.

48. W. Douglas Home *Half Term Report* (1954), p.149; *New Leader* 9 May 1942.

49. NAC Minutes 27/28 February 1943.

50. *Left* October 1942.

51. *WIL Internal Bulletin* September 1942. The WIL's request for a United Front on industrial issues was rejected (NAC Minutes 31 October 1942) because the NAC believed the WIL wanted to destroy the ILP (NAC Minutes 27/28 February 1943).

52. *New Leader* 25 July 1940.

53. Ibid., 19 September 1940.

54. Ibid., 14 and 30 November 1940.

55. H. Pelling, *The British Communist Party* (1958) and *Tribune* 14 February 1941.

56. *New Leader* 19 April 1941 for decision establishing this committee and ibid., 13 September 1941 when it was acted upon.

57. Ibid., 13 September 1941.

58. Ibid., 20 September 1941.

59. Ibid., 6 December 1941.

60. Carmichael and Taylor criticised the ILP's 'excessive involvement in union affairs to the detriment of the ILP's other work' (*New Leader* 11 April 1942).

61. East Anglia Division Minutes 29 June 1941.

62. James Griffiths MP (1890–1975), member of the NEC, and later minister in the third and fourth Labour governments.

63. *Labour Party Conference Report 1942*, p.105.

64. A. Calder, *The People's War* (1971), pp.497–512 and *New Leader* 31 January 1942.

65. *The Miners' Case.*

66. *New Statesman and Nation* 18 July 1942; Joseph Hall, the Yorkshire Mineworkers Federation President, claimed men were being paid £10

per week to distribute Trotskyist literature to miners!

67. *Daily Worker* 29 December 1942.
68. *Militant Scottish Miner* January, April and May 1943 and *Militant Miner* (the name had changed) July and August 1943.
69. E.g., *Militant Miner* October 1943.
70. *Glasgow Evening Citizen* 29 September 1943.
71. See LAB 10/483 'Reports of alleged contraventions of the 1AA regulations in the coal mining industry of Lanarkshire and the Scottish Constabularies'.
72. CAB WP (44) 202 memo from Home Secretary 5 April 1944, 'The Trotskyists in Great Britain'.
73. Privately the ILP claimed that it was active in the South Yorkshire Miners' 'unrest' (NAC Minutes 27 April 1943).
74. *New Leader* 20 February 1943. For details of this programme see P. J. Thwaites, 'The Independent Labour Party 1938–1950', Ph.D. thesis (1976), p.137.
75. CAB WP (44) 202 5 April 1944, 'The Trotskyists in Great Britain'.
76. The 'Bevin Boys' scheme; see LAB 10/451 passim and Report 22 February 1944.
77. Ernest Bevin (1881–1951), trade union leader, minister of Labour 1940–1945 and Foreign Secretary 1945–1951.
78. Over the 'Porter Award' which increased basic wages but threatened to cut piece rates (R. Page Arnot, *The Miners: In Crisis and War* [1961], pp.395–96.)
79. *Daily Worker* 8 and 9 April 1944 and *Labour Monthly* May 1944.
80. E.g., *Manchester Guardian* 5 April 1944, *Daily Herald* 6 April 1944 and *Reynolds News* 9 April 1944. See, however, *Daily Mail* 4 April 1944, which agreed with the CPGB.
81. See HC 392 col. 666 29 September 1943 and CAB 66 43 (44) 7 3 April 1944 for his fixation with political agitators; A. Bullock (*The Life and Times of Ernest Bevin* vol. 2 [1960], p.270) blames the strain of war.
82. They were convicted and later acquitted on appeal (LAB 10/451 press cuttings).
83. *New Leader* 15 April 1944 and *RCP Conference Report 5/6 August 1945*.
84. Some Trotskyists considered the ILP fertile ground for gaining recruits (e.g., J. Hasten, *WIL Internal Bulletin* 12 March 1942), but could not spare people to work in the ILP, as they were committed to industrial work and other activities (*RCP Bulletin* April 1946 pp.15–16).
85. CAB 66 WP (44) 202 13 April 1944, 'The Trotskyists in Great Britain'.

86. Interview D. Bateman, who claimed that some of the branches may even have been fictional.
87. Standing Orders Committee, *ILP Conference Report 1945*, p.5.
88. Ibid., and NAC Minutes 24/25 February 1945. The enquiry found that the numbers of delegates from branches to the North East divisional conference were 'illegally' allocated on different affiliation-fee-paying periods, with some branches allowed to count periods up to 26 months so as to appear to have more branch members than they really had.
89. For a discussion of the ILP 1945 conference and the expulsion of the Trotskyists see *RCP Bulletin* April 1946, pp.20–21.
90. *Socialist Appeal* June 1945.
91. John McNair and John Hatch, ILP National Organiser, spent months reviving the North East Divisional Council and the local branches (NAC Minutes 3 April 1945, and 9/10 February 1946).

Chapter 13

1. My emphasis. *New Leader* 22 November 1941 found it necessary to state that the ILP still opposed the war!
2. *Peace News* 28 February 1942 letter from Jack Gibson, ILP pacifist (my emphasis).
3. *New Leader* 29 August 1942.
4. See P. Addison, 'By-elections of the Second World War', Chapter 7 in C. Cook and J. Ramsden (eds), *By-elections in British Politics* (1973), pp.165–190, and A. Calder, 'The Common Wealth Party 1942–45', D.Phil. thesis (1968) vol. 2, pp.175–89.
5. See Calder op. cit., on which these two paragraphs are based.
6. *New Leader* 1 August 1942 and *Left* October 1942, and his memo in NAC Minutes 27/28 February 1943.
7. *New Leader* 28 November 1942.
8. Ibid., 9 January 1943.
9. Edwards and Ballantine in NAC Minutes 31 October 1942.
10. *Bristol Evening Post* 22 and 24 December 1942 and 11 January 1943.
11. Jennie Lee had refused to join CW (Calder op. cit., Vol. 1, p.126).
12. Interviews F. Brockway and W. Padley. See *New Leader* 30 January 1943 for McNair's biography.
13. *New Leader* 16 and 30 January 1943. Maxton may have wanted McNair to contest this seat because he shared Maxton's anti-war views; see Maxton in *New Leader* 6 February 1943.

14. Sir William Beveridge (1879–1963), civil servant, Director of LSE and Liberal MP 1944–1945.
15. A. Calder, *The People's War* (1971), pp.608–10.
16. J. Beveridge, *Beveridge and his Plan* (1954), pp.111–51.
17. *Bristol Evening Post* 18 January 1943.
18. MO Report No. 1649, p.14.
19. Her meetings were addressed by amongst others Tom Wintringham (1898–1949) First World War and International Brigade veteran, ex-member of the CPGB and of the 1941 Committee, and Michael Foot (1913–2010) journalist, author, Labour Party MP, government minister and Leader of the Labour Party 1980–1983 (MO Report No. 1649, p.6).
20. He had an audience of one for one meeting (*Bristol Evening World* 29 January 1943). For a report on this contest see *New Statesman and Nation* 27 February 1943. McNair was a very experienced public speaker, but not a firebrand like Jennie Lee.
21. *New Statesman and Nation* 27 February 1943.
22. McNair criticised her for becoming a 'Liberal' (see MO Report No. 1649, 7–8), and McGovern accused Lee and Nye Bevan of cowardice because they were not in the armed forces although they supported the war (Calder [1968] op. cit., vol. 1, p.126).
23. *Bristol Evening World* 16 February 1943.
24. MO Report No. 1649, p.4.
25. *New Leader* 27 February 1943 and see MO Report No. 1649, p.6, p.7, p.11.
26. See *Socialist* January 1943 and *Socialist Standard* January 1943.
27. Executive Committee Minutes 8 December 1942.
28. *New Leader* 5 December 1942.
29. Ibid., 1 May 1943. On 19 January 1944 Brockway, Edwards and Padley met Beveridge during his 'Full Employment Enquiry' and tried unsuccessfully to persuade him that full employment could not be achieved under capitalism; that socialist planning was essential for Britain's future, and that legislation to introduce the ILP's living wage policy was needed (LSE file Beveridge/9A/15/7).
30. HC 386 col. 16 18 February 1943. Arthur Greenwood had introduced a motion welcoming the report. On the amendment 119 out of 121 backbench Labour MPs voted against the government.
31. *New Leader* 3 April 1943.
32. NAC Minutes 27/28 February 1943 and *New Leader* 1 and 22 May 1943. The 'Jubilee' conference marked the 50th anniversary of the foundation of the ILP.

33. *Labour Party Conference Report 14–18 June 1943*, pp.127–36.
34. *The Times* 12 October 1943.
35. Maxton was forced to defend the by-election committee's decision (NAC Minutes 13 October 1943).
36. *Daily Worker* 10 December 1943.
37. Calder (1968) op. cit., vol. 1, pp.187–9. See NAC Minutes 13 October 1943 for the claim that the ILP wrote the election address.
38. *The Times* 27 September 1943.
39. Calder (1968) op. cit., vol. 1, p.223.
40. Interview Padley. *New Leader* 13 November 1943 called it a quiet campaign!
41. *The Times* 26 September 1943 noted Colyer's overtures to the Old Age Pensioners Association which was supposed to be a non-political organisation.
42. *New Leader* 6 November 1943.
43. Ibid., 12 and 20 November 1943 hardly mentioned the campaign or the result.
44. Interview Padley.
45. *New Leader* 27 November 1943.
46. Calder (1968), op. cit., vol. 1, p.223.
47. Herbert Morrison (1888–1965), MP, minister in second Labour government, Home Secretary 1940–1945, deputy prime minister 1945–1951.
48. MO Report No. 1990 'Mosley and After', quoted in Calder (1968) op. cit., vol. 1, p.144.
49. See *Acton Gazette* 10 December 1943, interview Padley, and H. Longhurst, *I Wouldn't Have Missed It* (1945), pp.170–72.
50. MO Report No. 1943, p.3.
51. NAC Minutes 6/7 November 1943. The NAC intended to raise an election fund of £5,000, but its by-election contests normally cost at least £250 each, so that war chest would only have covered a third of the seats it proposed to fight.
52. E.g., *New Leader* 13 November 1943 and 3 June 1944.
53. Calder (1968) op. cit., vol. 1, p.222.
54. HC 395 col. 993–1039 8 December 1943 and *Left* February 1944.
55. But at this time *Tribune* was supporting Left Unity, e.g., *Tribune* 17 December 1943 and 15 December 1944.
56. *New Leader* 18 March 1944 and NAC Report 1943–4, p.8.
57. *New Leader* 5 February 1944.
58. Ibid., 15 April 1944. For NAC response see NAC Minutes 10 April 1944.
59. Letter to Divisional Council from Barking Branch 26 April 1944 (copy

in Barking Branch Minutes), and Calder (1968) op. cit., Vol. 1, p.266.

60. *Left* April 1944.
61. E.g., *Left* May 1944 and August 1944, and NAC Minutes 10 April 1944.
62. J. McNair (*Life Abundant*, p.301) claims ILP opposition to unconditional surrender was aimed at giving the German people hope and encouraging those German political forces 'even then hostile to the Fuhrer' to deal with him themselves. The NAC also believed harsh terms would lead to another world war (NAC Minutes 12/13 August 1944).
63. *New Leader* 3 June 1944.
64. Ibid., 16 September 1944 and 28 October 1944, and *Bilston and Willenhall Times* 9 September 1944.
65. See Calder (1971) op. cit., p.651.
66. Birmingham Federation held a similar meeting in the Bull Ring (Minutes 14 December 1944, DBC DM 1532/Q1/5).
67. *New Leader* 30 December 1944 and 13 January 1945.
68. Ibid., 20 January 1945.
69. Ibid., 12 May 1945.
70. *Tribune* 25 April 1945, *South Wales Argus* 14 May 1945, *Daily Worker* 16 May 1945, and *New Leader* 2 June 1945.

Chapter 14

1. *New Leader* 14 August 1943; after that the growth rate decreased (*NAC Report 1945*, p.2).
2. For ILP membership numbers, see P. J. Thwaites, 'The Independent Labour Party 1938–1950', PhD thesis (1976), pp.25–27. A. Calder, 'The Common Wealth Party 1942–45', D.Phil. thesis (1968) vol. 1, p.234 says the Labour Party increased by 30,000 individual members during 1944–45!
3. *New Leader* 12 November 1943.
4. See Brockway NAC Minutes 6/7 November 1943.
5. *New Leader* 28 March 1940. Only Taylor and Padley voted in favour.
6. *Between Ourselves* March 1941.
7. *New Leader* 19 April 1941.
8. Ibid., 11 April 1942.
9. Ibid., 1 May 1943.
10. E.g., one conference resolution put the blame for the war on *all* the German people not just the Nazis.
11. *New Leader* 17 July 1943 and Maxton, Ibid., 14 August 1943.
12. Ibid., 5 and 12 February 1944.

13. Ibid., 14 April 1944.

14. F. A. Ridley in *New Leader* 30 September 1944.

15. See Carmichael, *Between Ourselves* September–October 1944, and W. Padley, *Left* January 1945.

16. See Attlee's speech in Leeds 1 April 1944, reported in *Tribune* 7 April 1944.

17. *Labour Party Conference Report 11–15 December 1944*, p.116, p.118.

18. *New Leader* 30 December 1944 and NEC Minutes 23 January 1945. The NAC had already decided to approach the NEC re electoral arrangements and reaffiliation (NAC Minutes 11/12 November 1944).

19. NEC election sub-committee Minutes 14 February 1945 No. 32, and NAC Minutes 24/25 February 1945.

20. There is no extant copy of this letter but its contents and the election sub-committee recommendations are summarised in NEC election sub-committee Minutes 21 March 1945 No. 48.

21. *New Leader* 3, 10 and 24 February 1945.

22. NAC Minutes 24/25 February 1945 and *New Leader* 3 March 1945. For affiliation were Brockway, Johnson, Ballantine, Padley, Bateman, Williams, Thomas and Edwards; against were Spurrell, Gibson, Barton, Reed and Smith.

23. *New Leader* 7 April 1945.

24. NEC Policy Committee Minutes, No. 6, 11 May 1945.

25. *The Times* 22 May 1945 and *Labour Party Conference Report 25 May 1945*, p.144.

26. *RCP Bulletin* October 1945 claimed that Brockway and Harold Laski of the NEC held meetings on this matter at the beginning of the year.

27. NEC Minutes, No. 20, 30 May 1945. It chose Morgan Phillips (1902–1963), (General) Secretary of the Labour Party 1944–1961, and G. R. Shepherd, National Agent.

28. For instance in Widnes the ILP only had a tiny, inactive branch (letter from J. Ashley to the author 16 June 1975).

29. Candidates were already chosen for these seats. On the day this meeting was held Trevor Williams, the Barking branch candidate, withdrew because he did not wish to challenge the Labour Party (Barking Branch Minutes 31 May 1945). The Norwich candidate was withdrawn two weeks later (*Norwich Mercury* 16 June 1945).

30. It seems to me unclear why the NEC had agreed to this meeting when its representatives were claiming that they could not, in effect, offer the ILP any electoral deals. Moreover the claim that the NEC could not force local parties to drop candidates was a little disingenuous given that the

NEC had refused to endorse candidates against Maxton and Stephen (see note 32).

31. NEC election sub-committee Minutes 14 February 1945.
32. NEC Minutes 4 June 1945 Supplement.
33. NEC Minutes 16 May 1945.
34. *Glasgow Eastern Standard* 19 May 1945.
35. Letter to author from branch secretary, D. Marshall, 30 September 1975.
36. Though a pro-affiliationist, McGovern often attacked the Labour Party leaders and complained if the *New Leader* did not carry these attacks (B. Hunter, *RCP Internal Bulletin* 19 October 1945).
37. NEC Minutes 4 June 1945 No. 7.
38. *NAC Report 1946*, p.6.
39. *New Leader* 16 June 1945.
40. *The Times* 18 June 1945.
41. *New Leader* 23 June 1945.
42. See *Left* July 1945.
43. *New Leader* 23 June 1945.
44. Election address in the David Gibson papers. Fred Jowett held this seat 1922–24, 1929–31.
45. *New Leader* 7 July 1945.
46. R. B. McCallum and A. Readman, *The British General Election of 1945* (1947), p.119.
47. McCallum and Readman op. cit., p.118 and *Glasgow Eastern Standard* 19 May 1945.
48. *New Leader* 30 June 1945 and 'Report by A. Readman' in McCallum and Readman op. cit., p.167, p.297.
49. *New Leader* 30 June 1945.
50. *Glasgow Catholic Herald* 6 July 1945. Roman Catholics composed a large proportion of the working-class voters in the East End of Glasgow. McGovern had written a pamphlet in 1938 called *Why the Church Supports Franco*.
51. *New Leader* 30 June 1945.
52. *Yorkshire Observer* 14 June 1945.
53. *Bradford Telegraph* 27 June 1945 and interview W. Ballantine.
54. *Yorkshire Observer* 15, 16 and 21 June 1945.
55. *Bilston and Willenhall Times* 28 July 1945.
56. Ibid., 16 and 23 June 1945.
57. *Glasgow Herald* 27 July 1945.
58. The Birmingham Federation Executive Committee blamed the failure of its Federation to act as a unit, the inconsistent policies of its branches,

and the inactivity of many local ILPers for the electoral defeat in Bilston (Minutes 11 July 1945).

59. CW won one seat from 23 contests; the CPGB won two seats from 21 contests.

Chapter 15

1. Letter of resignation from Trevor Williams (Barking Branch Minutes 1 August 1945).
2. Letter to author from E. Milne (1915–1983) 2 June 1975. His resignation was noted in the Birmingham Federation Minutes 14 June 1945.
3. Letter to author from J. Ashley (1922–2012) 3 June 1975.
4. J. McNair, *Life Abundant*, p.306; he hints that some were motivated by 'careerism'.
5. NAC Minutes 11/12 August 1945.
6. Edwards declared that 'the gradualism of a Labour Government will not deal with the world shattering events to follow' (NAC Minutes 11/12 August 1945, and see *RCP Bulletin* articles by J. Goffe and G. Healy, September 1945).
7. *Glasgow Eastern Standard* 25 August 1945. G. Brown (*Maxton* [1988], p.306) says Maxton confessed to McGovern that it was partly the hostility of Maxton's wife and his sister, Annie, to the Labour Party which stopped him joining it. Brown also suggests that as Maxton knew he was dying he was content to remain the emblematic head of the ILP.
8. *New Leader* 18 August 1945.
9. NAC Minutes 11/12 August 1945 and *New Leader* 25 August 1945. Edwards the ILP Chairman also called for 12 months free from internal controversy re affiliation (Organising Committee Minutes, 12 August 1945).
10. *RCP Bulletin* October 1945, p.10.
11. HC 413 col. 958 24 August 1945.
12. E.g., McGovern, HC 420 col. 232 5 March 1946; Maxton, HC 416 col. 2424 5 December 1945; Stephen, HC 420 col. 1742 19 March 1946; and 420 col. 1747 for Sir Thomas Moore's attack on the ILP. Brown (op. cit., pp.304–5) suggests that Maxton, at least, was willing to give the new government a chance.
13. *New Leader* 15 December 1945.
14. NEC Minutes 23 January 1946.
15. *New Leader* 9 February 1946.
16. *NAC Report 1946–7*, p.6. This had been carried by eight votes to four.

17. See *New Leader* 3 and 24 February 1945 and 16 February 1946.
18. *New Leader* 6 April 1946.
19. Ibid.; NAC Minutes 19 April 1946 and *NAC Report 1947–8*, p.13.
20. *Labour Party Conference Report 10–14 June 1946*, p.174.
21. G. D. H. Cole, *A History of the Labour Party From 1914* (1948), p.112, p.125, p.144, passim.
22. Cole op. cit., p.407; R. Miliband, *Parliamentary Socialism* (1961), p.384 and H. Pelling, *The British Communist Party* (1958), p.135.
23. Letters from Ellen Wilkinson to E. Mackay December 1944 and Harold Laski to Sybil Wingate 12 January 1945, quoted in A. Calder, 'The Common Wealth Party 1942–45', D.Phil. thesis (1968) vol. 1, p.294.
24. NEC Minutes 27 February 1946 No. 149 and 150; also NEC Minutes 27 March 1946. No. 173, 174 (decision), 175 (ILP application).
25. *Labour Party Conference Report 10–14 June 1946*, p.14, pp.169–174. *Manchester Guardian* 28 March 1946 claimed there was a feeling in the Labour Movement that the ILP's application might have been accepted if it had not come at the same time as that of the CPGB.
26. *New Leader* 6 April 1946. ILPers could, since May 1940 (NAC Minutes 25/26 May 1940), belong to the Co-operative Party; many were paying dues to the Labour Party in their union fees, and in some cases attending Labour Party branch meetings as representatives of other affiliated bodies when the ILP expected them to put forward ILP policies 'as far as possible' (Birmingham Federation Minutes 11 May 1944).
27. The NAC had no form of 'cabinet collective responsibility' and members were free to present their minority views to conference. Kate Spurrell, a member of the NAC, wrote to James Maxton on 6 May 1946 praising Gibson for his speech in favour of maintaining the ILP's independence (FJC ILP/4/1946/8).
28. J. McNair, *New Leader* 4 May 1946.
29. Brockway op. cit., p.35.
30. Ibid.; Brockway claims he resigned when he could not get the NAC to concur with him. NAC Minutes 23 April 1946 show he resigned because of the conference decision, and earlier Minutes e.g. NAC Minutes 9/10 February 1946, indicate the majority of the NAC actually agreed with him. He announced his resignation in *The Times* 20 June 1946.
31. Brockway op. cit., pp.35–6. Brockway wrote to James Maxton on 27 April 1946 explaining his actions (FJC ILP/4/1946/3).
32. *New Leader* 7 and 14 April 1945.
33. *New Statesman and Nation* 11 May 1946.

34. *New Leader* 4 May 1946 and 1 and 29 June 1946.
35. *Socialist Leader* 29 June 1946 (*New Leader* had changed its name the week before).
36. Letter to author from H. Dewar 24 September 1975.
37. NAC Minutes 4/5 August 1946.
38. *Socialist Leader* 29 June 1946.
39. E.g. that he referred to himself as Corporal Dewar (see *News Chronicle* 24 July 1946 and *Daily Express* 24 July 1946).
40. See *Battersea Borough News* for July 1946.
41. Ibid., 2 August 1946.
42. George Stone (1907–2001), editor of the *Socialist Leader* in 1947–48.
43. *Socialist Leader* 3 August 1946.
44. NAC Minutes 4/5 August 1946.
45. See *James Maxton: An Appreciation*, ILP publication (1946); Brown op. cit., p.303, pp.306–7.
46. HC 426 col. 2 24 July 1946.
47. Quotations from W. J. Brown and John Paton in Brown op. cit., pp.308–9.
48. Cohen op. cit., p.45 and R. E. Dowse, *Left in the Centre* (1966), p.161.
49. HC 398 col. 1101 23 March 1944.
50. Maxton numbered Winston Churchill, the socialists' favourite bogey-man, amongst his friends, and see Brown op. cit., p.306. However, both Maxton and Stephen had been in poor health for several years. It is possible, therefore, that their apparent loss of fervour may have been due in part to their failing health.
51. *The Word* July and August 1946. A former ILP colleague, R. E. Muirhead, President of the SNP, claimed in 1948 that Maxton had 'been contaminated' by his contact with the House of Commons (letter to F. Johnson, 29 April 1948, FJC ILP/4/1948/8).
52. Interviews N. Carmichael and H. Brown.
53. *Socialist Leader* 17 August 1946.
54. Interview D. Bateman.
55. Who was still a member of the Party though not of the NAC.
56. Interview B. Edwards.
57. Interview H. Sergeant.
58. Interview Sergeant. Carmichael apparently did have a strong personal following in Bridgeton (J. Taylor letter to F. Johnson 22 December 1946, FJC ILP/4/1946/29). See P. J. Thwaites, 'The Independent Labour Party 1938–1950', PhD thesis (1976), p.173 note 51 for a more detailed discussion of the rival claims regarding what Carmichael said at this

meeting. I have, on what I believe is the balance of evidence, accepted the Carmichael 'faction''s version.

59. *The Times* 26 August 1946.
60. J. McNair, *James Maxton: The Beloved Rebel* (1955), p.95. The Catholic organ, the *Glasgow Observer and Scottish Catholic Herald* 9 and 23 August 1946, gave considerable coverage to Wheatley's campaign but did not mention Carmichael!
61. *Glasgow Herald* 2 August 1946.
62. *Socialist Leader* 7 September 1946.
63. *Glasgow Herald* 2, 17 and 31 August 1946.
64. *Socialist Leader* 24 and 31 August 1946.
65. Ibid., 7 and 14 September 1946.
66. *Glasgow Eastern Standard* 17 August 1946.
67. *Economist* 7 September 1946, p.368.
68. *Socialist Leader* 22 November 1946. He had already resigned from the NAC (NAC Minutes 4/5 August 1946). He joined the PLP in July 1947. McGovern's loss was not regretted by every ILPer (J. Taylor letter to F. Johnson 20 November 1946, FJC ILP/4/1946/27).
69. J. McGovern, *Neither Fear Nor Favour* (1960), p.166.
70. *Glasgow Eastern Standard* 7 September 1946 and 23 November 1946.

Chapter 16

1. J. McNair, *Life Abundant*, p.306.
2. *RCP Bulletin* April 1946. Head Office circulars in Saltcoats Minute Book show *New Leader* sales falling from 11,000 to 10,000 between November 1945 and April 1946.
3. Barking Branch Minutes 27 February 1947.
4. E.g., *Tribune* 17 January 1947 and 14 February 1947; *Socialist Appeal* April 1946; and *RCP Bulletin* April 1946.
5. The 1914 ILP manifesto talked of the establishment of a United States of Europe (A. J. B. Marwick, 'The Independent Labour Party 1918–32', B.Litt. thesis [1960], p.10).
6. B. Edwards and F. A. Ridley, *United Socialist States of Europe* (1944), and W. Padley, *The Economic Problem of the Peace* (1944).
7. See *A Socialist Plan for Peace* (1945).
8. Edwards in *Yarmouth Mercury* 29 October 1945 and Padley in *Left* December 1945.
9. E. Meehan, 'The British Left and Foreign Politics 1945–51' PhD thesis (1954), p.191, p.195, and passim, and P. S. Gupta, *Imperialism and the*

British Labour Movement (1974), p.285. This idea of a United Europe as a force for peace, or defence, was gaining ground on the Right as well; see Winston Churchill's speech in Zurich 19 September 1946.

10. *Tribune* 24 May 1946.
11. *Socialist Leader* 21 December 1946.
12. Ibid., 8 March 1947.
13. E.g., *An appeal to the European peoples by the Committee of study and action for the USSE* (1947).
14. A. Calder, 'The Common Wealth Party 1942–45' D.Phil thesis (1968) vol. 1, p.341, and vol. 2, p.296.
15. *The Times* 3 June 1946. The ILP contingent was Edwards, Percy Williams and McNair (letter Williams to James Maxton 5 June 1946, FJC ILP/4/1946/14).
16. See Calder op. cit., vol. 1, p.304 and p.341 and *Socialist Leader* 5 October 1946 and 20 November 1946.
17. *Socialist Leader* 10 August 1946, interview C. Smith, and *The Times* 27 August 1946.
18. *The Times* 7 April 1947 and NAC Minutes 7 April 1947.
19. *NAC Report 1946–7*, p.15.
20. E.g., ILP Woolwich branch held joint meetings with the Eltham CW but refused to advertise them! Calder op. cit., vol. 2, p.296.
21. See *Between Ourselves* May 1946.
22. *Socialist Leader* 12 April 1947. The results were: (1) 27 for, 82 against; (2) carried 60 to 48; (3) 41 for, 63 against.
23. Calder op. cit., vol. 1, p.304, p.341. *CW National Committee Report 1947*.
24. *NAC Report 1947–8*, p.12.
25. *Socialist Appeal* Mid-April 1947. The Birmingham Federation Council claimed this call for a special conference was unconstitutional (Minutes 11 March 1947).
26. *Socialist Leader* 14 June 1947.
27. *Socialist Leader* 12 July 1947 and *Glasgow Eastern Standard* 12 July 1947. Stephen joined the PLP in October, one week before he died.
28. Edwards resigned and appealed for support from the Party because the NAC opposed this decision, which Edwards believed amounted to a heresy hunt against Stone (McNair letter 28 August 1947 and aftermath in NAC Minutes 20/21 September 1947).
29. E.g., *Socialist Leader* 30 August 1947.
30. Barking Branch Minutes 9 September 1947.
31. *Socialist Leader* 6 September 1947.
32. *Liverpool Evening Express* 22 August 1947.

33. *Liverpool Echo* 9 September 1947.
34. *Liverpool Daily Post* 20 August 1947.
35. *Liverpool Echo* 12 September 1947.
36. *Glasgow Eastern Standard* 1 November 1947. Apparently Carmichael's earlier letter of resignation had either been withdrawn or not accepted.
37. NAC Minutes 20/21 September 1947.
38. Interview N. Carmichael. He left the ILP on hearing of her nomination.
39. *Glasgow Eastern Standard* 31 January 1948 reports she asked the electors to send another Maxton to the House of Commons.
40. *Daily Worker* 30 December 1947 and *Socialist Leader* 3 January 1948.
41. *Glasgow Herald* 22 January 1948.
42. E.g., Ridley in *Socialist Leader* 29 June 1946, and F. Brockway, *Outside the Right* (1963), p.35.
43. See *News Chronicle* 8 May 1947.
44. *Socialist Standard* July 1947.
45. *Socialist Leader* 30 December 1947 and *Daily Telegraph* 21 January 1948.
46. *Daily Telegraph* 27 January 1948.
47. *Glasgow Herald* 20 January 1948.
48. *Socialist Leader* 10 January 1948.
49. *The Times* 30 January 1948. The Liberal and two Independents also polled over 2,000 votes between them and the Conservative held his party's 1945 votes whereas Inglis dropped 5,000 of the votes that Stephen had won in 1945, but the ILP was the obvious scapegoat.
50. See 'Rob Roy' in *Forward* 7 February 1948.
51. *Socialist Leader* 7 February 1948. The writing style suggests that the article was written by F. A. Ridley. The Birmingham Federation protested that the *Socialist Leader*'s editorial policy was 'hindering implementation of the conference decision of building a socialist alternative to the Labour Party' (Minutes 12 February 1948).
52. *NAC Report 1947–8*, p.2 passim.
53. Calder op. cit., vol. 2, p.77. N.B.: CW HQ expected the ILP to either break up or become just a movement if the Southport conference voted to cease electoral activity and it wanted to poach ILP members (see HQ letters 21 and 22 March 1948, CW Archive ILP General File 31/3).
54. J. Higgins, 'Ten Years for the Locust', *International Socialism* No. 14 (1963), p.30.
55. H. Pelling, *The British Communist Party* (1958), p.192.
56. *NAC Report 1947–8*, p.2.
57. Interview D. Bateman.
58. See note 37 above and *Between Ourselves* November 1948 for Ridley's

defence of his new position.

59. *Socialist Leader* 3 April 1948.
60. *Glasgow Herald* 2 February 1948.
61. *Socialist Leader* 3 April 1948. Surprisingly this newspaper did not carry a report of that debate.
62. This is based on reports in *The Times* and *Manchester Guardian* 29 March 1948.
63. *NAC Report 1948–9*, p.2.
64. *Daily Worker* 29 March 1948. See also *Daily Express* 29 March 1948 and *News Chronicle* 24 March 1948.
65. Labour Correspondent, *Manchester Guardian* 29 March 1948.
66. *Socialist Leader* 10 April 1948.

Chapter 17

1. See K. Eaton, *Between Ourselves* November 1948.
2. C. Driver, *The Disarmers* (1964), p.16 notes that the Gallup poll in December 1945 found that only 4 per cent of those asked about the potential effects of the atom bomb mentioned changes in military techniques and international relations.
3. J. McNair (*Life Abundant*, p.313) claims the ILP's anti-nuclear weapons campaign was well supported, and that CND was 'indirectly its off-spring'.
4. NEC Minutes 21 November 1948.
5. *NAC Report 1947–48*, p.22. McNair (op. cit., p.311) later claimed this was partly agreed so that the ILP did not continue to act in isolation.
6. *Socialist Leader* 15 and 22 May 1948.
7. *Sunday Times* 25 May 1975 article by P. Knightley and P. Kellner claims that the CIA was secretly funding the Hague Congress!
8. *NAC Report 1947–8*, p.22.
9. *Socialist Leader* 22 May 1948.
10. Ethel Mannin (1900–1984) became an anarchist at the time of the Spanish Civil War, but remained a member of the ILP for many years (see E. Mannin, *Privileged Spectator* [2nd ed. 1948] and *Brief Voices* [1959]). Her articles were described by one ILPer as 'the best thing in the SL nowadays' (H. Bryan to F. Johnson 8 January 1949, FJC ILP/4/1949/1).
11. D. Gibson, *Shall 20,000,000 Die?*
12. *A Call to the People of Britain* (1948), p.1, and NAC Minutes April 1948.
13. *NAC Report 1949–50*, p.9.

14. *Socialist Leader* 6 August 1949.

15. K. Eaton, *Between Ourselves* November 1948.

16. *Socialist Leader* 2 April 1949.

17. NAC Minutes 7/8 August 1948 and 20/21 May 1950.

18. McNair op. cit., p.311.

19. Barking Branch Minutes 2 September 1948.

20. J. Darragh, *Between Ourselves* November and December 1948 and articles by D. Kepper and M. Harrison in *Between Ourselves* December 1948.

21. *NAC Report 1948–49*, pp.2–3.

22. NAC Minutes 7/8 August 1948 and *Socialist Leader* 14 August 1948.

23. E.g., P. C. King in *Socialist Leader* 28 August 1948.

24. Some ILPers noted a Russophobic 'tendency' in the *Socialist Leader* (Birmingham Federation Minutes 11 November 1948 and H. Bryan letter to F. Johnson 8 January 1949, FJC ILP/4/1949/1). See *Socialist Leader* 23 April 1949 for the culmination of this dispute re the causes of world tension.

25. *Glasgow Eastern Standard* 17 April 1948.

26. *Socialist Leader* 25 September 1948.

27. Saltcoats Branch Minutes 22 October 1948 and *Socialist Leader* 6 November 1948.

28. Barking Branch Minutes 9 December 1948.

29. See *Socialist Leader* 8 January 1949 and 19 February 1949.

30. *Glasgow Eastern Standard* 19 January 1949.

31. Ibid., 27 November 1948. J. Darragh, Secretary of the Bridgeton ILP, stood for this body. For some unknown reason, despite the electoral ban, Welsh ILPers had the NAC's approval to stand as independents for municipal seats (NAC Minutes 7/8 August 1948).

32. *Glasgow Eastern Standard* 5 December 1948.

33. *NAC Report 1948–9*, pp.2–3. The NAC had received a damning report from Percy Williams, its National Treasurer, blaming the Party's decline on its anti-Labour Party tactics (NAC Minutes 7/8 August 1948). The decline of the ILP at a local level is graphically illustrated in the Birmingham Federation Minutes 1947–1950.

34. Francis Johnson (1878–1970), long-time Financial Secretary of the ILP and HO manager.

35. Dr Don Bateman (1919–2010), printer and lecturer.

36. *Socialist Leader* 23 April 1949.

37. If the ILP stopped electoral activity it was unclear what its branches/members would do. Indeed, R. E. Dowse (*Left in the Centre*

[1966] p.38) argues that the post 1918 ILP held on to its independent electoral activity because that gave its branches part of their raison d'être.

38. *Socialist Leader* 30 April 1949.
39. The Scottish Division was disappointed by Gibson's defeat but had not expected to win the other seats (letter from J. Taylor to Francis Johnson 15 May 1949, FJC ILP/4/1949/5). Seats were also fought in England; two seats were held, one won, one lost.
40. *Socialist Leader* 21 May 1949 '18 wickets, no runs'.
41. Ridley resigned as joint editor in September 1948 (see *Socialist Leader* 4 September 1948) because the 1948 ILP conference reiterated the 1945 constitution rule that Party officials could not simultaneously be members of the NAC.
42. *Forward* 4 June 1949.
43. *Socialist Leader* 11 June 1949.
44. Ibid., 3 October 1949.
45. Ibid., 17 September 1949.
46. H. G. Nicholas, *The British General Election of 1950* (1951), p.252.
47. *Peace News* 20 January 1950. Barton and Duncan were members of the PPU.
48. Ibid., leaflet 20 January 1950.
49. Ibid.
50. *Burnley Express and News* 8 February 1950.
51. *Socialist Leader* 3 January 1948. The CPGB did not approve of the Labour Party's 'anti-Soviet foreign policy'; see *Labour Monthly* February 1950 concerning the CPGB and the 'split vote'.
52. *Glasgow Herald* 22 February 1950. The ILP knew this change weakened their chances (letter from J. Taylor to F. Johnson 20 February 1950, FJC ILP/4/1950/22).
53. See *Socialist Leader* 19 November 1949.
54. E.g., *Glasgow Evening News* 21 February 1950.
55. *Glasgow Herald* 23 February 1950.
56. Interview Mrs M. Brown.
57. *Glasgow Eastern Standard* 10 March 1950.
58. Ibid., 3 March 1950. This paper, founded by John Wheatley in 1922, usually gave the ILP 'comradely' coverage.
59. E. J. Meehan, in 'The British Left and Foreign Policy' PhD thesis (1954), p.371, says the Left viewed the 1950 election defeat as a vindication of their demand for more socialism (see *Tribune* 3 and 10 March, and *New Statesman and Nation* 4 March 1950). The *Socialist Leader* 4 March 1950

saw it as the result of a 'bitter Tory attack against socialism'. In fact the Labour Party's vote went up compared to 1945, but a redistribution of seats and swings in favour of the Conservatives in many constituencies cost it seats.

60. There were probably now less than 1,500 members in the Party; see P. J. Thwaites, 'The Independent Labour Party 1938–1950' PhD thesis (1976) Appendix 1 p.26. CW certainly believed the ILP only had 8 or 900 members; see report on the 1950 ILP conference in CW Archive, ILP General 31/3.

61. The *Socialist Leader's* loss was £13 per week. See Dick Barnes, East Anglia Division Minutes 6 February 1950.

62. *NAC Report 1949–50*, p.3 passim and editorial note in *Between Ourselves* November 1950.

63. *Socialist Leader* 15 April 1950.

64. Edwards left to join the Labour Party in October 1950, and Ballantine just after when his work took him to an area in which there was only a 'pacifist branch' of the ILP (interview W. Ballantine).

65. See *ILP Conference Report 1951*, also its election propaganda for 1955.

66. See R. Mahon in *Glasgow Evening News* 18 October 1950.

67. *Socialist Leader* 29 July 1950 and 5 August 1950.

Chapter 18

1. D. Rubenstein, *Socialism and the Labour Party: The Labour Left and Domestic Policy, 1945–50* (1979) claims the Labour Left 1945–50 lacked organisation and leadership and so was unable to push the Labour government towards socialist policies. This suggests that there might have been a place for an ILP ginger group within the Labour Party. Yet if Michael Foot, Richard Crossman, Ian Mikado, and their allies, who had a voice via *Tribune*, could not move the Labour Party leftward, there is no guarantee that the ILP could have done so.

2. HC 435 cols. 1721–26 31 March 1947, 437 cols. 269–90 6 May 1947 and cols. 570 7 May 1947.

3. He blamed the Russians for the outbreak of the Second World War; see HC 351 col. 296 3 September 1939. And see HC 397 col. 736 22 February 1944 and 400 col. 849 24 May 1944 for his wartime attacks on the Soviet Union.

4. HC 450 col. 1162 4 May 1948.

5. HC 456 col. 973 22 September 1948.

6. HC 458 col. 2089 1 December 1948.

7. HC 477 cols. 534–6 5 July 1950.
8. HC 535 col. 649 6 December 1954 and J. McGovern, *Neither Fear Nor Favour* (1960), p.183.
9. *The Times* Obituary 15 February 1968.
10. *The Times* 12 February 1959.
11. *The Times* Obituary 15 February 1968.
12. Interview Mrs M. Brown.
13. HC 458 col. 2126 1 December 1948.
14. E.g., HC 480 col. 256 1 November 1950.
15. E.g., HC 457 col. 1436 9 November 1948.
16. Interviews Carmichael, H. Sergeant and *The Times* Obituary 20 January 1966.
17. See his maiden speech (HC 472 cols. 188–93 7 March 1950), also interview F. Brockway, and L. Gardner, 'The Fringe Left', in G. Kaufman (ed.), *The Left* (1966), p.118. Dr Charles Smith attacked Brockway in a letter to Don Bateman, 25 November 1971, for Brockway's 'misleading selection' of the facts in his autobiography *Inside the Left* (1942). Smith claims Brockway also later privately admitted that his opposition to the Second World War was a mistake (DBC DM1532 Q4/8).
18. HC 478 cols. 1452–5 15 September 1950.
19. C. Driver, *The Disarmers* (1964), p.25. Brockway was named as a KGB contact by Oleg Gordievsky in his memoirs describing running KGB operations in London in the 1980s, see C. Andrew, *Defence of the Realm* (2009), and P. Anderson and K. Davey, *Moscow Gold?* (2014), p.142. By that time Brockway was in his 90s and may well not have known he was lunching with a KGB agent.
20. Interview Brockway.
21. R. Segal, *The Race War*, p.322, quoted in P. S. Gupta, *Imperialism and the British Labour Movement 1914–1964* (1974), p.394.
22. F. Brockway, *Outside the Right* (1963), p.43.
23. Interview Brockway, and see *The Guardian* Obituary 29 April 1988.
24. Interview W. Padley.
25. HC 472 cols. 416–20 8 March 1950.
26. Driver op. cit., p.96.
27. Gardner op. cit., p.118, and *The Times* Obituary 17 April 1984.
28. Driver op. cit., p.45.
29. E.g., see the pamphlet by B. Edwards, *After Franco Who?* (1963).
30. Edwards was named in Andrew op. cit and Anderson and Davey, op.cit. p.122 and p.125 as a paid KGB agent, a claim repeated in R. Aldrich and R. Cormac, *The Black Door* (2016). Edwards admired the Soviet Union

in his youth, but given his experiences in Spain in 1937, and his known hostility to the CPGB (he fought off an attempted takeover of the Chemical Workers Union by that party) this seems to me unlikely. Moreover, his modest position as a backbench MP and reputation as a political loner does not suggest that he would have been a valuable KGB asset.

31. *Daily Telegraph* Obituary 7 June 1990.
32. *Daily Telegraph* Obituary 24 September 1993.
33. *Independent* Obituary 17 October 1993.
34. See T. D. Smith (1915–1993), *An Autobiography* (1970) and *The Times* Obituary 28 July 1993.
35. He did contact the ILP in 1974 but nothing came of this approach (interview D. Bateman).
36. Driver op. cit., p.233.
37. J. Ashley letter to the author 3 June 1975.
38. Interview T. Taylor.
39. Interviews N. Carmichael, H. Brown, Edwards, Brockway and Taylor.
40. Interviews W. Ballantine, A. Nicholls, H. Sergeant, R. Jobson.
41. (J.) Emrys Thomas (1900–1990(?)), schoolteacher and long-time NAC representative for Wales.
42. Bateman was National Treasurer for many years and Thomas was National Chairman from 1962–1971.
43. Treasurer's Report Annual General Meeting Scottish Division, April 1951. Gibson got just 680 votes (1.87 per cent) in the Scotstoun by-election.
44. E.g., *Forward* 4 November 1950.
45. Duncan polled 1,796 votes (5.36 per cent of the poll); Graham 1,195 votes (2.82 per cent) and Barton 1,006 votes (2.52 per cent).
46. *The Times* 14 April 1952.
47. Ibid., 19 April 1954.
48. In 1955 Stone polled 2,619 votes (7.38 per cent) and Birkett 715 votes (2.53 per cent).
49. *The Times* 26 March 1951 and *Socialist Leader* 30 June 1951 and 7 July 1951.
50. See *The Times* 24 May 1955.
51. Solidarity was originally formed by Trotskyists in 1960 and survived until 1992.
52. The Committee of 100 (1960–1968) was set up to achieve similar aims to CND but by direct action.
53. *The 100 versus the State.*

54. G. Thayer, *The British Political Fringe* (1965), p.147.
55. See Friendly Society File No. 5774R and Companies House Files Nos. 106263 and 141267.
56. Gardner op. cit., p.119, and see the scathing attack on the ILP in the 1960s in Thayer op. cit., pp.146–148.
57. See S. Christie and A. Metzer, *The Floodgates of Anarchy* (1970), p.125.
58. E.g., *The Times* 19 April 1965 and 9 January 1967.
59. Interview J. Morel.
60. *The Times* 4 February 1974.
61. D. Widgery (*The Left in Britain 1956–1968* [1976], p.485) said that the ILP had developed a revolutionary socialist tendency post-1968 but was 'largely content to vegetate in abstract utopianism'.
62. B. Winter, 'The ILP: a century for socialism' in D. James et al. (eds), *The Centennial History of the Independent Labour Party* (1992), pp.366–367. According to its website www.independentlabour.org.uk, 'Independent Labour Publications (ILP) is an educational trust, publishing house and pressure group committed to democratic socialism and the success of a democratic socialist Labour Party.'

Appendix

1. G. Cohen, *The Failure of a Dream* (2007), p.73. By 1899 there were ten ILPers on the Glasgow Council and one on the Norwich School Board. *ILP Conference Report 1925* p.21 noted that there were approximately 5,000 ILP councillors in Britain in 1924 (A. J. B. Marwick, 'The Independent Labour Party 1918–1932' B.Litt. thesis [1960], p.238).
2. Cohen op. cit., pp.73–80.
3. *New Leader* 7 October 1932 and 13 October 1945.
4. E.g. L. Kaye, ILP candidate for the Barnsley Council, in *New Leader* 18 August 1933.
5. *New Leader* 6 October 1933, *ILP Glasgow Municipal Election Address November 1934* and *New Leader* 22 April 1938.
6. E.g., ibid., 7 October 1932, and *Merthyr Express* 7 February 1948.
7. *New Leader* 7 October 1932.
8. See *Norwich Mercury* 20 October 1945 for a comparison of the ILP and Labour Party views on rates.
9. E.g., Yarmouth ILP councillors objected to expenditure on the Pleasure Gardens (*Yarmouth Mercury* 23 June 1938).
10. See Cohen op. cit., p.77, and for some of its relatively few electoral

successes 1932–1938 pp.75–76.

11. See *Barrhead News* and *Perthshire Advertiser* 13 October 1945 and 4 May 1946.

12. NAC Minutes 22/23 October 1946. The Northern Ireland branch only contributed £3.12.0d in total fees in 1948–49 (equating to less than 40 members).

13. E.g., *Forward* 31 August 1935.

14. *Forward* 1 September 1934 and see *ILP Glasgow Municipal Election Address November 1934*, p.3.

15. Letter from J. Taylor to F. Johnson 18 October 1947 (FJC ILP/4/1947/25).

16 He disagreed with what he believed to be the ILP's turn to the politics of revolutionary violence; see his letter of resignation published as part of his obituary in *Merthyr Express* 6 May 1934.

17. See ibid., 18 March 1933, 13 January 1934, 10 March 1934, 14 August 1934 and 22 December 1934 for reports on the formation and activities of the ILP Council group.

18. In the 1935 general election Stanfield stood for the ILP against the official Labour Party candidate and polled 9,640 votes. In a 1934 by-election for the same seat Campbell Stephen only polled 3,508 votes.

19. *Merthyr Express* 29 April 1950.

20. *Eastern Evening News* 5 December 1949.

21. East Anglia Division Minutes 4 September 1932, 1 February 1940 and 2 February 1946.

22. Interview R. Spraggins, ILP Norwich Secretary in the 1930s, who estimated that in the early 1930s branch meetings attracted nearly 100 members, but that the figure had halved by 1938.

23. Interview J. Morel who admitted that during the Second World War several US servicemen were therefore enrolled as members of the ILP! Kier Hardie Hall became a working men's club and finally closed in 2014.

24. Interviews A. Nicholls, A. South and G. Davison.

25. E.g., *Norwich Mercury* 17 September 1932.

26. Ibid., 24 November 1934.

27. Ibid., 14 March 1936.

28. Interviews South and Nicholls. See, however, *Norwich Labour Gazette* vol. 1 no. 43, January 1949 for an article attacking the 'irresponsible' ILP council group.

29. Interview Nicholls and *Eastern Evening News* 5 December 1949.

30. East Anglia Division Minutes 6 February 1950.

31. Ibid., 1 July 1933.

32. *Yarmouth Mercury* 1 April 1933 and interviews L. F. Bunnewell and Nicholls. For an account of the ILP's pre–1932 electoral record see *Yarmouth Mercury* 8 February 1936.
33. *Yarmouth Mercury* 24 November 1934, 15 December 1934 and 25 May 1935.
34. Ibid., 8 February 1936, 20 June 1936, and 31 October 1936.
35. Ibid., 20 November 1937.
36. Ibid., 12 February 1938.
37. HC 352 col. 758 17 October 1939.
38. Particularly re social services, e.g., *Yarmouth Mercury* 7 February 1942.
39. The ILP retained Stone's seat and won 3 others.
40. Interview F. H. Stone and *Yarmouth Mercury* 17 March 1950.
41. Interview Bunnewell and East Anglia Division Minutes 6 February 1950.
42. East Anglia Division closed down in 1960 (letter to the author from E. Burgess 20 January 1976).
43. G. F. Johnson claimed that at local elections people voted for the individual and not the party (*New Leader* 2 April 1937).
44. 'North Westerner' in *Lancashire Daily Post* 10 December 1940, and P. L. Budge, 'May Edwards: Councillor 1929–1935', unpublished dissertation, Chorley Public Library (1972).
45. Some ILPers objected to having their municipal programme dictated to them by annual conference (see Barking Branch Minutes 12 July 1945), while Bunnewell wanted the *New Leader* to give firmer pointers to municipal policy (see East Anglia Division Minutes 30 January 1944).
46. NAC Minutes 30 July 1938, 24/25 February 1945 and 11 December 1945. Input for the Municipal Programme was sought from local councillors and 'experts', such as Annie Maxton on education, David Gibson on housing and James Carmichael on social welfare. Federations might also have some input into the programme locally, e.g., see Birmingham Federation Minutes 14 January 1945.
47. E.g., Glasgow had housing and unemployment problems while Merthyr wanted to attract new industries to diversify from mining, and Yarmouth ILPers tried to turn the council's attention away from the holiday trade towards industry.
48. E.g. Stanfield on unemployment, *Merthyr Express* 30 October 1943.
49. *Norwich Mercury* 23 May 1936, *Yarmouth Mercury* 18 June 1938 and *New Leader* 5 June 1936.
50. Introduced by Labour Party Alderman Sam Jennings. Only he and the ILPers voted for it (*Merthyr Express* 4 November 1939).

51. HC 352 col. 758 17 October 1939.

52. E.g., Barking Branch Minutes 7 February 1943 and 30 February 1944, and Birmingham and District Federation Executive Committee Minutes 14 January 1945.

53. *Yarmouth Mercury* 6 July 1940.

54. *Merthyr Express* 25 April 1945; Morrison supported the ILP's claim.

55. *Norwich Mercury* 30 September 1939.

56. *Forward* 18 November 1933, apparently so that they would not be compromised by being associated with decisions over which they had no control.

57. *Glasgow Eastern Standard* 16 October 1940 and NAC Minutes 14/15 December 1940.

58. *Forward* 21 November 1936.

59. *Merthyr Express* 30 November 1945 and 30 July 1949.

60. *Yarmouth Mercury* 17 November 1945 and 8 December 1945 and interviews Stone and Bunnewell. They refused to wear aldermanic dress.

61. *Yarmouth Mercury* 5 January 1946 and interview Bunnewell.

62. *Merthyr Express* 4 March 1950 and *Yarmouth Mercury* 12 November 1948.

63. *Merthyr Express* 15 November 1947 and 22 June 1948. He also refused to appoint a chaplain or become a magistrate.

64. E.g. like Stone at the Annual Meeting of Yarmouth Hoteliers, *Yarmouth Mercury* 7 February 1948.

65. W. W. Hubert, *Merthyr Express* 9 February 1948.

66. Ibid., Editorial 20 November 1948.

Bibliography

ILP Documentary Sources

The British Library of Political and Economic Science holds the main ILP Archive (ILP/1–17/-) including NAC Minutes and annual conference reports, the Francis Johnson Correspondence, copies of ILP pamphlets, *New Leader, Socialist Leader, Between Ourselves*, the Barking Branch Minute Book 1942–1949 and the Birmingham Branch Minute Book 1948–1958.

The University of Glasgow Library's Broady Collection contains the papers of David Gibson including ILP annual conference reports, pamphlets and election addresses.

The Mitchell Library, Glasgow, holds the Maxton papers (though very few relate to the period covered here), the Bridgeton Branch Minute Book 1951–1963, Finance Book 1943–1962 and Social Committee Cash Book 1935–1953, together with the Glasgow Federation Invoice Book 1935–1939, Cash Book 1936–1939 and *New Leader* Accounts Book 1944–1946.

The University of Bristol Library Special Collections contains the Don Bateman Collection of ILP and related papers, including pamphlets, both Bristol and Birmingham Branch and Federation Minute Books (DM1532/Q1/4 & 5), and *Life Abundant*, the unpublished memoir of John McNair (DM1532 P5/9/1).

The Imperial War Museum holds a few papers of David Gibson, Stan Iveson and L. F. Bunnewell, as well as some material on the ILP contingent in the Spanish Civil War.

The North Ayrshire Museum has the Saltcoats Branch Minute Book 1941–1948.

Official and Political Unpublished Sources

The Keep, Brighton holds the papers of the Common Wealth party, and the
Mass Observation (MO) diaries, reports etc.
Labour Party Archive has NEC Minutes, reports, papers, and the James
Middleton ILP File.
The Modern Records Centre, University of Warwick holds the Revolutionary
Communist Party (RCP) and Workers' International League (WIL)
internal bulletins, reports etc.
The Public Record Office contains Cabinet Minutes and Papers (CAB 66, 67,
68), Metropolitan Police Papers (MEPOL2), and Ministry of Labour
Papers (LAB 10).

Official Published Sources

Hansard: House of Commons Debates 5th Series.

Interviews

Will Ballantine (7 March 1974); Don Bateman (9 February 1974 & 2 March
1976);
Fenner Brockway (15 January 1974); Hugh Brown (5 June 1974); Mary
Brown (5 June 1974);
L. F. Bunnewell (11 September 1975); Mary Carmichael (5 June 1974);
Neil Carmichael (29 March 1974); George Davison (9 September 1975);
Bob Edwards (5 February 1974); Ann Hambly (3 May 1974);
Douglas and Ruby Jobson (3 May 1974); Jenny Morel (16 June 1975);
Alf Nicholls (9 September 1975); Walter Padley (28 January 1974);
Harry Sergeant (5 June 1974); Dr Charles Smith (26 February 1974);
Arthur South (8 September 1975); Reg Spraggins (9 September 1975);
F. H. Stone (10 September 1975); Edna Sword (9 September 1975);
Tom Taylor (20 March 1974); J. Emrys Thomas (9 February 1974).

Letters

Jack Ashley (3 and 16 June 1975); E. Burgess (20 January 1976); Hugo
Dewar (24 September 1975); Bert Lea (28 June 1975); D. Marshall (30
September 1975); Eddie Milne (2 June 1975).

Unpublished Theses

Budge, P. L., 'May Edwards: Councillor 1929–1935', Chorley Public Library, 1972.

Calder, A. L. R., 'The Common Wealth Party 1942–1945', D.Phil. University of Sussex, 1968.

Jupp, J., 'The Left in Britain 1931–1941', M.Sc. University of London, 1956.

Marwick, A. J. B., 'The Independent Labour Party 1918–1932', B.Litt. University of Oxford, 1960.

Meehan, E., 'The British Left and Foreign Policy 1945–1951', Ph.D. University of London, 1954.

Thwaites, P. J., 'The Independent Labour Party 1938–1950', Ph.D. University of London, 1976.

Newspapers and Periodicals

National newspapers and periodicals
Daily Express
Daily Herald
Daily Telegraph
Economist
Independent
Manchester Guardian
News Chronicle
New Statesman and Nation
Reynolds News
Sunday Times
The Times

Political newspapers and periodicals
American Militant
Between Ourselves
Controversy/Left
Daily Worker
Forward
Labour Monthly
Militant
Militant Miner
New Leader
Norwich Labour Gazette

Peace News
Socialist
Socialist Appeal
Socialist Leader
Socialist Standard
Tribune
The Word

Local newspapers
Acton Gazette
Barrhead News
Battersea Borough News
Bilston and Willenhall Times
Bradford Telegraph
Bristol Evening Post
Bristol Evening World
Burnley Express and News
Cardiff and Suburban News
Cardiff Times
Eastern Evening News
Edinburgh Evening Dispatch
Glasgow Eastern Standard
Glasgow Evening Citizen
Glasgow Herald
Glasgow Observer and Scottish Catholic Herald
Lancashire Daily Post
Lancaster Guardian
Liverpool Daily Post
Liverpool Echo
Liverpool Evening Express
Merthyr Express
Newcastle Journal
Norwich Mercury
Perthshire Advertiser
Renfrew Press
South Wales Argus
Stretford Borough News
Stretford Guardian
Stretford and Sale Advertiser
Western Mail

Yarmouth Mercury
Yorkshire Observer

Books, Articles and Pamphlets

Addison, P., 'By-elections of the Second World War', in Cook, C., and Ramsden, J. (eds), *By-elections in British Politics*, London, Macmillan, 1973.

Aldrich, R., and Cormac, R., *The Black Door*, London, William Collins, 2016.

Anderson, P. and Davey, K., *Moscow Gold?: The Soviet Union and the British Left*, Ipswich, Aaaargh! Press, 2014.

Arnot, R.P., *The Miners: In Crisis and War*, London, Allen and Unwin, 1961.

Barker, R., *Education and Politics 1900–1951*, Oxford, Clarendon Press, 1972.

Barltrop, R., *The Monument: The Story of the Socialist Party of Great Britain*, London, Pluto Press, 1975.

Beckett, F., *Enemy Within: The Rise and Fall of the British Communist Party*, London, John Murray, 1995.

Beveridge, J., *Beveridge and His Plan*, London, Hodder and Stoughton, 1954.

Brockway, F., *The Workers' Front*, London, Seeker and Warburg, 1938.

  The Way Out, ILP pamphlet, 1942.

  Inside the Left, London, Allen and Unwin, 1942.

  Socialism Over Sixty Years: The Life of Jowett of Bradford, London, Allen and Unwin, 1946.

  Outside the Right, London, Allen and Unwin, 1963.

Broue, P., and Temime, E., *The Revolution and the Civil War in Spain*, London, Faber and Faber, 1972.

Brown, G., *Maxton*, London, Fontana, 1988.

Brown, M., 'ILP Centenary: Still Making Socialists', *Bulletin of the Marx Memorial Library*, No. 124, pp.3–7, London, Autumn 1995–Spring 1996.

Brown, W. O., *The Hypocrisy and Folly of War*, SNP pamphlet, (n.d.).

Bullock, A., *The Life and Times of Ernest Bevin*, London, Heinemann, 1960.

Bullock, I., *Under Siege: The Independent Labour Party in Interwar Britain*, Edmonton, AU Press, 2017.

Calder, A. L. R., *The People's War*, London, Panther Books, 1971.

Callaghan, J., *The Far Left in British Politics*, Oxford, Basil Blackwell, 1987.

Campbell, J. R., *Socialism through Victory: A Reply to the Policy of the I.L.P.*, CPGB (n.d.).

Camrose, Viscount, *British Newspapers and their Controllers*, London, Cassel and Co. Ltd., 1947.

Cantrill, H., *Public Opinion 1935–46*, Boston, Princeton University Press, 1951.

Carr, E. H., *The Bolshevik Revolution*, Harmondsworth, Penguin Books, 1953.

Challinor, R., *The Struggle for Hearts and Minds: Essays on the Second World War*, Whitley Bay, Bewick Press, 1995.

Christie, S., and Metzer, A., *The Floodgates of Anarchy*, London, Sphere Books Ltd., 1970.

Clayton, J., *The Rise and Decline of Socialism in Great Britain 1884–1924*, London, Faber and Gwyer, 1926.

Cohen, G., *The Failure of a Dream: The Independent Labour Party from Disaffiliation to World War II*, London, Tauris Academic Studies, 2007.

Cole, G. D. H., *A History of the Labour Party From 1914*, London, Macmillan, 1948.

The Second International 1889–1914, London, Macmillan, 1956.

Crick, B., *George Orwell: A Life*, Harmondsworth, Penguin Books, 1982.

Cross, C., *The Fascists in Britain*, London, Barrie and Rockcliff, 1961.

Deutscher, I., *Stalin*, Harmondsworth, Penguin Books, 1970.

Dowse, R. E., 'The ILP and foreign politics 1918–23', in *International Review of Social History*, Vol. VII, 1962.

Left in the Centre: The Independent Labour Party 1893–1940, London, Longmans, 1966.

Driberg, T., *Beaverbrook: A Study in Power and Frustration*, London, Weidenfield and Nicholson, 1956.

Driver, C., *The Disarmers: A Study in Protest*, London, Hodder and Stoughton, 1964.

Edwards, B., *Workers! Freedom or Servitude*, ILP pamphlet, 1941.

War on the People, ILP pamphlet, 1943.

After Franco Who? ILP pamphlet, 1963.

Edwards, B., and Ridley, F. A., *United Socialist States of Europe*, ILP pamphlet, 1944.

Estorick, E., *Stafford Cripps*, London, Heinemann, 1949.

Gardner, L., 'The Fringe Left', in Kaufman, G. (ed.), *The Left*, London, Anthony Blond, 1966.

Gibson, D., *Shall 20,000,000 Die?*, ILP pamphlet, 1948.

Groves, R., *The Balham Group: How British Trotskyism Began*, London, Pluto Press Ltd., 1974.

Gupta, P. S., *Imperialism and the British Labour Movement 1914–1964*, London, Macmillan, 1974.

Hall, C., 'Not Just Orwell': *The Independent Labour Party Volunteers and the*

Spanish Civil War, Barcelona, Warren & Pell Publishing, 2009.

Higgins, J., 'Ten years for the locust: British Trotskyism 1938–1948', in *International Socialism*, No. 14, 1963.

Hill, C., *Puritanism and Revolution*, London, Panther Ltd., 1968.

Home, W. D., *Half Term Report: An Autobiography*, London, Longmans Green, 1954.

Hyde, D., *I Believed*, London, Heinemann, 1950.

ILP pamphlets: *ILP Constitution and Rules*, 1933, 1936 and 1942.
What the Party Stands For, 1935, 1936 and 1945
A Socialist Plan for Britain, 1935 and 1945.
Socialist Britain Now, 1942.
Shop Steward pamphlets, 1943.
ILP 1893–1943: Jubilee Souvenir, 1943.
A Socialist Plan for Peace, 1945.
James Maxton 1885–1946: An Appreciation, 1946.
A Call to the People of Britain, 1948.

James, D., Jowitt, T., and Laybourn, K. (eds), The *Centennial History of the Independent Labour Party*, Halifax, Ryburn Academic Publishing, 1992.

Jupp, J., *The Radical Left in Britain 1931–1941*, London, Frank Cass, 1982.

Kirkwood, D., *My Life of Revolt*, London, George G. Harrap and Co., 1935.

Knox, W., *James Maxton*, Manchester, Manchester University Press, 1987.

Lee, J., *This Great Journey: A Volume of Autobiography, 1904–1945*, New York, MacGibbon and Kee, 1963.

Lenin, V. I., *Collected Works*, Moscow, Progress Publishers, 1966.
Socialism and War, Moscow, Progress Publishers, 1972.
Imperialism, the Highest Stage of Capitalism, Moscow, Progress Publishers, 1970.

Lewis, C. Day, *Buried Day*, London, Chatto and Windus, 1960.

Longhurst, H., *I Wouldn't Have Missed It*, London, Dent, 1945.

McCallum, R. B., and Readman, A., *The British General Election of 1945*, Oxford, Oxford University Press, 1947.

MacCormick, J. M., *Flag in the Wind: The Story of the National Movement in Scotland*, London, Gollancz, 1955.

McGovern, J., *Why the Church Supports Franco*, ILP pamphlet, 1938.
Neither Fear Nor Favour, London, Blandford Press, 1960.

McNair, J., *James Maxton: The Beloved Rebel*, London, Allen and Unwin, 1955.

Mannin, E., *Privileged Spectator*, London, Jarrolds, 2nd ed., 1948.
Brief Voices, London, Hutchinson, 1959.

Martin, D., *Pacifism*, London, Routledge and Kegan Paul, 1965.

Marwick, A. J. B., 'The ILP in the 1920s', in *Institute of Historical Research Bulletin*, Vol. XXXV, 1962.

Miliband, R., *Parliamentary Socialism*, London, Merlin Press, 1961.

Morrison, S., *I Renounce War: The Story of the Peace Pledge Union*, London, Sheppard Press, 1962.

Nicholas, H. G., *The British General Election of 1950*, London, Macmillan, 1951.

Nicholls, D., *The Pluralist State*, London, Macmillan, 1975.

Orwell, G., *Homage to Catalonia*, Harmondsworth, Penguin Books, 1983 edition.

Orwell, S., and Angus, I. (eds), *The Collected Essays, Journalism and Letters of George Orwell*, Harmondsworth, Penguin Books, 1968.

Padley, W., *The Real Battle for Britain*, ILP pamphlet, 1943.
The Economic Problem of the Peace: A Plea for World Socialist Union, London, Victor Gollancz, 1944.

Paton, J., *Left Turn*, Martin Secker and Warburg Ltd., 1936.

Pelling, H., *The British Communist Party: An Historical Profile*, London, A and C Black, 1958.
A Short History of the Labour Party, London, Macmillan, 1961.
A History of British Trade Unionism, Harmondsworth, Penguin Books, 1963.
'The Story of the ILP', in *Popular Politics and Society in Late Victorian Britain*, London, Macmillan, 1968.
Britain and the Second World War, Glasgow, Fontana, 1970.

Pimlott, B., *Labour and the Left in the 1930s*, London, Allen and Unwin, 1986.

Pollitt, H., *How to Win the War*, CPGB pamphlet, 1939.

Priestley, J. B., *Postscripts*, London, Heinemann, 1940.

Qualter, T. H., *Propaganda and Psychological Warfare*, New York, Random House, 1962.

Ridley, F. A., *Socialism and Religion*, ILP pamphlet, 1948.

Rubenstein, D., *Socialism and the Labour Party: The Labour Left and Domestic Policy, 1945–1950*, Leeds, ILP Square One Publications, 1980.

Shinwell, E., *I've Lived Through It All*, London, Gollancz, 1973.

Smith, T. D., *An Autobiography*, Newcastle-upon-Tyne, Oriel Press, 1970.

Stafford, D., 'The Detonator Concept: British Strategy SOE & European Resistance After the Fall of France', *Journal of Contemporary History* Vol. 10, No. 2, 1975.

Taylor, A. J. P., *English History 1914–45*, Oxford, Clarendon Press, 1965.

Beaverbrook, London, Hamilton, 1972.

Thayer, G., *The British Political Fringe: A Profile*, London, Anthony Blond, 1965.

Thwaites, P. J., 'Revolutionary Opposition to the Second World War' in *Review*, No. 1, London, Imperial War Museum, 1986.

'The Independent Labour Party Contingent in the Spanish Civil War', in *Review* No. 2, London, Imperial War Museum, 1987.

Widgery, D., *The Left in Britain 1956–68*, Harmondsworth, Penguin Books, 1976.

Winter, B., *The ILP: A brief history*, Leeds, Independent Labour Publications, 1982.

Winter, N., *Workers' Control*, ILP pamphlet, 1947.

Wiskemann, E., *Europe of the Dictators*, London, Fontana, 1966.

Wood, N., *Communism and British Intellectuals*, London, Gollancz, 1959.

Index

Lightning Source UK Ltd.
Milton Keynes UK
UKHW050702061220
374527UK00013BA/905/J

9 781789 631302